W9-CZU-327

CURRICULUM ANALYSIS AND DESIGN FOR RETARDED LEARNERS

**Nancy Krow Klein, Marvin Pasch,
Thomas W. Frew**

Cleveland State University

Charles E. Merrill Publishing Company
A Bell & Howell Company
Columbus   Toronto   London   Sydney

106186

Dedication

To the retarded children who have taught us so much

Published by
Charles E. Merrill Publishing Company
A Bell and Howell Company
Columbus, Ohio 43216

This book was set in Optima, Fifth Avenue Outline.
The production editor was Susan Herten.
The cover was prepared by Will Chenoweth.

Copyright © 1979, by Bell & Howell Company. All rights reserved. No part of this book may be reproduced in any form, electronic or mechanical, including photocopy, recording, or any information storage and retrieval system, without permission in writing from the publisher.

Cover photograph by Tom Hutchinson.

Library of Congress Catalog Card Number: 78–78035

International Standard Book Number: 0–675–08273–0

Printed in the United States of America

1 2 3 4 5 6 7 8 9 10/ 85 84 83 82 81 80 79

Foreword

Special education for the mentally retarded has had a checkered career, swinging between the poles of optimism and pessimism. In 1846, Seguin developed a program for the "moral treatment, hygiene and education of idiots," which emphasized training of the senses. The first public institution in the United States was the Walter Fernald State School in Massachusetts, established in 1847. In the beginning, admissions to state residential institutions were restricted primarily to the more capable youth and young adults who showed promise of social rehabilitation and release to communities.

About the turn of the century, special classes for the mildly retarded or educable children at the elementary school level began to appear in the larger school systems throughout the country. It was not until the late 1930s that legislatures began to recognize the importance of this program by amending the special education laws to include provisions for the mentally retarded, and by providing financial support to the schools so that this program expanded rapidly. The movement to establish special class programs for moderately retarded or trainable children in the community developed some 20 years later. The decade 1948 to 1958 witnessed an unprecedented rise of 132% in special education enrollments in the public day schools across the nation, but nonetheless it was estimated that only about 25% of the mentally retarded children were enrolled in a special education program. During this period, it was believed that expansion of special classes was the only solution to the problems of educating the mentally retarded. It was thought that smaller class size and specially trained teachers would permit individualized attention and a more functional curriculum would allow retarded children to experience success in school and to be better prepared for adult employment.

The changing pattern of services was paralleled by changing views on the nature of mental retardation. For the first half of this century, the IQ was the hallowed instrument for the diagnosis of mental retardation. It was viewed as a fixed attribute of the person, determined largely by heredity. With this assumption, social segregation and sterilization were advocated in order to prevent retardation, and of course, the goals of education or treatment were minimal. In the *Proceedings of the Second Annual Conference on the Problem of the Exceptional Child* in 1911, it was stated that "All that society can do for the feeble-minded is to take care of them under custodial conditions, so that they may be out of harm's way and that those capable of such training may be developed sufficiently to reimburse society for the cost of their maintenance, wholly or in part." Some 30 years later, most professional workers used Edgar Doll's definition of *mental deficiency,* which included the diagnostic criteria of incurability and social incompetence obtaining at maturity. However, follow-up studies of graduates of special class programs proved that many were quite competent as adults, despite their below-average IQ. In 1959, the American Association on Mental Deficiency produced a *Manual on Terminology and Classification in Mental Retardation* (edited by Heber), which revolutionized the concept of mental retardation as well as substituting the term "retardation" for "deficiency." Mental retardation was now defined as a functional characteristic of the individual that might well change in the course of time, so that a person might be judged retarded at one age and not at another. This manual also introduced the importance of assessing the social-adaptive skills of the person and required that a person be considered retarded on the basis of two concomitant criteria, subnormal intelligence accompanied by significant impairment in adaptive behavior. This opened the door to a much more optimistic view of the potential of retarded persons.

Since 1960, there has been a growing and painful awareness that our good intentions have fallen far short of the mark. Studies of the efficacy of special classes in public schools suggested little, if any, benefit for the enrollees when compared with similar-IQ children who were maintained in regular classes. The special class graduates felt little gratitude; indeed, they experienced social isolation, shame, and stigmatization. Jane Mercer's studies showed that a disproportionate number of special class students came from poverty and minority groups and raised the question of discrimination based on the nature of the IQ test and system of placement. Many of these children were "6-hour retarded children" who were independent and competent outside the classroom. Simultaneously, the warehouse conditions of state institutions and the negative effects of institutionalization were forcefully brought to public attention. All this led to efforts to break with the past and search for new solutions.

With the passage of Public Law 94–142 in 1975, public education was mandated to serve all handicapped children in the least restrictive environment appropriate for their needs. Essentially the authors of this book are trying to bring the education of the retarded into the mainstream of educational thinking. They review the basic knowledge about cognitive and emotional development and use this to understand how retarded children are the same and how they differ. Similarly, educational models to classroom design and curricular planning are examined for their relevance to the retarded. They suggest modification to make the "normal" fit the retarded, as opposed to an alternative, segregated system of special education. They suggest that the retarded child is no less a whole person than the normal-IQ child, and that motivational and emotional parameters must be considered along with the cognitive limitations. This book should serve to reassure regular classroom teachers of their ability to meet the needs of the retarded child and thus reduce the gap between regular and special education. Tolerance for differing rates and styles of learning is one important part of the story; the other is ingenuity in teacher planning to choose instructional objectives and devise materials and methods that will present the material in small, sequential steps for real mastery. The time has come for special education to share some of their pedagogical philosophy and techniques—not only for the better education of retarded children but towards the goal of more individualization of instruction for all children.

Jane W. Kessler, Ph.D.
Leffingwell professor of psychology, and director of Mental Development Center
Case Western Reserve University

Preface

The concept *mainstreaming*—placing of handicapped children in a "least restrictive environment" as mandated by P.L. 94–142—is a process encompassing far more than many educational fads that have been relegated to brief mention in educational history textbooks. The typical educational innovation has a clear life cycle. It begins with a period of intense activity, where supporters of the innovation seem to include everyone but a hesitant few. As the enthusiasm for the innovation peaks, believers design research and evaluation studies to provide empirical evidence of success. When completed, the investigators are puzzled by confounding conclusions, at best. On the stormy side of the cycle, the criticism multiplies and overwhelms the support.

If this sounds unpromising and grim, consider the roster of discarded or disabled innovations during the last 20 years—New Math, team teaching, open education, flexible scheduling, and so on and on. How is the process of mainstreaming, as a concept and an educational practice, different from earlier attempts to alter existing procedures? First, mainstreaming is the process of educating children in the least restrictive environment. At the heart of the matter, it states a belief about the process of education for *all* children. We believe that integrating handicapped and nonhandicapped children in a classroom has educational value for all. Furthermore, we believe that the focus on the needs of each indivdual, a basic tenet in special education, is important for having the best education for all children. The process of mainstreaming holds promise for personalizing school experiences. Consequently, mainstreaming is not just another fad and is not predestined to be added to the list of unfulfilled educational innovations.

This book, then, is dedicated to the belief that special education and regular education can be intertwined, can become interdependent and complementary. That two of the three authors (Frew, Klein) are special educators and that the third (Pasch) is a curriculum and instructional development specialist demonstrates a commitment to integrated education.

This book also represents our attempt to bring together theoretical and classroom-tested knowledge of how special chlidren learn and to focus on mildly and moderately mentally retarded youngsters along with how to select, design, implementation, and evaluate their classroom instruction. We espouse a position that testifies to the "right of every child to learn whether he or she learns easily or with great difficulty. Without this focus on the individual, rhetoric about mainstreaming has no substance.

In the mainstreaming process we feel that the individual teacher chiefly determines educational success or failure. Mainstreamed education cannot rest on a cadre of teachers who perceive their role as only to teach from 9:00 to 3:00. There are no substitutes for knowledgeable, alert, caring, secure, active, creative, and dedicated classroom teachers. Transforming teachers into technicians who deliver "canned learning programs" will not produce a focus on the individual child. Selecting teachers who let others make decisons for them is a prime ingredient in a recipe for educational impotence.

We are committed to a clear set of principles. The book is our best effort to create a product that will be useful to teachers who work with or are concerned about children, all children.

Acknowledgments

We are fortunate to have worked in the protective environment of the College of Education at Cleveland State University, where creative activity is respected. We have received assistance from many sources. In particular, our department chairpersons, Floyd Adams, Diana Jordan, and Dean Richard McArdle, have encouraged and supported us.

Our dissertation professors, Frederick Smith at Indiana University, Philip Safford at Kent State University, and Thomas M. Stephens at The Ohio State University, through their spirit and examples, taught us the value of communication through the written word. We have tried to apply the principles they taught us; whatever success we have achieved in communicating ideas is due, in no small part, to their skill and patience.

We have been influenced by many persons whose original principles and concepts form the basis for the book's content. The following individuals, among others, inspired us by the quality of their thinking: Benjamin Bloom, Jerome Bruner, Robert Gagné, Robert Glaser, John Patrick, Burton Blatt, Seymour Sarason, Jane Kessler, Florence Stratemeyer, and Ralph Tyler.

A number of contributions to the book were made by our colleagues and students at Cleveland State University and by the Cleveland educational community. Dave Adams offered his ideas on LAP's and listened to us when we were elated or depressed. Darryl Smith contributed his best thinking in developing learning hierarchies.

Acknowledgments

The Cleveland Heights Board of Education and the Cuyahoga County Board of Mental Retardation wilingly assisted us in securing pictures and children's work.

The Instructional Support Services at Cleveland State University assisted us in the production of photographs and graphic services. Our thanks to Nate Eatman and Mike Ludwig. Our patient and talented secretary, Linda Juzkiewicz, typed and retyped drafts of each chapter until she could recite a substantial segment of the book.

We could not have completed the book without the understanding, encouragement, patience, and assistance we received from our spouses and children. To Judy, Dawn, and Bob our love and appreciation. Knowing that they were with us lightened the burden of rewriting and increased the glow of pride when we were successful.

Yet, in a very real sense, the individuals who have had the most profound influence on our thinking, teaching, and learning are the numerous mentally retarded persons with whom we have interacted during the past 20 years. They have shown us the importance of fine teaching and given us the opportunity to learn with and from them. To all these people, we say thank you. We hope that this book is an appropriate expression of our gratitude.

Contents

106186

The Functional Life Curriculum (see pages 140-153) aims to help learners understand themselves and others, become responsible adults, and prepare for independent living. Lisa (pictured on the front cover and again here) attended a high school special class where these aims were important in the curriculum. William Berger, her high school teacher (shown with her here), helped her write these reflections about being handicapped. Lisa went on from high school to attend a local community college, and is now working in a sheltered workshop.

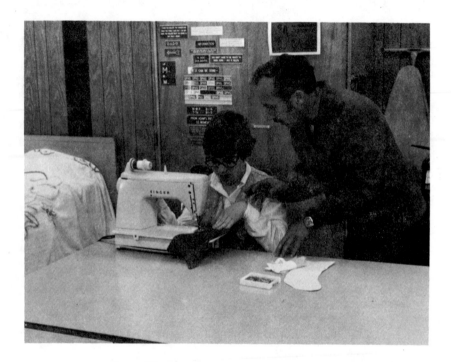

Being handicapped means being faced with physical limitations... It means that there will be difficulties such as marriage and raising a family. It means not walking or running with my friends, except in dreams. This is where frustrations of a handicap come in. Nevertheless, it is a necessity that when I find myself faced with these facts, I cannot change to adapt myself accordingly. An example of this is that while I think of the tremendous effort it takes for a mountain climber to climb a mountain. Yet it takes as much time and effort for me to walk one length of the parallel bars in therapy. Something most people not having experienced what I have had would take it for granted. But it is my mountain that I have climbed in success. And it means just as much.

A Starting Place

A Philosophical Position

Although history suggests that mentally retarded persons have been among the most victimized of American citizens, during the last half of the 20th century there have been dramatic improvements in their treatment. The growth of self-contained classes and special schools for retarded learners during the 1940s and 1950s resulted in a separate educational stream for retarded learners. More recently, judicial actions such as *Brown vs.* the *Topeka Board of Education,* efficacy studies, and group action by parents and professionals led society to think further about educational opportunities for retarded students. Although class size was smaller than regular classes and teachers were specially trained and materials specially designed, these separate classes did not meet the expectations of those who advocated for mentally retarded students. One major negative consequence was the separation of regular and special education students. Special education became the stream for the children whom regular education could not teach.

On the positive side, special education research and development produced increased knowledge about how to teach children with special needs. The major thrust of special education has been the development of an instructional technology. Individualization of instruction is a basic tenet. Regular education, on the other hand, has directed its attention to subject matter content analysis and related materials development. The curriculum reformers in regular education during the 1950s and 1960s searched for patterns of relationship that organize subject matter.

Thus, two separate fields developed in the public school system. Special education stressed methodology and a focus on individual needs; regular education stressed subject matter and group instruction. These two streams maintained separate classrooms, separate teachers, separate students, and separate administrators.

New federal and state mandates now require educators to rethink and reorganize their practices. The "least restrictive alternative" principle in P.L. 94-142, the Education for All Handicapped Children Act of 1975, mandates that regular and special education personnel assume new roles. Special education no longer will be totally separate from the rest of the school community.

The purpose of this book is to integrate regular and special education, through curriculum analysis and design. The focus is on both content analysis and individualizing instruction for the retarded learner. It is our position, as two special educators and one regular educator, that through collaboration such as ours, meaningful curriculum revision is possible.

P.L. 94-142 is a challenge to both regular and special educators. Our task as professional teachers is to create appropriate, exciting, relevant learning experiences that will help retarded students achieve success. This success will be determined by the degree to which these students are able to lead normal, productive lives in their communities.

The normalization principle, now widely accepted, serves as a guide in developing school experiences. Normalization means that

Learning about your family is an important part of the school curriculum.

services to mentally retarded people must resemble those available to nonretarded people. In addition, these services must be provided to handicapped youngsters in as unrestrictive an environment as possible.

The school curriculum is the vehicle for developing least restrictive, normalizing educational experiences for retarded students. Underlying this position are several assumptions:

1. Mentally retarded students, like their nonretarded peers, will benefit from carefully planned learning experiences.
2. Curriculum development for retarded learners is a systematic process that requires collaboration among regular and special educators, parents, and students when possible.
3. A curriculum that does not take into account the needs and interests of the learner, the needs of society, and subject matter content can result in an inadequate education for retarded students.

4. The attitudes of school personnel affect both program development and ultimately the learning outcomes of retarded students.
5. The public schools must provide education that enables retarded students to accept the responsibilities and risks inherent in normalization.

It is our hope that through the collaboration of educators, administrators, parents, and students, education will transcend the limits of the self-fulfilling prophecies (Rosenthal & Jacobson, 1968) that have held back retarded students.

Completing assignments correctly is important to these students.

Curriculum Theory

Underlying Analysis

Teachers are repeatedly confronted by difficult curriculum issues. Often, these issues focus on "what to teach" to create a useful curriculum for mentally retarded learners. Chapter 1 suggests that, whatever the subject area, a useful curriculum must be built upon the results of a comprehensive analysis of the particular students to be taught. The analysis considers the psychological, physiological, and intellectual maturity of students. It should forecast the knowledge, skills, and attitudes that will be useful when formal schooling ends. Finally, it should accurately diagnose each student's present

Learning together builds skills and friendships.

level of knowledge and ability. Consequently, instruction must begin where students can gain the greatest benefit.

Useful curriculum analysis must also include the instructional setting and its accompanying physical and emotional environment. Appreciating an educational setting today means understanding how radically treatment of the retarded has changed since the period before World War II. At that time most retarded people were institutionalized; they were rarely educated. Fortunately, during the last 20 years, special education has moved from obscurity and neglect into a period of positive change. Today we are attempting to integrate normal and handicapped children wherever and whenever possible. Integrated environments will inevitably accelerate the pressure to diagnose and prescribe individual treatment for each student. This is in stark contrast to our all-too-common homogenized style of group instruction. Most of all, the focus on the educational setting implies a concern for the important effects on learning that can be attributed to environmental factors. For example, the physical arrangement of the furniture in the classroom, the temperature and the lighting, and the distractions of movement and sound are quite important. Equally important is the emotional environment. Although it is not tangible, it can be felt and assessed by any capable observer. There are some classrooms where inquiry and problem solving are respected and encouraged, where the climate is marked by warmth and honesty. Others are sterile, with no student participation and activity. There, education is trivialized, and students learn with subdued hostility or indifference that obedience is the only expected outcome.

Finally, understanding the educational setting means understanding the role of supportive personnel. Psychologists and counselors may assist the student in coping with needs that extend beyond the learning realm, while tutors and curriculum personnel can assist in the diagnosis and prescription for individual children. In addition, when the teacher actively cultivates a strong relationship with the students' parents, the students benefit through deeper and broader learning experiences.

Selecting Curriculum Goals

Chapter 4 introduces the curriculum development process. Curriculum content may be generated from three sources: (a) the expressed and implicit needs of students; (b) the mastery of useful subject matter based on the traditional disciplines such as math, language,

Learning to use tools is an important skill for the home handyperson.

and science; and (c) timely and urgent needs of the society, such as employment, education, citizenship, drug and alcohol abuse (Tyler, 1950). Also in Chapter 4, we will introduce our concept of a curriculum that we believe meets the needs of mentally retarded learners. This curricular theory synthesizes the work of Tyler (1950) Stratemeyer, Forkner, McKim, and Passow (1957), and Bruner (1963). The result of this analysis is the Functional Life Curriculum, designed to enable the retarded learner to cope with the demands of our complex, modern society.

The examples included within this book integrate crucial subject matter content, the needs of the learner, and the demands of the society. Economic education is used to demonstrate the application of this theory to curriculum development.

The Curriculum Development Process

The organizational divisions within the process of curriculum development structure this and subsequent chapters in the book. In diagram form, the process appears in Figure 0–1.

This chapter reflects the overall pattern of curriculum development process (see Figure 0–1). The first step is analysis of the learner and the environment. Next comes content: choosing what to teach. Once a curriculum is developed, the teacher uses instructional theory to implement it.

Instructional Theory

Questions concerning the organization and implementation of curriculum goals surface in instructional issues. Throughout this book we use a *systems approach* to instruction. This approach has been applied to solve educational, technological, and human services problems for many years.

A systems approach to problem solving has the following characteristics.

1. It focuses on the *achievement of a stated goal* or purpose.
2. It attempts to *integrate the component* of the system to provide efficient operation.
3. It encourages *feedback* at critical points in the system's operation.
4. It provides for *modification or redesign* of the system when feedback or new developments warrant.

Instruction has been affected by the systems approach through new models of instruction based upon psychological principles. One

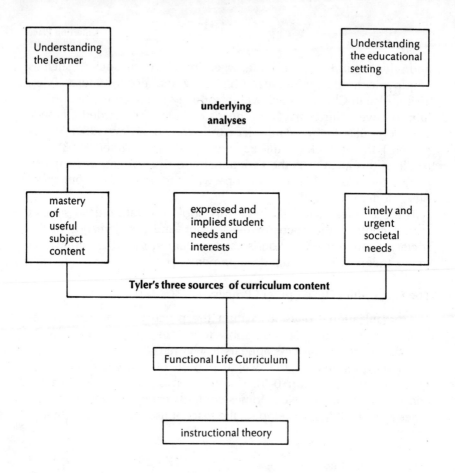

Figure 0–1   *The Curriculum development process**

* Drawn from *Basic Principles of Curriculum and Instruction* by Ralph Tyler. Chicago: University of Chicago Press, 1969. Used by permission.

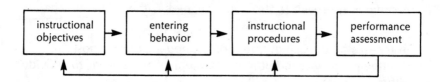

Figure 0–2   *The Glaser model of instruction**

* Reprinted from "Psychology and Instructional Technology" by R. Glaser, in *Training Research and Education*, Robert Glaser, editor. New York: Wiley, 1965, p. 6. Originally published in 1962 by the University of Pittsburgh Press. Used by permission.

notable example is the model created by psychologist Robert Glaser (see Figure 0–2). The Glaser model displays only the core elements in the instructional process. Our own conception, displayed in Figure 0–3, is somewhat more detailed, although it is obviously related to the Glaser model. Both are patterned as a flowchart of instruction.

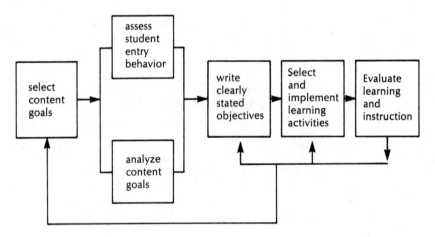

Figure 0–3   *Instructional process model*

A systems approach to instruction is effective with any student population. Applications of this approach have been used successfully for primary grades through university settings, with normal and exceptional students. Because the clarity of the instructional objectives, the integration of components, and the feedback combine to establish a structured, sequenced learning environment, the systems approach to instruction is most appropriate for mentally retarded learners. In Chapter 1, the importance of matching the learning environment to the needs of the mentally retarded is described.

The remaining chapters of the book are constructed around the components of the instructional process model. In Chapter 3, the curriculum development process is introduced and developed. Chapter 2 discusses how to assess the individual pupil. The process of goal setting is the central issue in Chapter 4. Chapters 5 and 6 focus on translating content goals into clearly stated objectives. Chapters 7 through 9 extend the process through activities and evaluation procedures.

Teaching mentally retarded learners is both an art and a science. The scientific aspects of teaching are reflected by the systems approach to curriculum and instructional planning. The interaction between the teacher and the students is the art. Because teaching is a human endeavor, a positive student-teacher relationship is potentially one of the most intimate and thus rewarding of all human relationships.

REFERENCES

Bruner, J. S. *The process of education.* New York: Vintage, 1963.

Glaser, R. Psychology and instructional technology. In R. Glaser (Ed.), *Training research and education.* New York: Wiley, 1965.

Rosenthal, R., & Jacobson, L. F. *Pygmalion in the classroom.* New York: Holt, Rinehart & Winston, 1968.

Stratemeyer, F., Forkner, H. L., McKim, M., & Passow, A. H. *Developing a curriculum for modern living* (2nd ed.). New York: Columbia University Press, 1957.

Tyler, R. *Basic principles of curriculum development.* Chicago: University of Chicago Press, 1950.

The Development of
Retarded Learners

Viewing the Retarded Learner

The history of education and treatment of mentally retarded students is tarnished by societal attitudes toward them. One example of how these attitudes work in a school setting is the self-fulfilling prophecy, in this case that teachers' expectations affect how well retarded students learn. Although the work of Rosenthal and Jacobson (1968) has been criticized, our experience shows clearly that a teacher's negative expectations can be devastating for retarded students. Its effects are reflected in administrative decisions, curriculum development, teacher education, teacher attitudes, and school organization.

The practice of labeling children *mentally retarded* is derived from a medical model. This model begins with a diagnosis of a condition, thus implying that something is wrong with the child. The label pinpoints the child or the condition as the source of the problem. In the case of retardation, the child is called *retarded;* that condition is used to explain school failure.

Recently, there has been a departure from the medical model approach in studying retardation. Goffman (1963), Edgerton (1967), Farber (1968), and Mercer (1973) describe mental retardation as a social phenomenon. They have broadened our perspective on mental retardation; they view the retarded person as part of a larger social context. More recently, Taylor and Bogdan (1977) suggest a particular sociological approach, a phenomenological perspective, as still another way of understanding the retarded individual. As they state:

> From the phenomenological perspective, mental retardation, like beauty, is in the eyes of the beholder. The phenomenologist distinguishes between intellectual or neurological conditions and societal definitions of mental retardation. As a concept, mental retardation exists in our own minds, rather than in the minds of those so "labeled." (p. 194)

A phenomenological perspective on mental retardation has implications for both understanding and teaching retarded learners. It has implications for job training, employment, and residential alternatives within a community.

Another significant departure from previously held views of the retarded individual is the "developmental view." Based on the developmental model (Roos, 1974), this view maintains that mentally retarded persons are more like their nonretarded counterparts than not. They go through the same sequences of development, although at a slower rate, as all children. They can and do learn. Because their development proceeds more slowly than normally expected, it is important that teachers understand developmental stages. The teacher's adaptation of the developmental view, a belief that retarded children have the potential to learn, and a firm understanding of the relationship of growth and development to learning are essential prerequisites for creating appropriate education experiences for retarded learners.

This book is about the millions of children who have or will be labeled *mentally retarded*. It is about those children who frequently experience school failure. It addresses both the process and products of education for mildly and moderately retarded children in America's public schools.

What Is Mental Retardation?

Who are the children we call *mentally retarded?* Approximately 6,000,000 Americans will be labeled *mentally retarded* at some time in their lives, about 2% to 3% of the population of this country. Some will always need some degree of care and supervision. Others, perhaps 75% to 80% of all mentally retarded persons, will be able to lead relatively independent lives if professional educators meet their responsibility for educational program planning, implementation, and evaluation.

Mental retardation has been defined by many scholars from different perspectives, and it is important that we launch our discussion from a common viewpoint. The most widely used, current definition of mental retardation was written by Grossman (1973) and published by the American Association on Mental Deficiency. According to this definition:

> Mental Retardation refers to significantly subaverage general intellectual functioning existing concurrently with impairments in adaptive behavior and manifested during the developmental period. (p. 11)

Mental retardation denotes a level of behavior without reference to cause. As a result, it does not distinguish between retardation associated with psychosocial or environmental influences and retardation associated with biological deficits. *Mental retardation* describes current behavior; it does not imply a prediction of the person's future status.

Intellectual functioning may be assessed by one or more of the standardized tests (typically the Stanford-Binet [Terman & Merrill, 1973] or Wechsler Intelligence Scale for Children [Wechsler, 1974]). *Significantly subaverage* refers to performance that is two or more standard deviations from the mean or average of that test. However, despite current practice, a low IQ is not sufficient to make the diagnosis of mental retardation.

The upper age limit of the developmental period is placed at 18 years and distinguishes mental retardation from other disorders of human behavior.

Adaptive behavior is defined as the effectiveness with which the standards of personal independence and social responsibility expected of an age and cultural group are met. Because these expectations vary for different age groups and cultures, deficits in adaptive behavior will also vary. These developmental expectations include the following areas.

During infancy and early childhood in:
1. Sensorimotor development,
2. Communication skills, including speech and language,
3. Self-help skills,
4. Social development—the ability to interact with others.
During childhood and early adolescence in:
5. Application of basic academic skills in daily life activities,
6. Application of appropriate reasoning and judgment in mastery of the environment,
7. Social skills—participation in group activities and interpersonal relationships.
During late adolescence and adult life in:
8. Vocational and social responsibilities.

During infancy and early childhood, sensorimotor, communication, self-help, and socialization skills ordinarily develop sequentially as the child matures. Delays in the acquisition of these skills represent potential adaptive behavior deficiencies associated with mental retardation. Of course, there can be developmental delays not associated with mental retardation such as those in children with sensory impairment. For instance, most deaf children have severe language delays. Only if developmental lags are also associated with intellectual impairment is mental retardation present.

Note that the definition does not involve predictions or potential intellectual level. Instead, this current definition is concerned with intellectual performance as representative of the current level of behavioral functioning.

The 1973 AAMD definition departs from previous definitions in the uppermost IQ score classified as mentally retarded. Heber (1959) defined subaverage intellectual functioning as one standard deviation below the mean. The 1973 definition places the retardation boundary at two standard deviations below the mean (see Figure 1–1).

Assessments of intelligence involve the administration of one or more standardized tests by a qualified clinician. After an IQ score is obtained, the individual is assigned to a level of retardation. The level assigned depends only upon IQ score (see Figure 1–1).

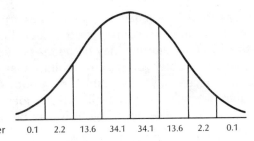

percentage of cases under each portion of curve	0.1	2.2	13.6	34.1	34.1	13.6	2.2	0.1
standard deviations								
	−3	−2	−1	0	+1	+2	+3	
Wechsler deviation IQ scores	55	70	85	100	115	130	145	
Stanford-Binet deviation IQ scores								
	52	68	84	100	116	132	148	
Percentiles (rounded)	0.1	2	16	50	84	98	99.9	

Figure 1–1   *The theoretical normal probability curve of intelligence test scores showing the distribution of deviation IQ scores and percentages of cases under each segment of the curve*

From *Exceptional Children in the Schools,* Second Edition, edited by Lloyd Dunn, p. 66. Copyright © 1963, 1973 by Holt, Rinehart and Winston, Inc. Reprinted by permission of Holt, Rinehart and Winston.

The scores are translated into intelligence quotient (IQ) values. The IQs correspond to levels of retardation as established by the AAMD (see Table 1–1).

Mild retardation is roughly equivalent to the educational term *educable; moderate retardation* includes those individuals who are likely to fall into the educational category *trainable; severe retardation* includes individuals once termed *dependent retarded;* the

Table 1–1   *IQ ranges and levels of mental retardation*

Level   *Obtained intelligence quotient*

	Stanford-Binet* Cattell	Wechsler Intelligence** Scales
Mild	67–52	69–55
Moderate	51–36	54–40
Severe	35–20	39–25
Profound	19 and below	24 and below

*The standard deviation on the Stanford-Binet (Terman & Merrill, 1973) and Cattell (1960) scales is 16 points.

**The standard deviation on the Wechsler (1974) scales is 15 points.

profound retardation level is sometimes called *life-support level.* These terms are, of course, neither absolute nor static. A child classified *mildly retarded* may be better served in a "trainable" class than an "educable" one; some children at the severe level may function successfully in a "trainable" group; children may move up or down between categories. The level does not necessarily dictate the particular service needed, but it may be helpful as one criterion in planning needed services.

To be considered mentally retarded, a person must have both subaverage measured intellectual functioning and impairment in adaptive behavior. Unfortunately, accurate measurements of adaptive behavior are difficult to obtain for several reasons. Adaptive behavior involves what a person does every day, in his or her normal surroundings. Therefore, measures of adaptive behavior cannot be administered directly in offices, but must be determined on the basis of several observations in many places over considerable periods of time. Rating scales and interview data often are used to provide data for assessing adaptive behavior. These measures consistently show lower reliability than standardized intelligence and achievement tests. For example, two people interviewed may give different evaluations on self-help skills for the same child. And one rating scale may indicate higher functioning levels than another because of the scale's wording or format. Some scales provide an overall general index (the Vineland Social Maturity Scale Social Quotient, Doll, 1947); others provide separate data for each of several areas (the AAMD Adaptive Behavior Domains, Nihira, Foster, Shellhaas, & Leland, 1969). To be as thorough as possible, both a published scale and clinical judgments should be used to evaluate adaptive behavior. The selection of techniques and instruments will be determined by the proposed use of the data. To determine a child's training level, a general combined index is undoubtedly less useful than indicators of the level of functioning in specific areas. To group individuals for statistical purposes, a wiser choice would be to use a standardized measure for better accuracy and communication of the results.

Despite these difficulties, assessment of adaptive behavior is indispensable if mental retardation is to be validly identified. Table 1–2 describes the highest levels of adaptive behavior that can be expected for different ages within the classifications of mental retardation. These behavioral descriptions will vary because they are expectations and not firm predictions. The behaviors, which are classified into subject areas, can be both directly and indirectly related to formal education.

Table 1–2   *Illustrations of highest level of adaptive behavior by age levels*

Level	Age	Illustrations
Profound*	3 years and above	*Independent functioning:* Drinks from cup with help; cooperates by opening mouth for feeding. *Physical:* Sits unsupported or pulls self upright momentarily; reaches for objects; has good thumb-finger grasp; manipulates objects (e.g., plays with shoes or feet). *Communication:* Imitates sounds, laughs or smiles back (says "da-da," "buh-buh" responsively); no effective speech; may communicate in sounds and/or gestures; responds to gestures and/or signs. *Social:* Indicates knowing familiar persons and interacts nonverbally with them.
Severe Profound	3 years 6 years and above	*Independent functioning:* Attempts finger feeding; cooperates with dressing, bathing, and with toilet training; may remove clothing (e.g., socks) but not as act of undressing as for bath or bed. *Physical:* Stands alone or may walk unsteadily or with help; coordinates eye-hand movements. *Communication:* One or two words (e.g., "Mama," "ball") but predominantly undifferentiated vocalizations. *Social:* May respond to others in predictable fashion; communicates needs by gestures and noises or pointing; plays "patty-cake" or plays imitatively with interaction; or occupies self alone with toys few minutes.
Moderate Severe Profound	3 years 6 years 9 years and above	*Independent functioning:* Tries to feed self with spoon; considerable spilling; removes socks, pants; cooperates in bathing; may indicate wet pants; cooperates at toilet. *Physical:* Walks alone steadily; can

Level	Age	Illustrations
		pass ball or objects to others; may run and climb steps with help. *Communication:* May use four to six words; may communicate many gestures (e.g., pointing). *Social:* Plays with others for short periods, often as parallel play or under direction; recognizes others and may show preference for some persons over others.
Mild Moderate Severe Profound	3 years 6 years 9 years 12 years and above	*Independent functioning:* Feeds self with spoon (cereals, soft foods) with considerable spilling or messiness; drinks unassisted; can pull off clothing and put on some (socks, underclothes, boxer pants, dress); tries to help with bath or hand washing but still needs considerable help; indicates toilet accident and may indicate toilet need. *Physical:* May climb up and down stairs but not alternating feet; may run and jump, may balance briefly on one foot; can pass ball to others; transfers objects; may do simple form-board puzzles without aid. *Communication:* May speak in two- or three-word sentences ("Daddy go work"); name simple common objects ("boy," "car," "ice cream," "hat"); understands simple directions ("put the shoe on your foot," "sit here," "get your coat"); knows people by name. (If nonverbal, may use many gestures to convey needs or other information.) *Social:* May interact with others in simple play activities, usually with only one or two others unless guided into group activity; has preference for some persons over others.
Mild Moderate Severe Profound	6 years 9 years 12 years and above 15 years and above	*Independent functioning:* Feeds self with spoon or fork, may spill some; puts on clothing but needs help with small buttons and jacket

zippers; tries to bathe self but needs help; can wash and dry hands but not very efficiently; partially toilet trained but may have accidents.

Physical: May hop or skip; may climb steps with alternating feet; rides tricycle (or bicycle over 8 years); may climb trees or jungle gym; play dance games; may throw ball and hit target.

Communication: May have speaking vocabulary of over 300 words and use some grammatically correct sentences; if nonverbal, may use many gestures to communicate needs; understands simple verbal communications including directions and questions ("put it on the shelf," "Where do you live?"); some speech may be indistinct sometimes; may recognize advertising words and signs ("ice cream," "Stop," "Exit," "Men," "Ladies"); relates experiences in simple language.

Social: Participates in group activities and simple group games; interacts with others in simple play ("store," "house") and expressive activities (art and dance).

Level	Age
Mild	9 years
Moderate	12 years
Severe	15 years and older

Independent functioning: Feeds self adequately with spoon and fork; can butter bread (needs help with cutting meat); can put on clothes and can button and zipper clothes; may tie shoes; bathes self with supervision; is toilet trained; washes face and hands without help.

Physical: Can run, skip, hop, dance; uses skates or sled or jump rope; can go up and down stairs alternating feet; can throw ball to hit target.

Communication: May communicate in complex sentences; speech is generally clear and distinct; understands complex verbal communication including words such as

Level	Age	Illustrations
		"because" and "but"; recognizes signs, words, but does not read prose materials with comprehension. *Social:* May participate in group activities spontaneously; may engage in simple competitive exercise games (dodgeball, tag, races); may have friendship choices maintained over weeks or months. *Economic activity:* May be sent on simple errands and make simple purchases with a note; realizes money has value but does not know how to use it (except in coin machines). *Occupation:* May prepare simple foods (sandwiches); can help with simple household tasks (bedmaking, sweeping, vacuuming); can set and clear table. *Self-direction:* May ask if there is "work" for him to do; may pay attention to task for 10 minutes or more; makes efforts to be dependable and carry out responsibility.
Mild Moderate	12 years 15 years and over	*Independent functioning:* Feeds, bathes, dresses self; may select daily clothing; may prepare easy foods (peanut butter sandwiches) for self or others; combs/brushes hair; may shampoo and roll up hair; may wash and/or iron and store own clothes. *Physical:* Good body control; good gross and fine motor coordination. *Communication:* May carry on simple conversation; uses complex sentences; recognizes words, may read sentences, ads, signs, and simple prose material with some comprehension. *Social:* May interact cooperatively and/or competitively with others. *Economic activity:* May be sent on shopping errand for several items

Level	Age	Illustrations
		without notes; makes minor purchases; adds coins to dollar with fair accuracy. *Occupation:* May do simple routine household chores (dusting, garbage, dishwashing); prepare simple foods that require mixing. *Self-direction:* May initiate most of own activities; attend to task 15 to 20 minutes (or more); may be conscientious in assuming much responsibility.
Mild**	15 years and adult	*Independent functioning:* Exercises care for personal grooming, feeding, bathing, toilet; may need health or personal care reminders; may need help in selection of purchase of clothing. *Physical:* Goes about home town (local neighborhood in city, campus at institution) with ease, but cannot go to other towns alone without aid; can use bicycle, skies, ice skates; uses trampoline or other equipment requiring good coordination. *Communication:* Communicates complex verbal concepts and understands them; carries on every-day conversation, but cannot discuss abstract or philosophical concepts; uses telephone and communicates in writing for simple letter writing or orders but does not write about abstractions or important current events. *Social:* Interacts cooperatively or competitively with others and initiates some group activities, primarily for social or recreational purposes; may belong to a local recreation group or church group, but not to civic organizations or groups of skilled persons (e.g., photography club, great books club, or kennel

club); enjoys recreation (e.g., bowl-
ing, dancing, TV, "checkers"), but
either does not enjoy or is not
competent at tennis, sailing, bridge,
piano playing, or other hobbies
requiring rapid or involved or complex planning and implementation.
Economic activity: Can be sent or go
to several shops to make purchases
(without a note to shopkeepers) to
purchase several items, can make
change correctly, but does not use
banking facilities; may earn living
but has difficulty handling money
without guidance.
Occupation: Can cook simple foods,
prepare simple meals; can perform
everyday household tasks (cleaning,
dusting, dishes, laundry); as adult
can engage in semiskilled or simple
skilled job.
Self-direction: Initiates most of own
activity; will pay attention to task
for at least 15 to 20 minutes;
conscious about work and assumes
much responsibility but needs
guidance for tasks with responsibility
for major tasks (health care, care of
others, complicated occupational
activity.)

*Note: All behaviors at greater degree of impairment would also indicate PRO-
FOUND deficit in Adaptive Behavior for persons 3 years of age or above.

**Note: Individuals who routinely perform at higher levels of competence than
illustrated in this pattern should NOT be considered as deficient in adaptive behavior. Since, by definition, an individual is not retarded unless he shows significant
deficit in both measured intelligence and in adaptive behavior, those individuals
who function at higher levels than illustrated here cannot be considered retarded.

From *Manual on Terminology and Classification in Mental Retardation,* by H. J.
Grossman. American Association on Mental Deficiency Special Publication No. 2,
1973 Revision. Pp. 25–33. Used with permission.

Scheerenberger (1964) has suggested a different classification system for retarded individuals that uses educational expectations as
the parameter. As illustrated by Chinn, Drew, and Logan (1975),
Scheerenberger's approach (see Table 1–3) is a statement of predicted achievement and can be used as a guide for curriculum development.

Table 1–3 *Classification by educational expectation*

Level	Approximate IQ range*	Educational expectations
Dull-normal	IQ 75 or 80 to 90	Capable of competing in school in most areas except in the strictly academic areas where performance is below average. Social adjustment which is not noticeably difficult from the larger population although in the lower segment of adequate adjustment. Occupational performance satisfactory in nontechnical areas, with total self-support highly probable.
Educable	IQ 50 to 75 or 80	Second- to fifth-grade achievement in school academic areas. Social adjustment that will permit some degree of independence in the community. Occupational sufficiency that will permit partial or total support when an adult.
Trainable	IQ 20 to 49	Learning primarily in the areas of self-help skills; very limited achievement in areas considered academic. Social adjustment usually limited to home and closely surrounding areas. Occupational performance primarily in sheltered workshop or an institutional setting.
Custodial	IQ below 20	Usually unable to achieve even sufficient skills to care for basic needs. Will usually require nearly total care and supervision for duration of lifetime.

*IQ ranges represent approximate ranges, which vary to some degree depending on the source of data consulted.

From *Mental Retardation: A Life Cycle Approach*, by P. C. Chinn, C. J. Drew, and D. R. Logan. St. Louis: C. V. Mosby, 1975. Used by permission.

This class-constructed collage illustrates social studies concepts.

Both the Grossman and the Scheerenberger classifications combine levels of predicted competency and real-life situations, in and out of school. Analyzing the skills from both sources reveals the importance of education in decreasing the effects of impaired adaptive behavior. But educating for competence in mentally retarded persons has cognitive as well as adaptive behavioral goals. Competence must be measured both by academic achievement and by high levels of adaptive behavior. Thus curriculum development and learning experiences must be directed toward two objectives. Academic achievement alone is not sufficient. The mentally retarded person's ability to use the knowledge he has acquired and to integrate it in his work, social, and personal life is the true test of his school success.

Causes of Mental Retardation

Mental retardation can be attributed to both social-environmental and the biological causes. Although the specific role of environmental factors is less clear than are biological ones, significant data support that both these factors affect intellectual development.

Biological factors. Some instances of biological mental retardation are genetically determined at the time of conception. The results of these chromosomal aberrations manifest themselves in conditions such as Down's syndrome, Turner's syndrome, and Kleinfelter's syndrome. Other biologic causes of mental retardation can be found in prenatal conditions such as drug ingestions and maternal infection during the first trimester of pregnancy. Several studies have attempted to analyze the relationship between low birth weight and gestational age with later developmental delays. For example, Rubin, Rosenblatt, and Balow (1973) report a study on infants born at the University of Minnesota Hospital between 1960 and 1964. Controlling for socioeconomic status, they found that low birth-weight, preterm males and low birth-weight, full-term infants of both sexes constitute a *high-risk* group of children in terms of eventually developing difficulties in school.

The biological effects of poverty on the developing fetus, newborn infants, and children are serious. Prematurity, poor maternal nutrition, lack of adequate prenatal care, and vulnerability to lead poisoning are found more frequently among lower socioeconomic groups. These children are considered to be in the *at risk* or *high risk* categories associated with mental retardation.

Social-environmental factors. In addition to these biological conditions, there are several socio-environmental conditions generally recognized as directly affecting the early development of children. The work of D.O. Hebb (1949) provides a theoretical framework for analyzing these effects. According to Hebb, the human brain is made up of genetically determined sensorimotor tissue and environmentally stimulated associative tissue, which is nurtured and developed particularly in the first 2 years of life. The sensorimotor tissue provides for the motor, reflexive, and sensory functions of the body; associative tissue provides for cognitive functioning. The extent to which both the sensorimotor and associative tissue have developed determines an individual's future intellectual capacity.

The largest subgroup, about two-thirds of the total retarded population, are labeled *cultural-familial mentally retarded.* This diagnostic term describes individuals who have no organic problems that could account for their mental retardation and who come from families where at least one other sibling and one or both parents are similarly affected (MacMillan, 1977). This degree of retardation is usually mild, with IQ scores between 50 and 75, although incidences of moderate retardation have been included in this group. The specific cause of this form of retardation is unknown, but it

25

appears to be the result of a combination of heredity and extremely adverse environmental conditions. Parental inadequacy often accounts for the presence of cultural deprivation, although it is not usually severe enough to warrant the conclusion that the retardation is caused solely by the lack of stimulation. In those cases where the deprivation is severe, a child is classified as a cultural-familial retardate if there is a family history of intellectual subnormality.

The following case description exemplifies the situation.

> The "R" family gives a . . . picture of the multiproblem home associated with cultural-familial mental retardation but here is a mother who, in spite of her limitations, is devoted to her children. There is a question as to whether she can effectively meet their needs but there is no doubt of her sustained interest and concern for their well-being.
>
> There are three children, two girls and a boy, and both girls are residents of an institution for the retarded. There appears to be retardation in parents, the father's siblings, and the father's mother. Amid all of this mental subnormality, rural isolation, and deprivation, one child, the boy, has managed to achieve normal if not above-average ability.
>
> Troy, age 22, is a biology major in a college in a neighboring state. He understands the problems of his parents and siblings and serves as a liaison person between the family and the social agencies with which they've been involved. While still living at home with his mother, Troy had attended a community college. He wanted to continue his education, but with no 4-year college within commuting distance he feared the impact that his departure would have on the home. Troy finally decided that he must try to build a life for himself and he did leave home to attend college though the institution is not too far from his home.
>
> Emma, age 19, with tested IQ ranging from 46 to 66, has been in an institution for the retarded since age 11. She repeated first grade in a rural school where she was described as restless, having difficulty in concentrating, excessively demanding of the teacher's attention, and not getting along well with classmates. Various kinds of nonsexual aggressive behavior were displayed toward boys in her class and she is seen as immature, having a childlike self-image, and excessively seeking of adult attention. She has not done well in a program that prepares residents for community return but eventually she'll return home. She wants to live with her mother and her mother is anxious to have her back.
>
> Teresa, age 17, with tested IQ ranging from 35 to 45, was institutionalized with Emma when Teresa was 9 years old. She also had much difficulty in school—the description of her behavior is almost identical to that of her older sister and, in the absence of a special program, she too was removed from school. Some

106186

sense of her degree of immaturity and lack of readiness for school is gained by realizing that at the time of her entry into first grade, her mental age was surely less than 3 years. In effect, a child with the mental and emotional development of a 2- to 3-year-old was placed in a group setting appropriate to 6-year-olds. It is not surprising that she couldn't cope with it and was seen as disruptive. At the institution, Teresa is seen as a fairly attractive and shy girl who gets along well with others. Like her sister, Emma, she is in an "exit cottage" program from which community return is the next step. For her this will involve temporary residence in a group home and work training experience in a sheltered workshop. She is capable of employment in repetitive unskilled work but community living without some supervision will always be precarious.

Mr. R., age 44, attended school to the third grade and has been variously employed in unskilled jobs. His mother and his siblings are retarded and a younger brother was in a correctional facility. Mr. R. is said to have whipped his children excessively and to have regularly beaten his wife. He has served a prison term for theft.

Mrs. R., age 38, has had only a fourth grade education, was married at age 15, is described as "very erratic" and has had at least one psychiatric hospitalization. In spite of her limitations, Mrs. R. represents the kind of socially impoverished parent who cares about her children. At the time that Emma and Teresa were institutionalized, Mrs. R. was viewed as genuinely interested in the children but unable to provide proper guidance and training for them. During the years of their institutionalization, the mother has maintained a continuous interest in them as shown in frequent correspondence and in a direct request to have the children back in her home. With son Troy now out of the house, the mother's recent strong wish to have her daughters back may be at least as much a function of her needs as theirs. . . .

The experience of these children and of their parents has been one of cultural isolation and deprivation. They were always very poor and lived in a remote rural area. They often lacked the barest necessities and were long known to social agencies. Both parents are seen as "very limited"; the father is said to have squandered his meager earnings and frequently left the family without food or adequate clothing. Some sense of the family's cultural isolation is that prior to the institutionalization of the girls, not only was the home without television, a not necessarily fatal flaw, but the children had never seen a movie. (Baroff, 1974, pp. 88–89)

Thus you can see that the causes of retardation are complex and hard to pinpoint. More to the point here is another question: What can be done to teach them effectively?

Personality Development

To be motivated to achieve their full potential, people must be understood and have opportunities to satisfy their basic needs. Without such opportunities, they will become frustrated and be unable to function fully. This is true for retarded as well as "normal" people.

Allport (1961) defines personality as "the dynamic organization within the individual of those psychological systems that determine his characteristic behavior and thought (p. 38).

According to Allport, the interaction of constitutional characteristics and environment determines personality. The personality development of a mentally retarded person follows the same principles and patterns as that of the ordinary person. However, a person who is retarded has unique problems and frequently excessive stress. Because society is geared for the person of average intelligence, a person who is retarded has more difficulty in daily life.

The parents' response to the retarded child can also be a source of stress. Studies indicate that the parents' attitudes toward their retarded child have a direct bearing on the child's development of a healthy self-concept. Therefore, it is important to help the parents and other significant persons in the young child's life to understand the dynamics of healthy personality development.

The retarded child may also find that a younger sibling can succeed at tasks with which he is as yet unsuccessful. A retarded child with language delays may withdraw or act in anger and frustration. All these factors affect the development of the personality. In most cases, it is not retarded mental development that leads to personality problems, but rather stress, frustration, and negative experiences. Retarded children, like their normal peers, need a variety of early positive experiences to gain a self-identity in relation to the world around him.

Unfortunately, however, the parents of retarded children are not always stable, healthy people who have the power to provide nurturing and supportive early experiences. The President's Panel on Mental Retardation stated:

> The majority of the mentally retarded are children of the more disadvantaged classes of our society. The extraordinarily heavy prevalence in certain deprived population groups suggests a major causative role, in some way not fully delineated, for adverse social, economic and cultural factors . . . Deprivation in childhood of opportunities for learning intellectual skills, childhood emotional disorders which interfere with learning or obscure motivational factors appear somehow to stunt young people intellectually during their developmental period. (President's Panel on Mental Retardation, 1962)

To provide a context for the effects of early home experiences on the growth of the young retarded child, we will now examine three different theories of human development: the psychodynamic view, the cognitive view, and the behavioral view. Each theory attempts to explain how children develop and mature.

Psychodynamic view of development

Psychoanalytic theory, spearheaded by Sigmund Freud, offers one explanation for the profound influences of the home and family upon the child's development during his early years. In fact, according to psychoanalytic theory the major influence upon the child during these years begins with the mother, followed by the father and other family members. And although child-rearing practices vary according to culture, the impact of significant persons in the life of a child holds across cultures.

Personality structure. Freud posited three distinct aspects of the personality that are interdependent, yet have their own specific characteristics. They are the *id,* the *ego,* and the *superego.*

The *id* is the central core of the personality of an individual. The id is the basis of all newborn instinctual drives; the source of all the psychic energy of the child and the basis of all sexual drives.

As the child develops, a second structure, the *ego,* emerges from the basic core of the id. This new dimension modifies id impulses and relates id forces to the outside world. The ego mediates the strong forces of the id with the reality imposed by the demands of the society. The ego has two major functions: (a) to gratify the impulses of the id, and (b) to induce the id to modify or inhibit impulses.

The weak ego of the infant becomes strengthened through interactions with the surrounding world. These interactions demand the delay of the gratification of id impulses. Because of undeveloped ego control, young children are frequently observed to be uncontrolled in their expression of id forces. There is, however, a balance that must be met between the delay of gratification, which results in healthy ego development, and severe deprivation which prevents the healthy development of intact ego structures. By the age of 5 or 6 years, the child begins to gain a sense of identity, to control more primitive personality forces, and to establish the components of the ego structure.

Ego development for the retarded child is frequently complicated by several factors. The retarded infant is usually slower in some aspects of development, such as social, mental, motor, and language development, than the average infant. The retarded child may be frustrated by his inability to meet the expectations established by the culture. The frustrations and anxiety of the mother who expectantly awaits the mastery of developmental benchmarks further complicates the child's frustrations. As a result, these mutual frustrations can potentially damage the mother-child relationship and impair the child's personality.

The third basic structure of the personality, the *superego,* is derived from the ego and begins to develop at about the age of 5 or 6 years. Primarily, this structure functions as a "watchdog" and is often called the individual's *conscience.* The superego incorporates the values of the culture and the society into the personality. The child learns what behaviors are acceptable, valued, and unacceptable from the way the parents respond to his actions. Through this process, the structure of the superego becomes formed, and the child internalizes parental and societal values.

Personality development of the retarded child. What, then, is the relationship of retarded mental development to the maturation of the personality? There is no reason to believe that mildly or moderately retarded children have id drives that are different from those of ordinary children. However, while there has been no evidence that the basic drives of retarded and nonretarded persons differ qualitatively, there may be quantitative differences of psychic energy or libido present in the id. Limited evidence suggests that retarded people have more energy than their nonretarded peers.

Ego development in retarded children follows the same patterns and requires the same supports as in ordinary children. However, retardation frequently has a significant effect on the process. For a child to develop a strong grasp of reality and of his place in the world, he must have adequate language skills. Because language develops slowly in the retarded, ego development is delayed. Even at maturity, the ego of the retarded is at a lower level than the average person's.

Because of their immature egos, it is difficult for many retarded children to delay gratification or to keep from expressing primary id drives. Children with immature egos may be subject to their own inner drives because of a limited ability to understand cause and effect relationships, to predict consequences, or to understand the needs of other persons in their environment. Although these children may choose to be aggressive and uncontrolled at times, the limits imposed by delayed development may make the mastery of societal demands difficult. However, this does not alter the child's desire for success or the desire to please the adults in the environment.

The immature ego structures of the mentally retarded child may also result in an overdependence on adults. This may result in dependence upon teacher attention before tasks are undertaken, prolonged separation anxiety, or demands for excessive attention during school or home activities.

The lack of a mature ego structure also prevents the mentally retarded child from gaining a sense of his own separateness from other people. For example, mentally retarded children sometimes cry when a classmate cries or act out when a peer is acting out.

The effects of retarded development are also evident in the structure of the superego. Even at maturity, the superegos of many mentally retarded people are immature. The immature superego results from the immature ego, out of which the superego has derived in addition to cognitive deficits that prevent more abstract levels of reasoning.

Everyone, included retarded children, wants to succeed, and to receive the rewards that accompany success. Most of us can meet our aspirations, at least in part, because we can set realistic goals that are within our capacity. Further complications for the mentally retarded child arise when they have aspiration levels, a function of the superego, that are higher than their capability. The mentally retarded child may have goals that are beyond reach and, thus, may not be achieved. As a consequence, the child's failures end in self-blame and lowered self-esteem. All children, of course, experience failures. However, the ability to deal with failure and to put it into proper perspective depends upon self-concept and upon the degree of success the child has experienced to counter the effects of failure. A healthy ego and superego enables a child to try again or persist, because remembered successes motivate continued striving toward success. These strivings, characteristic of healthy children, are frequently lacking in mentally retarded children and must be encouraged by supportive adults.

Mentally retarded children frequently experience more failure during their early years than their nonretarded peers. They may have delayed speech and language skills and, an immature ego that results in a lack of inhibition. They may take longer to learn the rules established by the home. In some cases, these children have pronounced behavior problems that result in repeated negative interactions with their parents.

One possible consequence of negative early experiences for young children, particularly unsatisfactory emotional experiences, is that the children avoid new learning situations, avoid attempts to cope with problems, and over time, begin to withdraw from active learning experiences. Some writers have described mentally retarded persons as being *rigid;* they tend to settle on one way of believing or engaging in an activity and continue to do it that particular way. Some retarded children have been known to perseverate on a task for weeks or even months and seem to refuse to move on to another task. Zigler (1966) has described personality characteristics of mentally retarded persons from a developmental perspective. He explains this rigidity as a fear of failure. Once they find a task at which they can succeed, they tend to repeat the task over and over again to experience success. The possibility of failure associated with a new task is very threatening; thus, new tasks are avoided, not because of the task, but because of the perceived potential failure.

The personality development of mentally retarded children, like their nonretarded peers, depends upon a supporting, nurturing environment both at home and at school. Theories of personality development serve as guides to understanding how children grow. There are obvious implications for the classroom. It is important to help the young child to gain ego strength, and develop a healthy self-concept. Successful classroom experiences can lead to an enhanced self-image. The teacher can help the child attempt new tasks by directing his attention to earlier successes; the teacher's support and encouragement can help the child to master the fear of failure.

The Cognitive-Developmental View

A second theory of child development focuses on cognitive development as a vital area for study and research. Jean Piaget, a Swiss psychologist, is a leader in this movement. His developmental theory deals with the process of intellectual development, focusing on how abstract thinking develops from its origins in the sensorimotor behaviors of infants to the logic used by adults. Piaget views intelligence as an adaptive process that spans a lifetime. There are three basic elements that are required to promote this adaptive process: (a) the genetic make-up of the child, (b) the environment, and (c) the experiences of the child. The child's active involvement with persons and objects in the environment nurtures the adaptive process, because intelligence is born of action. Learning is an active, not a passive activity.

Piaget describes two basic methods of adaptation: *assimilation* and *accommodation.* During assimilation, the child uses something in the environment and easily incorporates this new experience or new learning into his developing structures. During accommodation, the child interacts with the environment but is faced with new learnings that are not easily assimilated; his internal structures themselves must be altered several times. Thus, the child must act upon the new learning by operating on it, modifying it, or transforming it so that she can understand it. These modifications of existing structures as the result of new learnings are the essence of intelligence. The child constantly seeks equilibrium by striving for a balance between assimilation and accommodation. Thus, children seek activities that can be easily assimilated as well as those that require them to expand their present knowledge to again achieve a balance.

The cognitive-developmental view stresses the environment while acknowledging that the child's mental structures undergo self-growth.

> Development is dependent upon experience; practice does not necessarily accelerate it but lack of an environment suited to the stage of the learner will handicap it. Growth is marked by stages which occur in an inexorable sequence, each a necessary prelude to the next and absorbed into the next. The pace of growth will vary among children for both natural and cultural reasons. (Meyers & MacMillan, 1976)

According to Piaget (1952), every act of intelligence, from early sensorimotor through formal operations, presumes some type of underlying cognitive structure. The structures are described as stages that begin immediately at birth. The stages are fixed and hierarchical; the emergence of the second stage depends on the development of the first. Table 1–4 summarizes the stages.

Table 1–4   *Piaget's stages and substages of intellectual development*

Stage 1   *Sensorimotor period (Birth to 2 yr.)*
   Reflex—exercising the ready-made sensorimotor schema (0–1 mo.)
   Primary circular reactions (1–4 mo.)
   Secondary circular reactions (4–8 mo.)
    Intention
    "Motor Meaning"
    Incorporation of new objects into existing schemata
    Object permanence and construction of space
   Coordination of the secondary schemata (8–12 mo.)
    Intention and means-end relations
    Sign meaning
    Incorporation of new objects into existing schemata
    Object permanence and the construction of space
    Causality
   Tertiary circular reactions (12–18 mo.)
    Intention and means-end relations

> Object permanence, space, and time
> Causality
> Invention of new means through mental combinations (18–24 mo.)
>> Intention and means-end relations
>> Object permanence, space, and time
>> Causality

Stage 2   *Preoperational period (2–7 yr.)*
> Concreteness
> Irreversibility
> Egocentrism
> Language to express thought

Stage 3   *Concrete operations period (7–11 yr.)*
> Conservation of number
> Conservation of quantity weight and volume
> Composition of classes

Stage 4   *Formal operations period (11–15 years)*
> Operations on operations
> The real us—the possible

From *The Origins of Intellect: Piaget's Theory,* 2nd edition, by J. L. Phillips. San Francisco: W. H. Freeman, 1975. Used by permission.

Stage 1   Sensorimotor period.   Stage 1, the sensorimotor period, contains 6 substages. During substage 1, the intelligence of the infant is essentially characterized by the reflexes of sucking, grasping, and undifferentiated motor activities. During primary circular reactions, infants begin to repeat an action for its own sake. In secondary circular reactions, children accidentally repeat responses that provide new experiences. Children are interested in the results of their actions and swing, rub, or hit in order to obtain a desired result. During the fourth substage, the coordination of secondary schemata, children begin to play simple games, use verbal signs, and imitate others in the environment. In the fifth substage, tertiary circular reactions, children begin to experiment with objects. They move and shake them and become interested in their actions upon them. At this substage children begin to differentiate themselves from their environment. They begin to sense themselves as being separate from objects. It is this differentiation, during tertiary circular reactions, that Piaget describes as the beginning of true intelligence.

The primary characteristic of the sensorimotor stage is that children lack symbolic function. In other words, children are unable to internalize representations or visual images that represent objects or persons in their absence. Out of sight is literally out of mind to the child in the sensorimotor stage.

As structures develop that allow for symbolical representation, object permanence emerges for the child. For example, an object such as a penny may be placed in front of the child; if that object is hidden from view, the child will look for it because she now has a symbolic representation of the object. Object permanence, a basic substructure of the sensorimotor period, is the foundation for later affective and intellectual development. For example, when children have acquired object permanence, they realize that their mother's absence from view does not mean that she will never return.

Stage 2   Preoperational period.   The child has undergone an "intellectual revolution" during the substages of the sensorimotor period. The primary task during the preoperational period is the conquest of the symbol and the development of language, which expresses the international symbols or thought. Children begin to use words for images and to engage in primitive verbal exchanges. Further, socialization allows children to use their newly acquired words. Through symbolic play or deferred imitation, children re-create situations such as dress-up, playing school or house, and having tea parties. Children at this stage learn by role practice and through imitation. At this stage, however, there are important qualitative as well as quantitative differences between the child's thought and the logical thought of adulthood. For example, preoperational children believe anything that moves is alive, including toy animals and other objects. Also, they want to know why everything is what it is and how it is, because they believe that all things have a concrete and specific purpose. The preoperational child is unable to make a general rule and apply it in other situations. Perceptual dominance characterizes his thinking. Without the ability to synthesize bits of data to form concepts, things are exactly as they look, sound, or feel. The most significant aspect of this child's thinking is called *egocentrism*. Children see themselves as the center and are unable to take the perspective of another individual. This egocentrism is the result of an intellectual immaturity.

Preoperational children are unable to perform conservation tasks. Their thinking is dominated by perception with the inability to hold quantitative concepts constant. For example, if a 4-year-old child is shown two clay balls of equal size and shape, he will agree that they have the same amount. When one ball is elongated into a sausage shape, he will then say they have different amounts, because he is unable to hold the amount "constant" when the shape changes. Also, the child is unable to classify multiple dimensions, because attention can be focused on only one dimension at a time. These

35

characteristics have educational implications that we shall discuss later.

Stage 3   Concrete operational period.   The third stage of development conceived by Piaget is concrete operational thought. Children can now overcome perceptional dominance and develop concepts. In this stage, children can reverse the order in their thinking. They have developed a grasp of cause and effect relationships. For example, children can conserve weight, quantity, and number and use language to express these concepts.

Stage 4   Formal operations.   During this stage, the child uses formal logic and is able to use more abstract thought processes. Few, if any, retarded people are known to have reached this level of cognitive development.

Application of Piaget's theory to the mentally retarded learner. The diagnostic tools and techniques devised by Piaget to explore and analyze cognitive developmental processes are unique and distinctive. They allow the experimenter to gain insights into children's thinking. The most important aspect of Piaget's theory is the fixed sequence of intellectual stages, especially the *order* of stages, which is not a function of age. It is reasonable, therefore, to use the Piagetian stage model in research with children who are developing at a rate slower than normally expected. The investigator focuses on the characteristics of the thinking involved in problem solving, rather than right or wrong responses. The problem-solving abilities of the child indicate his level of cognitive development and sophistication of thought.

Although Piaget does not center his theory on individual differences or mental retardation per se, his ideas have caused something of a minor revolution in the field of mental retardation. Piaget's orientation involves understanding a retarded individual in terms of his cognitive development, rather than in terms of his deficiencies and inadequacies. This positive view encourages you to look at what retarded children are rather than what they are not; what they know rather than what they do not know.

Inhelder (1968) relates Piaget's theory to the development of retarded persons. She found that Piaget's stages are the same for mentally retarded children, although they pass through them at a slower rate. The chronological divisions established for nonretarded persons can be adjusted. The ultimate stage of cognitive development achieved by a mentally retarded individual is a function of his degree of retardation (Inhelder, 1968). Inhelder suggested the following scheme for viewing the ultimate developmental level with the classification level:

1. Severely and profoundly retarded: fixated at the sensorimotor stage
2. Moderately retarded: fixated at the preoperational stage
3. Mildly retarded: fixated at the concrete operations stage

Using the theory in the classroom. Much of the research in this area indicates that mentally retarded children may be less able to express their thoughts verbally than nonretarded learners. Thus, it is important for teachers to be sure that questions are appropriately stated and fully understood by the retarded child.

The cognitive-developmental view implies the idea of readiness to learn. Therefore, tasks must be selected for their appropriateness to the child's level of development. Learning experiences should be active so that they let children engage in the physical manipulation of materials. While curriculum should match content with appropriate grade level, it should also include social as well as cognitive activities.

The application of Piaget's theory to curriculum planning and instruction for mentally retarded children and adults holds promise for enhancing their learning. Many researchers (Klein & Safford, 1976, 1977; Stephens & McLaughlin, 1974) have studied the thinking of mentally retarded individuals using Piaget's theory; their work has provided useful insights into the cognitive-developmental aspects of mental retardation and its implications for educational planning.

Operant Conditioning and Behavioral Theory

Operant conditioning evolved from the early work of B. F. Skinner (1938), who shaped and modified the behavior of laboratory animals. *Behavioral therapy, behavior modification,* and *applied behavior analysis* are terms commonly associated with Skinner's operant conditioning.

Operant conditioning has been used in many studies, and the quality and quantity of this research has made it one of the most widely applied techniques for teaching mentally retarded persons. The following explanation more clearly defines Skinner's theory.

Operant conditioning is loosely defined as an operation whereby the probability or rate of a response is increased by the contingent presentation of a reinforcing stimulus. Behavior, which is both

> observable and measurable, is viewed as a product of its conse-
> quences in that its probability of occurrence, or response strength,
> is directly altered and maintained by the schedule or pattern with
> which reinforcing consequences are made available. (Mercer &
> Snell, 1977, p. 258).

Skinner proposed two types of responses, *operant* and *respondent*. Respondent behavior is present at birth and is unlearned. Holland and Skinner (1961) equate respondent behavior with reflexes. They present, as an example, the reflex response of the knee jerking when it is tapped with a mallet. The reaction is always the same, because a person has no control over this response.

Operant responses are learned and are a function of the consequences, not the antecedents of a behavior. By carefully selecting and controlling the consequences of certain behaviors and by reinforcing or punishing these behaviors, you can operantly condition a response to recur or to be extinguished.

Operant reinforcement is concerned with positive and negative reinforcers. Both types of reinforcement theoretically increase the probability of eliciting a recurring response. Punishment, on the other hand, decreases the probability of a response recurring. Table 1–5 outlines the effects of various consequences on operant behavior.

To further clarify the probability of response of positive and negative reinforcers, reinforcers are defined by their effect:

> It is not correct to say that operant reinforcement "strengthens
> the response that precedes it." The response has already occurred
> and cannot be changed. What is changed is the future probability
> of responses in the same class. It is the operant as a class of be-
> havior, rather than the response as a particular instance, which is
> conditioned. . . . Instead of saying a man behaves because of the
> consequences which are to follow his behavior, we simply say that
> he behaves because of the consequences which have followed
> similar behavior in the past. That is of course, the Law of Effect or
> operant conditioning. (Skinner, 1953, p. 87)

In other words, if a person is rewarded for doing something, he is more likely to do it again. The reward may take the form of the presentation of something pleasant (money, stars, a hug) or the removal of something unpleasant. In behavioral terminology, these two classes of consequences are called positive and negative reinforcers.

Reinforcers are generally grouped into primary and secondary reinforcers. *Primary reinforcers* include basic human needs such as food and water. *Secondary reinforcers* take many shapes and include verbal praise, toys, and physical contact. *Interim reinforcers,* which are secondary reinforcers, include tokens, checks, and contracts. In teaching and training moderately, severely, and profoundly retarded individuals, primary reinforcers have been used successfully. For example, the objective of a study done by Heindziak, Maurer, and Watson (1965) was to toilet train 29 severely retarded boys in an institutional setting. During a 27-day period, the operant conditioning group (Group 1) received candy, dispensed by a machine, contingent upon the use of the toilet for elimination. In addition, subjects were placed on the toilet every 2 hours or when the need was apparent. The conventional group (Group 2) received similar treatment but without the use of contingent primary reinforcements. Group 1 showed a significant increase in use of the bathroom, while Group 2 showed no significant increase. Similar studies using primary reinforcers for toilet training can be found in Kimbrell, Luckey, Barbuto, and Love (1967); Giles and Wolf (1966); and Azrin and Foxx (1971).

Punishment has been widely used to control certain behaviors of retarded individuals. The use of punishment as a technique is almost always employed as a last resort. The behaviors of some severely retarded patients may be so dangerous that punishment is the only tool for behavioral change. With profoundly retarded adults, Vukelich and Hake (1971) used time-out (restraint in a chair) to reduce aggressive attacks on others; however, they also gave positive reinforcement for all nonaggressive behaviors. Clark, Rowbury, Baer, and Baer (1973) also used time-out procedures to reduce attacks on other people from a moderately retarded 8-year-old boy. While most punishment techniques are useful only under controlled, clinical situations, time-out has been used extensively with much success in public school classrooms. It can take many forms, ranging from placing a child in a quiet corner of the classroom to isolation or total exclusion from the classroom environment. Unfortunately, punishment is often considered synonymous with behavior modification; it is not. Such misinterpretations have brought negative publicity to the use of operant conditioning in the classroom. Many educators have read the results of these individually prescribed punishments, generalized the techniques to classroom populations, and subsequently banned the use of operant conditioning in their school districts.

During the 1960s, however, many behavioral techniques stressing positive reinforcements were begun in public and private school classrooms for educable mentally retarded learners. By looking at

Table 1-5 *The effects of various consequences on operant behavior*

| | *I. Consequence of the operant* | | *II. Future strength of the operant* |
Presented	*Removed, withdrawn*	*Withheld*	
Positive reinforcement occurs when a stimulus (positive reinforcer) which is added to the situation causes a strengthening in the probability of the operant.			Increase in the operant strength or the probability of the response.
	Negative reinforcement occurs when a stimulus (negative reinforcer; aversive) which is removed from the situation causes a strengthening in the probability of the operant.		Increase in the operant strength or the probability of the response.

Punishment (aversive conditioning) occurs when an aversive stimulus or a negative reinforcer is presented following an operant.

Punishment (response cost) occurs when positive reinforcers are removed following an operant.

Immediate but temporary weakening of operant strength is due to elicitation of emotional responses incompatible with the operant and also results in

1. Aversive conditioning of response-produced stimuli
2. Negative reinforcement of escape behavior
3. Nonselective suppression of other responses

Extinction of an operant occurs when reinforcement is *no longer* forthcoming or withheld.

Gradual but permanent weakening of operant strength.

From C. D. Mercer and M. E. Snell. *Learning Theory Research in Mental Retardation: Implications for Teaching.* Columbus, Ohio: Charles E. Merrill, 1977, p. 261. Reprinted with permission.

environmental events and response patterns, teachers were effectively able to change children's behavior so that they could successfully participate in far more appropriate academic and social behaviors. By disregarding the cause of a behavior and working directly with the behavior itself, teachers were able to provide much quicker and, often more effective, remedial assistance to retarded students.

One of the most useful tools for teachers is token reinforcement. Tokens are made contingent upon specified behaviors. When the behavior has been appropriately emitted, a token is given to the subject. Tokens are usually saved and used to purchase some object or classroom privilege. Tokens may be used to strengthen both academic and social behaviors. Dalton, Rubino, and Hislop (1973) found that children rewarded with tokens made and maintained, one year later, a significant arithmetic gain over children receiving only praise. Iwata and Bailey (1974) found that tokens were effective in decreasing rule violations and off-task behavior. Another study found that when subjects were reinforced with tokens contingent upon daily performance in academic areas, the subjects displayed higher test performance than when reinforcement was noncontingent. (Tyler & Brown, 1968).

The use of behavioral techniques has also changed teachers. Some teachers have changed the ways they were responding to children. Instead of looking for inappropriate behaviors, and then punishing those behaviors, these teachers now tend to reinforce appropriate behaviors when they find a child performing appropriately. The conditioning processes, often debated by educators, are in fact helping both children and teachers to pinpoint behaviors, improve academic performance, and contribute to a much more profitable classroom atmosphere for all concerned.

Thus, operant conditioning, applied to teaching, contains many very useful techniques. *Applied behavior analysis* is being used to a great extent to identify and provide teaching strategies for academic and social behavior changes. It involves the direct observation of an individual's behavior, coupled with the continuous measurement of those behaviors. That is, the teacher sets a goal and then looks at where the learner is in relation to that goal. With these techniques, a teacher is able to arrange environmental events and plan teaching strategies appropriate to the retarded individual's needs.

Operant conditioning is seemingly more simplistic than the other theories discussed in this chapter; however, it is a complex process and should be used by individuals trained in its techniques. Misuse of operant conditioning can result in painful consequences for retarded learners. The work instituted by Skinner and other behaviorists for use with mentally retarded people has had a great impact on teachers and on the process of teaching. There are many questions still unanswered for retarded learners, but the success of operant techniques with this population provides the impetus for more research in this area.

Learning Characteristics of Mentally Retarded Students

As we have said, mentally retarded people are developing individuals who have a potential for growth, learning, and continued development. This "developmental model" (Roos, 1974) implies that the development of mentally retarded persons parallels that of nonretarded people, but at a slower rate. He also implies optimism about the potential learning of retarded students. Thus the custodial care that dominated the treatment and care of the retarded in the past has been replaced by a demand for individualized education and rehabilitation programs, focusing on selected skills. This new, positive viewpoint has characterized research and program development of the last 30 years. The optimism evolving from the belief that all people can change is a basic tenet of special education:

> The promise of special education was not a special curriculum, or special methods, or even special teachers. It was to demonstrate that each person can contribute to the larger society, that all people are valuable, that a human being is entitled to developmental opportunities; and that development is plastic. The gifts that this movement was to bestow were optimism and belief in the human ethos, charity and love for our brothers, and the conviction that our work is not to judge who can or cannot change, but rather to fulfill the hope that all people can change; each person can learn. (Blatt, 1977, p. 6)

The belief that people can change is supported by volumes of empirical data. Therefore, the question is no longer, "Can retarded children learn?" The issue that must be confronted is, "What can we learn from this body of accumulated knowledge that we can use to enhance the learning of children with special needs?"

Only recently have mentally retarded persons been subjects in research studies because they were interesting as a population to be studied in their own right. Historically, mentally retarded persons were employed as research subjects by theorists who were more interested in the universality of the learning processes than in the

As soon as Linda finishes her seatwork, she will join her friends at the Learning Center.

mentally retarded person as an individual (Robinson & Robinson, 1976). Recent learning research, however, reflecting a change in this practice, is now oriented toward the study of mentally retarded persons as learners (Mercer & Snell, 1977). One of the shortcomings of some research today is the tendency to view mentally retarded persons as a homogeneous group and even to generalize findings accordingly. In fact, mentally retarded people are a heterogenous group, and research findings can only be generalized with caution. Yet, some important insights into the learning characteristics of retarded learners are generally accepted.

Attention

Attention refers to the ability of an individual to focus on a specific stimulus. Much of the learning research with retarded subjects has been in discrimination learning involving discrimination tasks. In these tasks, a series of sets of two or three stimuli are presented to the subject. The subject is then asked to choose the correct one by using feedback from the correctness of choices made during previous trials. Obviously, attention is an important prerequisite in discrimination learning.

Zeaman and House (1963) studied the role of attention in discrimination tasks with mentally retarded subjects. First, they noted that the usual method of data plotting, which consists of averaging the performance of an entire group over a series of trials, hides individual performance characteristics. A traditional learning curve rises quickly at first, and then rises more slowly with continued trials. When they plotted the data on individual trials and constructed backward curves, a quite different picture became evident. The

Using both hands together correctly requires practice.

learning curves appeared to have two stages. At the first stage, the curves hovered near 50% for a varying number of trials. They then rose quickly to 100% (see Figure 1–2).

Based on this information, they posited a two-stage theory. The first stage can be interpreted as the attention stage and represents the subject's ability to attend to the task. During the second stage, the subject has identified the relevant stimulus, thus learning the

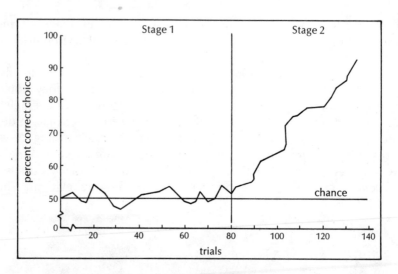

Figure 1–2 *Typical learning curve generated by a group of retardates performing discrimination tasks*

From "The Role of Attention in Retardate Discrimination Learning," by D. Zeaman and B. J. House, in *Handbook of Mental Deficiency,* edited by N. R. Ellis. New York: McGraw-Hill, 1963. Used by permission.

required discrimination task. Zeaman and House found that the difference between retarded children with mental ages (MA) of 2 to 4 years and those with MAs 4 to 6 years (mean chronological ages of both groups was 12 years) to be in the length of the initial portion of the curve. In other words, the lower the mental age of the individual, the longer the first stage of the process will be. However, when improvement begins at the second stage, it occurs rapidly for younger as well as older children. Among retarded subjects, Zeaman and House (1966) found that higher IQ was related to more efficient discrimination performance. Stage-two performance did not depend on mental age.

In a discrimination experiment, both relevant and irrelevant stimuli are present. The relevant dimensions of the stimuli provide information for the correct choice while the other dimensions provide no relevant information. After many discrimination task trials with retarded subjects, Zeaman and House (1966) concluded that retarded children enter the situation with a lower capacity to attend to the relevant, as opposed to the irrelevant, dimensions than non-retarded children.

The research conducted in the area of attention implies that learning deficits are the result of the retarded person's difficulty in attending to stimuli. However, once the retarded subjects have mastered the requirements of attending in the first stage, they are able to learn the requisite task.

Julie gives her full attention to writing details.

For classroom practice, these research findings can be used by the teacher to increase attention and to enhance learning for retarded students. The following guidelines are suggested:

1. Present stimuli that have clear and obvious dimensions.
2. Initial stimuli should vary on as few dimensions as possible (large circles, red and blue or large and small circles, all red).
3. Use of attention-gaining techniques will help the child attend to the desired dimensions. These techniques may include the use of verbal signals, gestures, or a combination of these cues.
4. A darkened room with a light focused on the stimuli may enhance the child's attention.
5. Placing work on a different colored background may enhance attention.
6. The use of audiovisual equipment such as an overhead projector or slide projector will focus the child's attention on the lighted stimuli in a darkened room.

7. The use of a bell or a buzzer may help focus the child's attention.
8. Only selected stimuli should be present. Remove all extraneous stimuli from the teaching situation.
9. Reward correct responses immediately.

Memory

Another important variable in the learning process is memory. Lerner (1971) has referred to *memory* as:

> The ability to store and retrieve upon demand previously experienced sensations and perceptions, even when the stimulus that originally evoked them is no longer present. (p. 299)

Two different aspects of memory—*short-term memory* (STM) and *long-term memory* (LTM)—have been studied. For mentally retarded subjects, Ellis (1963) found that STM was a problem area. This finding led to the development of the *stimulus trace theory* (Ellis, 1963), which states that an environmental stimulus generates a trace on the central nervous system. Lasting only a few seconds, this trace allows for a behavioral response. Ellis theorizes that mentally retarded individuals are deficient in the stimulus trace processes, which accounts for their STM difficulties. The intactness of the central nervous system influences the stimulus trace process; therefore, intelligence functions as a limiting factor in this process (Ellis, 1963). Ellis (1963, 1970) found that mentally retarded children are not deficient on LTM tasks.

Following this theoretical formulation, Ellis (1970) conducted extensive research on short-term memory in retarded subjects. His investigations led to the formulation of a *multiprocess model* to explain memory. In the multiprocess model, Ellis (1970) maintains that once an organism attends to a stimulus, the information is relayed to one of three memory storage mechanisms—*primary memory, secondary memory,* or *tertiary memory.* This relay process, termed a *rehearsal strategy,* transmits information from primary memory to secondary or tertiary memory. Furthermore, Ellis maintains that short-term memory varies directly with intelligence and may be a central factor in the intelligence inadequacy of the retarded.

Ellis (1970) found that the inadequate use of rehearsal strategies by retarded subjects may result from language deficiencies, which inhibit verbal rehearsal processes. Consequently, the impaired relay processes of rehearsal strategies may account for the memory deficits seen in retarded subjects.

Brown's (1974) work on rehearsal strategies supports Ellis'. Brown found that developmentally young children are deficient in the spontaneous use of rehearsal strategies. As a result, they do not spontaneously produce and use organizational strategies to purposely control memory.

In addition, mentally retarded children have been noted to make insufficient use of rehearsal strategies (Brown, 1974; Estes, 1970). Several studies, however, have shown that training in the use of

Evelyn types her work and then reads it to her classmates. She indeed has special skills.

rehearsal strategies is beneficial for retarded subjects (Brown, 1974). The results of these studies suggest the following guidelines for classroom practice:

1. Use labeling and verbal associations to enhance learning.
2. Repeat and practice skills to promote overlearning.
3. Break tasks down into small steps and present small amounts of information sequentially.
4. Select interesting and meaningful tasks so that the learner will remain involved in the learning process.
5. Teach the learner to use rehearsal strategies and practice them.
6. Provide an opportunity for the learner to practice skills in many contexts, through a multisensory approach and as an active process.
7. Use auditory and visual stimuli for rehearsal strategies.

Paired-Associate Learning

The ability to associate pairs such as people and places, pictures and objects, or words and pictures is called *paired-associate learning*. This ability has been found to be closely related to learning and school success.

In research involving paired-associate tasks, a series of pairs of stimuli are shown to the subject. The stimuli may be words, three-dimensional objects, or pictures. One item of each pair is designated as the stimulus item, and the remaining item is the response item. On the first trial, the subject is shown both items. On subsequent trials, he is shown the stimulus item first and is asked to indicate the response item before it is shown. The required task is to provide the appropriate response when given a stimulus. In many studies, the pairs are presented in a serial fashion; A is associated with B, B is associated with C, and the subject must make the association between A and C. For example, three lists of word pairs would be presented to the subject. List A might include a pair of words such as *apple–pear*. List B might include *pear–banana*, and list C might include *apple–banana*. Thus, the connection of A–C, *apple–banana*, can be learned as a paired-associate through the use of the facilitating word train.

Verbal mediation and mediation strategies appear to be central elements in the ability to do paired-associate learning tasks. Verbal mediation may be used by the subject so that verbalizations that are related to the stimuli result in the appropriate response.

Many paired-associate studies conducted with retarded subjects have addressed the use of mediational processes. Consisting of active strategies, these processes are used by subjects to establish connections between stimuli. Studies (Jensen & Rohwer, 1963; Milgram, 1967) indicate that experimentally developed mediators can be used by retarded children to facilitate paired-associate learning. For paired-associate tasks, as tasks become more difficult, verbal mediators play an increasingly important role. Without such mediation, mentally retarded persons are at a disadvantage and thus develop the language deficits frequently found in that population (Robinson & Robinson, 1976).

Other studies suggest that mentally retarded learners perform worse than their normal peers because they fail to use mediators, rather than because they are unable to use them. Although there are only speculative explanations for this failure, mentally retarded subjects tend not to be alert to cues that are available for solving problems.

Estes (1970) found that certain variables can enhance paired-associate learning with mentally retarded subjects. For example, the subject's familiarity with the stimulus-response pair enhances verbal mediation, and the meaningfulness of the material increases the effectiveness of learning.

The acquisition of paired-associate task skills is difficult for many retarded students. These skills are vitally important to school success. Practice in paired-associate learning can be provided by incorporating these tasks into subject areas. The following guidelines are suggested:

1. The content should be meaningful and interesting to the learner.
2. Materials and concepts should be concrete rather than abstract.
3. Begin with associations presently familiar to the child such as a mother's first name; dog or cat's name.
4. Reward successful approximations.
5. When necessary, provide the student with the verbal mediators until the student can use them independently.
6. Use a paired-associate teaching model in teaching reading. Choose pictures or objects that are familiar and interesting to the child; then pair the printed symbol or word with the object or picture.
7. Use a paired-associate training model to teach number concepts and written symbols. Give the child two objects, then the written symbol.
8. Use a paired-associate training model with food, clothing, and other innately interesting content.
9. Make the student aware of mediators that facilitate learning.
10. Actively involve the student by requiring that he move objects to symbol, outline word with his finger, etc.

Learning to Learn

Nonspecific transfer or general learning to learn has been called *transfer set* (Harlow, 1949). Learning through the use of transfer sets represents the effects of prior learning applied to current learning and has important consequences for learning ability. Research on the learning set of mentally retarded subjects has shown that the formation of the set to solve a particular problem proceeds more slowly than with normal children (Kaufman & Prehm, 1966).

Harter (1967) reported that the rate of learning-set formation improved with increases in both MA and IQ, which contributed independently to the improvement. She also found that higher MA subjects, who learn more rapidly, begin by using strategies that include training from previous trials. The young subjects, however, use strategies that are not related to previously presented information. The slower learning rates of retarded children seem to reflect that retarded children not only begin with inappropriate response sets but are also less responsive to the information the experimenter provides.

Zeaman and House (1963) described a reverse type of learning set, called a *failure set,* that has particular relevance for the retarded learner. Basic to all learning is the idea that a child's earliest attempts to succeed must be positively reinforced. However, mentally retarded children frequently find success difficult to attain in their daily lives. Thus, they may attempt problem solving and fail many times. Children who have such experiences are sometimes unable to solve easier problems rapidly (which they may have already mastered) due to this negative set.

There are some direct implications for classroom practice that emerge from research on learning-set formation:

1. Present learning tasks in order from easy to difficult.
2. Reward initial successful problem-solving attempts.
3. Present concrete, interesting tasks that are meaningful to the learner.
4. Facilitate the child's understanding of principles and rules governing problem-solving tasks.
5. Present many examples.
6. Use manipulative materials with clear dimensions.
7. Provide language for the child that describes the child's learning.

Problem Solving

Levine (1966) regards a discrimination learning problem as one involving a number of hypotheses, only one of which is correct. For example, stimuli may be presented that differ in form and color. The following hypotheses could be posed: blue is correct; red is correct; square is correct; circle is correct. After each trial, the child is given feedback until he has eliminated all but the correct hypothesis. Obviously, memory plays an important role in these discrimination tasks. Along with memory, the child's ability to attend to the relevant dimensions of a task will allow him to find the correct response.

Another aspect of problem solving can be tapped by asking questions intended to secure information. Eventually, this will enable the child to solve a problem. The old, standard game of *Twenty*

Questions is an example of a problem-solving task. In this game, the child may initially be told the possible solutions to the problem; then he is required to seek the necessary information by asking questions. For example, the child is shown a set of 16 items and told to discover, as quickly as possible, the item the teacher is thinking about. The teacher can only give "yes" or "no" answers to the questions. There are two possible sets of questions that the child may use—*constraint-seeking* or *hypothesis-testing* questions. According to Robinson and Robinson (1976), questions that refer to more than one alternative are constraint-seeking; questions that refer to an individual item are hypothesis-testing. Returning to the example of the 16 items, let's say that there are four cars, four boats, four kinds of fruit, and four animals. One possible constraint-seeking question would be, "Is it an animal?" If a negative response is given, this would eliminate four possibilities. In contrast, the hypothesis-testing question, "Is it a cat?" refers to a single item that would only eliminate one possibility at a time. Clearly, constraint-seeking questions are more efficient for solving problems.

Young children and mentally retarded children tend to perform poorly on this kind of problem-solving task because they ask hypothesis-testing questions. In part, this may be accounted for by their impulsive and frequently incorrect responses. As compared with reflective children, who tend to give slower, more accurate responses, Kagan (1965) found that impulsive children give quick and often incorrect responses. Mentally retarded children tend to be more impulsive in their responses, and thus often incorrect. Furthermore, retarded subjects fail to plan a strategy or course of action before making a response. These findings, too, have direct implications for classroom practice.

The ability to solve problems correctly and efficiently is essential for independent adulthood. This deficiency in mentally retarded persons necessitates the development of classroom activities that will enhance their problem-solving skills. Guidelines for classroom practice include the following:

1. Practice in constraint-seeking questions for problem-solving activities such as *Twenty Questions* and *Mystery Games*.
2. The level of difficulty of problem-solving experiences should be at the child's stage of development (activities in single, double, and triple classifications may be necessary).
3. Problem-solving tasks should focus on the development of a strategy or plan of action.

4. The child should design a plan of action in separate steps.
5. Students need practice in asking questions to solve problems; they need to evaluate the information gathered from the question.
6. Classroom procedures and teacher responses can modify incorrect impulsive responses.
7. Reward children for reflective responses that are correct.
8. Help students tolerate the ambiguity associated with solution-seeking.
9. Encourage students to present *new* solutions or ideas.
10. Use real-life situations or class problems as content for practice.

Concept Attainment

The world in which we live, both social and physical, contains many diverse stimuli. We use concepts to organize these diverse elements into a meaningful order:

> Concepts serve as crucial links between the total environment and the individual. They serve as tools man uses to organize and thereby adapt to his world. A concept functions as an organizer of the diverse stimuli which bombard an individual at every moment. The concept is an expression or a rule by which the diversity is brought together and thereby reduced. In this way, ambiguity is reduced and efficiency enhanced. Application of the concept means that there does not have to be relearning every time one encounters a member of that class. (Sigel, 1975, p. 67)

Piaget has described a series of stages that account for perceptual and cognitive stages of development. During the process of development, the child learns to identify an object and then learns to distinguish it from other objects (Inhelder & Piaget, 1964). He learns that the objects exist as separate entities and that they have permanence. He also learns that they share certain similarities and differences. Understanding the sameness and differences of objects is a crucial first step toward concept attainment.

Considerable research has been done with mentally retarded subjects to determine whether they follow the same process of concept attainment as their nonretarded peers. The evidence seems to support the conclusion that they do, indeed, follow the same pattern, although at a slower rate (Klein & Safford, 1977). From the work of Piaget, several implications for classroom practice can be inferred:

1. The child learns by doing. Develop learning experiences that allow the child to be an active participant in the classroom.

"Fishing with magnets," these children learn to understand the concept of magnetism.

2. Learning experiences that allow the child to manipulate concrete materials facilitate concept attainment.
3. Learning occurs in an ordered sequence; therefore, tasks should be presented in a step-by-step process.
4. Be sure the child has mastered each step before moving to the next higher step. For example, the child's comprehension of quantity comes before his comprehension of weight.
5. Recognize the logic characteristic of children, which may seem quite distorted to an adult. Observe the child's actions in order to understand his logic and meaning.
6. Expose children to a wide variety of experiences.
7. Encourage the use of verbal expression and, when required, provide the necessary language.
8. Encourage children to engage in activities with peers.
9. Provide a rich learning environment that contains interesting, manipulative materials.
10. Select tasks that are neither too easy nor too difficult but that interest and challenge the child.
11. The teacher can be viewed as the facilitator whose role is to organize a stimulating environment and facilitate the children's

interactions with it. Observations of children's performance is a rich data source.
12. Instructional experiences should be guided by the child's cognitive level.

Motivation

Motivation and personality directly affect learning. Some mentally retarded children have been characterized as uninterested in learning and unwilling to spend the effort to master difficult tasks. Although it is easy to cite the mentally retarded child as the source of the problem, such a conclusion is both inaccurate and misleading. It may avoid facing the real source of the difficulty. Each individual learns through a combination of ability and experience. By understanding the retarded person as a learner, reviewing the literature regarding the relationship of motivation to learning, and determining specific actions, the teacher can maintain the retarded student's interest in learning.

Even before coming to school, mentally retarded children have frequently experienced failure. This failure may result from the combination of the delayed achievement of developmental tasks such as walking and talking, and the responses of the family to this delayed development. Compounding this failure in the home, the effects of school failure have a negative impact on motivation and attitudes toward learning. Mentally retarded children, as all children, want to succeed and secure the approval of their teachers and parents. But because mentally retarded persons have a history of failure, they tend to put their energy into avoiding failure rather than striving to achieve success (Zigler, 1973). Retarded children may settle for a small degree of success and not aspire to goals that may be within their capabilities.

Children who have had much experience with failure tend to be ineffective in coping with it. Noonan and Barry (1967) call the behavior these children use to soften the failure *success deprivation*. Studies that employed retarded children and measured their response to failure found that these children react in one or a combination of the following ways: (a) learn to expect failure; (b) react passively and make stereotyped responses; (c) avoid situations that they perceive as potential failure; (d) become defensive and make excuses for their avoidance; (e) accept a low level of success (f) act out aggressively in response to a situation perceived as threatening failure; (g) respond impulsively and not expect success. None of these seven responses is desirable; successful school curricula will avoid them.

According to the social learning theory of Rotter (1954), the power of the expectancy of success or failure will determine an individual's behavior. Expanding this theory, Moss (1958) states simply that, if retarded children experience repeated failure, they will come to expect failure.

Group games encourage cooperation.

Competence, as delineated by White (1960), has relevance to the retarded students motivation for learning. White's biologically based definition includes concepts of fitness or ability. White characterizes childhood as a time when people engage in interesting and challenging experiences that enhance their abilities to deal effectively with the world. As children explore, question, manipulate, and investigate, they actively strive to master their environment. According to White, these behaviors are motivated by *effectance,* which is characterized by intense involvement, attention, and repeated trial and error. In children's play behavior, effectance can be seen when children experiment, master tasks, and then create new play situations. Behaviors motivated by effectance result in a heightened sense of

57

competence. As children gain competence in mastering new tasks, they also feel more competent. Repeated successes enhance children's feelings about themselves and their ability to cope with the complexities of the environment.

Because both objective and subjective competence play important roles in the child's view of himself as successful, Hunt (1961) discusses "the match," a problem critical to learning for young children. Matching the child to appropriately challenging tasks will optimize motivation and learning. Also supporting mastery as a desirable goal, Harter and Zigler (1974) found after reviewing much research that "the greatest pleasure is derived when a task is optimally challenging" (p. 169). And if such tasks are presented, intrinsic motivation is enhanced (Piaget, 1952). Montessori (1912) reported incidents of 3-year-old children working 40 or 50 minutes on a task in which they were interested. Thus, the time the child is willing to put into a task is determined to a large degree by the appropriateness of the task.

Although White did not deal with mentally retarded children per se, his work regarding the development of a sense of competence and effectance has implications for that population. In essence, White says that children who live in an environment that accepts their natural curiosities, and who engage in tasks of their own choosing develop a sense of competence. Conversely, if children are forced to do tasks for which they are not ready and at which they cannot succeed, their sense of competence will suffer.

When children fail, as many mentally retarded children often do, they begin to mistrust their own resources. Their faith in themselves is weakened, and they tend to look outside themselves for approval and support. Zigler (1966) describes the tendency of retarded persons to depend upon external cues for guides to action as *outer-directedness*. He suggests that a history of failure combined with a low mental age contribute to the retarded child's dependency on external cues. Yando and Zigler (1971) have found that, in experimental situations, the retarded children who were most deficient in requisite concepts tend to be the most outer-directed. These were the students who needed the most help, knew they needed it, and sought assistance.

In this finding, several factors have relevance to teaching mentally retarded children: (a) the child who seeks external cues may be unable to deal with the task presented; (b) tasks that are appropriate to the child's level of functioning enable him to work more independently; and (c) the child's response to a task is a combination of an active ability to do the task and a sense of competence (or the child's perceived ability) in regard to the task.

The role of the teacher looms large when assisting the child to be independent and to master effectance. Outer-directedness can be modified by presenting tasks carefully matched to the child's ability. The teacher can also facilitate independence by eliminating those teacher responses that reinforce dependence. She may be inadvertently maintaining dependence by responding to the child's request for help and attention each time it is sought. With appropriate tasks, the teacher can gradually wean the child from external cues in several ways. When the child asks for help, the teacher can look over and reinforce positive work. Next, she would suggest the child continue, and praise his work if he does so. Each time the child seeks cues, the teacher extends the time period between request and response, and praises the child for successful work. Positive feedback, when the child does not request it, can also support the child's growing independence. The exact formula that fosters

Feeling the sandpaper letters helps this student learn the letters in her name.

independence is a function of the needs of the individual child. Intermittent verbal, tactile, and visual responses are suggested.

Several implications from research related to motivation can serve as guidelines for classroom practice.

1. Provide children with tasks that are appropriate to their developmental levels.
2. Create a success-oriented classroom atmosphere.
3. Use attractive, manipulative objects and materials to gain and maintain the interest of the child.
4. Use familiar events and materials in classroom activities.
5. Provide learning activities that allow the child to be an active participant.
6. Encourage creativity and reward independent thought.
7. Allow children to participate in the development of rules governing the class.
8. Reward attempts at new tasks.
9. Provide external cues through verbal or nonverbal means.
10. Fade cues gradually to encourage independent functioning.
11. Encourage social rewards by having class members praise each other for efforts at success. This may be accomplished by establishing a "buddy system" or a "helper system" that encourages social interaction and provides an opportunity for additional social praise. This may also teach children how to have and be a friend. This approach is particularly helpful for a new child entering a classroom.
12. Provide opportunities for problem-solving activities commensurate with the child's level of ability. Begin with concrete, familiar situations and then move to more abstract "what if" situations according to the child's level.
13. Reward each child's attempts at unusual or innovative answers as opposed to just right or wrong ones.
14. When children make errors, put question marks on their papers that mean "think about it again."
15. Provide opportunities for children to demonstrate their particular areas of competence such as in art, music, dance or physical education.

Conclusion

In general, the research on development and learning for mentally retarded students suggests that they are slower at mastering tasks than their nonretarded peers. But the differences tend to be quantitative rather than qualitative. When special techniques and strategies are used, mentally retarded learners benefit.

Early experiences affect the overall development of retarded learners in the same way they affect others. The failure frequently experienced by young retarded children can affect their motivation to learn. Instruction designed to provide success experiences assists the child's developing sense of competence and enhances both motivation and learning.

Much research has been conducted using mentally retarded persons as subjects. These accumulated findings can be synthesized into instructional principles to guide classroom practice. The implementation of research-derived principles for retarded learners makes education for these learners special.

REFERENCES

Alport, G. *Pattern and growth in personality.* New York: Holt, Rinehart, & Winston, 1961.

Azrin, N. H., & Foxx, R. M. A rapid method of toilet training the institutionalized retarded. *Journal of Applied Behavior Analysis,* 1971, *4,* 88–99.

Baroff, G. *Mental retardation: Nature, cause and management.* New York: John Wiley, 1974.

Blatt, B. Issues and values. In B. Blatt, D. Biklen, & R. Bogdon (Eds.), *An alternative textbook in special education.* Denver: Love Publishing, 1977.

Brown, A. L. The role of strategic behavior in retardate memory. In N. R. Ellis (Ed.), *International review of research in mental retardation* (Vol. 7). New York: Academic Press, 1974.

Cattell, P. *The measurement of intelligence of infants and young children.* New York: Psychological Corporation, 1940; rev. ed., 1960.

Chinn, P., Drew, C., & Logan, D. *Mental retardation: A life cycle approach.* St. Louis: C. V. Mosby, 1975.

Clark, H. B., Rowbury, T., Baer, A. M., & Baer, D. M. Timeout as a punishing stimulus in continuous and intermittent schedules. *Journal of Applied Behavior Analysis,* 1973, *6,* 443–455.

Dalton, A. J., Rubino, C. A., & Hislop, M. W. Some effects of token rewards on school achievement of children with Down's syndrome. *Journal of Applied Behavior Analysis,* 1973, *6,* 251–259.

Doll, E. Vineland Social Maturity Scale. Minneapolis: Educational Test Bureau, 1947.

Dunn, L. (Ed.). *Exceptional children in the schools* (2nd ed.). New York: Holt, Rinehart, & Winston, 1973.

Edgerton, R. *Cloak of competence.* Berkeley: University of California Press, 1967.

Ellis, N. R. The stimulus trace and behavior inadequacy. In N. R. Ellis (Ed.), *Handbook of mental deficiency.* New York: McGraw-Hill, 1963. Pp. 134–158.

Ellis, N. R. Memory processes in retardates and normals. In N. R. Ellis (Ed.), *International review of research in mental retardation* (Vol. 4). New York: Academic Press, 1970. Pp. 1–32.

Estes, W. K. *Learning theory and mental development.* New York: Academic Press, 1970.

Farber, B. *Mental retardation: Its social context and social consequences.* Boston: Houghton Mifflin, 1968.

Giles, D. K., & Wolf, M. M. Toilet training institutionalized, severe retardates: An application of operant behavior modification techniques. *American Journal of Mental Deficiency,* 1966, *70,* 766–780.

Goffman, E. *Stigma.* Englewood Cliffs, N.J.: Prentice-Hall, 1963.

Grossman, H. (Ed.). *Manual on terminology and classification in mental retardation.* Washington, D.C.: American Association on Mental Deficiency, 1973.

Harlow, H. The formation of learning sets. *Psychological Review,* 1949, *56,* 51–65.

Harter, S. Mental age, IQ and motivational factors in the discrimination learning set performance of normal and retarded children. *Journal of Experimental Child Psychology,* 1967, *5,* 123–141.

Harter, S., & Zigler, E. The assessment of effectance motivation in normal and retarded children. *Developmental Psychology,* 1974, *10,* 169–180.

Hebb, D. O. *The organization of behavior.* New York: John Wiley, 1949.

Heber, R. F. A manual on terminology and classification in mental retardation. *American Journal on Mental Deficiency,* 1959, *64,* Monograph Supplement (rev. ed.), 1961.

Heindziak, M., Maurer, R. A., & Watson, L. S., Jr. Operant conditioning in toilet training of severely mentally retarded boys. *American Journal of Mental Deficiency,* 1965, *70,* 120–124.

Holland, J. G., & Skinner, B. F. *The analysis of behavior.* New York: McGraw-Hill, 1961.

Hunt, J. M. *Intelligence and experience.* New York: Ronald Press, 1961.

Inhelder, B. The diagnosis of reasoning in the mentally retarded. New York: John Day, 1968.

Inhelder, B., & Piaget, J. *The early growth of logic in the child.* New York: Harper & Row, 1964.

Iwata, B. A., & Bailey, J. S. Reward versus cost token systems: An analysis of the effects on students and teacher. *Journal of Applied Behavior Analysis,* 1974, *7,* 567–576.

Jensen, A. R., & Rohwer, W. D. The effect of verbal mediation on the learning and retention of paired associates by retarded adults. *American Journal of Mental Deficiency*, 1963, *68*, 80–84.

Kaufman, M., & Prehm, H. A review of research on learning sets and transfer of training in mental defectives. In N. R. Ellis (Ed.), *International review of research in mental retardation* (Vol. 2). New York: Academic Press, 1966. Pp. 123–149.

Kimbrell, D. L., Luckey, R. E., Barbuto, P. F., & Love, J. G. Operation dry pants: An intensive habit-training program for the severely and profoundly retarded. *Mental Retardation*, 1967, *5*, 32–36.

Klein, N., & Safford, P. Application of Piaget's theory to the study of the thinking of the mentally retarded. *Journal of Special Education*, 1977, *11*, 201–216.

Klein, N., & Safford, P. Effects of representational level of materials on transfer of classification skills in TMR children. *Journal of Special Education*, 1976, *10*, 47–52.

Lerner, J. W. *Children with learning disabilities.* Boston: Houghton Mifflin, 1971.

Levine, M. N. Hypothesis behavior by humans during discrimination learning. *Journal of Experimental Psychology*, 1966, *71*, 331–338.

MacMillan, D. *Mental retardation in school and society.* Canada: Little, Brown, 1977.

Mercer, C. D., & Snell, M. E. *Learning theory research in mental retardation: Implications for teaching.* Columbus, Ohio: Charles E. Merrill, 1977.

Mercer, J. *Labeling the mentally retarded.* Berkeley: University of California Press, 1973.

Meyers, C. E., & MacMillan, D. L. Utilization of learning principles in retardation. In R. Koch & J. Dobson (Eds.), *The mentally retarded child and his family: A multi-disciplinary handbook* (2nd ed.). New York: Brunner/Mazel, 1976. Pp. 339–367.

Milgram, N. Retention of mediation set in paired associate learning of normal and retarded children. *Journal of Experimental Child Psychology*, 1967, *5*, 341–349.

Montessori, M. *The Montessori method.* New York: F. A. Stokes, 1912.

Moss, J. W. *Failure avoiding and success striving behavior in mentally retarded and normal children.* Unpublished doctoral dissertation, George Peabody College, 1958.

Nihira, K., Foster, R. Shellhaas, M., & Leland, H. Adaptive Behavior Scale: *Manual.* Washington, D.C.: American Association on Mental Deficiency, 1969.

Noonan, J. R., & Barry, J. R. Performance and retarded children. *Science*, 1967, *156*, 171.

Piaget, J. *The origins of intelligence in children.* New York: International Universities Press, 1952.

Phillips, J. L. *The origins of intellect: Piaget's theory* (2nd ed.). San Francisco: W. H. Freeman, 1975.

President's Panel on Mental Retardation. *A proposed program for national action to combat mental retardation.* Washington, D.C.: U.S. Government Printing Office, 1962.

Robinson, N. M., & Robinson, H. B. *The mentally retarded child: A psychological approach.* New York: McGraw-Hill, 1976.

Roos, P. Trends and issues in special education for the mentally retarded. In S. Kirk & F. Lord (Eds.), *Exceptional children: Educational resources and perspectives.* Boston: Houghton Mifflin, 1974.

Rosenthal, R., & Jacobson, L. *Pygmalion in the classroom.* New York: Holt, Rinehart & Winston, 1968.

Rotter, J. B. *Social learning and clinical psychology.* New York: Prentice-Hall, 1954.

Rubin, R., Rosenblatt, C., & Balow, R. Psychological and educational sequelae of prematurity. *Pediatrics,* 1973, *52,* 352.

Scheerenberger, R. C. Mental retardation: Definition, classification and prevalence. *Mental Retardation Abstracts,* 1964, *1,* 432–441.

Sigel, I. Concept formation. In J. J. Gallagher (Ed.), *The application of child development research to exceptional children.* Reston, Va.: The Council for Exceptional Children, 1975.

Skinner, B. F. *Science and human behavior.* New York: Macmillan, 1953.

Skinner, B. F. *The behavior of organisms: An experimental analysis.* New York: Appleton-Century-Crofts, 1938.

Stephens, B., & McLaughlin, J. A. Two-year gains in reasoning by normals and retardeds. *American Journal on Mental Deficiency,* 1974, *79,* 116–126.

Taylor, S., & Bogdan, R. A phenomenological approach to mental retardation. In B. Blatt, D. Biklin, & R. Bogdan (Eds.), *An alternative textbook in special education.* Denver: Love Publishing, 1977.

Terman, L. M., & Merrill, M. A. The Stanford-Binet Intelligence Scale (3rd ed.). Boston: Houghton Mifflin, 1973.

Tyler, V. O., Jr., & Brown, G. D. Token reinforcement of academic performance with institutionalized delinquent boys. *Journal of Educational Psychology,* 1968, *59,* 164–168.

Vukelich, R., & Hake, D. F. Reduction of dangerously aggressive behavior in a severely retarded resident through a combination of positive reinforcement procedures. *Journal of Applied Analysis,* 1971, *4,* 215–225.

Wechsler, D. Wechsler Intelligence Scale for Children. New York: Psychological Corporation, 1949; rev. ed., 1974.

White, R. W. Competence and the psychosexual stages of development. In M. R. Jones (Ed.), *Nebraska symposium on motivation.* Lincoln: University of Nebraska Press, 1960.

Yando, R., & Zigler, E. Outerdirectedness in the problem solving of institutionalized and noninstitutionalized normal and retarded children. *Developmental Psychology,* 1971, *4,* 277–288.

Zeaman, D., & House, B. The role of attention in retardate discrimination learning. In N. R. Ellis (Ed.), *Handbook of mental deficiency.* New York: McGraw-Hill, 1963. Pp. 159–223.

Zeaman, D., & House, B. J. The relation of IQ and learning. In R. M. Gagne (Ed.), *Learning and individual differences.* Columbus, Ohio: Charles E. Merrill, 1966.

Zigler, E. Research on personality structure in the retardate. In N. R. Ellis (Ed.), *International review of research in mental retardation* (Vol. 1). New York: Academic Press, 1966. Pp. 77–108.

Zigler, E. The retarded child as a whole person. In D. K. Rowth (Ed.), *The experimental psychology of mental retardation.* Chicago: Aldine, 1973.

Pupil assessment

Children learn at different rates, use different styles, and give different responses to teaching materials. In fact, it is quite likely that two children of the same age, height, weight, and IQ would learn in totally different ways. Children with widely differing characteristics are found in every classroom. Most attempts to group children "homogeneously" result in groups of children who have "heterogeneous" learning characteristics.

Paying attention to individual differences has long been a basic concern in special education. Special educators look for differences among children (interindividual) and within a single child (intra-individual). These individual learning variations obviously affect the overall outcome of instruction. Optimizing each child's education requires systematic pupil assessment.

This chapter focuses on pupil assessment as it relates to two educational purposes: (a) identification and placement of children, and (b) instructional intervention and programming.

Assessment for Identification and Placement

One reason to assess students carefully is to determine who is "retarded" and who is not. This may be necessary for the school to qualify for government funding or for other administrative purposes. However, we must be quite cautious in identifying a child as retarded. For many children, the label *mental retardation* leads to a long series of problems. The stigma associated with that label comes from many sources—including parents, teachers, children, neighbors. A child might be recognized as being "slow," but once he is labeled "retarded" he is likely to be rejected, isolated, and devalued. Somehow calling a person "retarded" changes the ballgame.

We must constantly remind ourselves that mental retardation is a relative concept. A person may be retarded in one situation and not in another. For example, anyone of us might appear quite retarded among a group of Nobel laureates discussing high energy nuclear physics. Yet we may be quite knowledgeable and conversant about Chinese art or Middle Eastern politics. Mildly retarded children, too, have varying levels of difficulty or success depending upon the situation. The label *mental retardation* implies a global deficiency that often is not accurate. While mildly retarded children often have difficulty in academic subjects, they may leave school at the end of the day and perform successfully in jobs, play with friends in the neighborhood, and have ordinary life experiences. These children have been called "The Six-Hour Retarded Child" in that they are "retarded" only during school hours (President's Committee on Mental Retardation, 1970).

Most cases of mild mental retardation are first identified by the classroom teacher and later referred to the school psychologist for testing. In contrast to moderately, severely, and profoundly retarded children who are usually first identified by physicians before they reach school age, mildly retarded children are rarely identified before they begin school. The physical problems and extreme delays in development associated with more severe retardation are not characteristic of mildly retarded individuals.

For the most part, mildly retarded children are healthy, well-developed youngsters. They may walk and talk at a slightly later age than their nonretarded peers, but the lag usually goes unrecognized during the preschool years. They rarely have any outward physical symptoms or unusual behaviors. These children usually get along well with their neighbors, are accepted by friends, and are regarded by their parents as normal.

Only when these children enter school and have difficulty is their condition recognized. A child who is enrolled in a regular class may have prolonged and significant problems in either academic performance or social behavior. After the teacher decides that more information is needed, he refers the child to the school psychologist for testing.

Mercer (1973) describes how children have been labeled *mentally retarded* in the public schools. The process ends only when the child completes or withdraws from school. Only then does the child have the chance to get rid of the label. Although P.L. 94–142 will alter these stages, they are good examples of past practices.

Stage 1 Enrollment in public school. Children in private or parochial schools are rarely identified as being mildly retarded.

Stage 2 Normal student in regular classroom. As we have seen, most mildly retarded children are not identified until after they have had difficulty in the regular classroom.

Stage 3 Retained student status. Mercer found that some children who have academic difficulty are retained in the same grade because they fail to master the material, and others are referred for testing and possible special class placement. Whether the child is retained or placed in a special class depends in part upon the teacher's expectations for certain minority groups.

Stage 4 Referral to the principal. After the child has been retained for a year and has still not mastered the required material, the teacher has two options: social promotion, or referral for psychological evaluation. It is at this point that the principal is often consulted.

Stage 5 Psychological testing and evaluation. Most states require that children be tested by licensed psychologists before being labeled *mentally retarded*.* Not all children referred to psychologists are tested, however. Mercer found that of all children referred to psychologists by teachers and principals, about 70% are tested. Of those children referred for possible special class placement, 90% are tested. Of those referred for unspecified academic placement, 70% are tested. And 40% of those referred for behavior alone are tested. Thus a child has the best chance of being tested if he is referred for special classes, and the least chance if he is referred for behavior alone.

Mercer found that there are no differences between tested and untested children on the basis of sex or ethnicity. However, there is a problem when children are tested using standardized intelligence instruments. At the time of Mercer's study, 1973, the California IQ cutoff for placement in classes for the mentally retarded was an IQ of 80. When the children referred for testing were given commonly used intelligence tests, significantly more black and Mexican-American children scored below IQ 80 than white children. In addition, a significantly greater proportion of those scoring below 80 came from families of low socioeconomic status.

Mercer contends that the use of the intelligence test as a labeling device accounts for the disproportionate numbers of minority group children who become labeled *mentally retarded*.

Stage 6 Labeling. Following the psychological evaluation, the child is labeled *mentally retarded* depending upon the IQ cutoff established by the state and the child's score on the test.

Stage 7 Placement. After the child has been labeled, the case is referred to a "Placement Committee on the Handicapped" or a similarly named body. The composition of this committee varies; in most cases it is comprised of the special class teacher, regular class teacher, psychologist, principal, parent, and student (when appropriate). Other professionals, such as the school nurse, may be included when required. This committee studies the information, considers diagnosis and classification, and recommends placement in the best interests of the child. P.L. 94–142 requires that an individualized education program (IEP) be developed from diagnostic and assessment data as part of the placement process. Thus, placement decisions must be made on the basis of the best setting(s) to achieve the stated objectives. Mercer (1973) found that only

---

* The tests used for identification and placement are similar to those used for intervention and programming. They will be discussed in detail later in the chapter.

64% of the children with an IQ of 79 or below were placed in special classes. The 36% who were not placed in special classes tended to be white females or to come from homes of higher socioeconomic status.

Stage 8   Leaving the "Mentally Retarded."   The final stage of Mercer's labeling process is leaving behind the label of *mentally retarded*. Since most mildly retarded children are labeled by the schools, they can get rid of the label by leaving school—either graduating, completing a specified program, or simply dropping out. Often the role expectations outside of school are more easily mastered. The academic expectations that presented a problem to the child while in school no longer apply. However, students who were not able to master basic reading and other basic skills, and who have either minimal or no job skills, may continue to be considered retarded. This is increasingly true as our society becomes more technologically complex.

In a few cases, mildly retarded children make enough academic progress to get rid of the label while they are still in school, either during the elementary years or between elementary and junior high school.

Although the labeling process described by Mercer has been modified by a change in public attitudes toward the mentally retarded and expressed through judicial decisions and public law, the use of standardized tests for identification and placement remains controversial. Labeling a child *retarded* has serious consequences; it is not a decision to be taken lightly.

Assessment for Instructional Programming

The second purpose of pupil assessment, which we shall concentrate on for the remainder of the chapter, is the determination of appropriate and individualized instructional programming. Pupil assessment for programming involves the determination of: (a) what an individual is currently able to do; (b) what an individual might be able to do; and (c) in what instructional areas the pupil is or is not performing successfully. In other words, pupil assessment involves determining a student's aptitudes, skills, and competencies. If assessment information is to be both accurate and useful, the data-gathering process must be viewed as the initial component in a systems approach to learning.

A systems approach requires the statement of a precise learning goal, integration of instructional components, feedback concerning learning success or failure, and provision for modification or redesign when warranted by learning results or new developments. Instructional designers refer to a systems approach as possessing *purpose, integration, feedback,* and provision for *redesign.* The role of assessment in a systems approach is pivotal. Assessment provides the information that guides the process toward the solution of a particular instructional problem. Assessment permits the instructor to understand the dimensions of a problem relative to an individual learner before objectives are set and learning activities are chosen. In that way, the probability of success is increased.

A systems approach to learning can be used in both regular and special education. The concept of *mastery learning* espoused by Bloom and his colleagues (1976) and *diagnostic-prescriptive teaching* supported by Stellern, Vasa, and Little (1976) are examples of this approach to education for all children, including those with special educational needs.

Mastery Learning

Since the 1960s, there has been a movement for change in both regular and special education. The revolutionary changes that have altered the entire philosophy of special education have spilled over into general education, and several themes have emerged: (a) educators must be accountable for the learning of each individual child; (b) learners have individual needs and styles; (c) all children can learn under carefully designed conditions; (d) learning is crucial to overall development; (e) parents have an important role in the education of their children; and (f) effective techniques, which have been characteristic of special education teachers, can be used by regular education teachers as well.

All of these themes run through the work of Benjamin Bloom, Distinguished Service Professor of Education at the University of Chicago. His work (Bloom, 1976) emphasizes the importance of individualizing instruction through a rigorous program of educational assessment for all learners. Bloom's work justifies the use of educational assessment as an on-going instructional process. One significant implication of Bloom's work is that it can be applied to all learners, even those with handicapping conditions. The concept of *mastery* transcends labels and categories.

In his book *Human Characteristics for School Learning,* Bloom (1976) maintains that schools can and should move from a "sifting and sorting" function to one which encourages and facilitates "individual development." Research into mastery learning leads him to believe that "what any person in the world can learn, almost all persons can learn if provided with appropriate prior and current conditions of learning" (Bloom, 1976). He argues persuasively that assessment (diagnosis) is critical. It is the assessment, in the form of brief diagnostic instruments, that can identify a pupil's current level of performance on each learning task, and target what remains to be learned as the child progresses toward mastery. Continuing his analysis of learning performance, Bloom maintains that mastery can be determined through the operation of variables that explain school learning. Bloom attributes the greatest positive learning outcomes to three basic variables:

1. *Cognitive entry behaviors* (assessment of current levels of performance),
2. *Affective entry characteristics* (attitudes affected by self-concept, interest, health and well-being as well as previous learning performance),
3. *Quality of instruction* (see Figure 2–1).

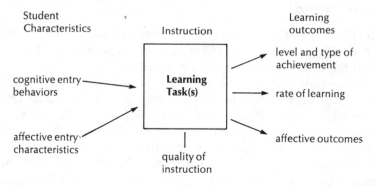

Figure 2–1 *The learning unit in mastery learning*

From *Human Characteristics and School Learning* by B. S. Bloom. New York: McGraw-Hill, 1976. Used by permission.

Together, these three variables affect a particular learning task and determine the nature of learning outcomes. Although Bloom argues that all three variables are important, it must be noted that "the research done by Bloom and his students suggests that learning success is largely determined by the extent to which students possess the necessary cognitive entry behaviors applicable to subsequent learning tasks" (Harvey & Horton, 1977, p. 190).

Bloom's work supports the notion of the individuality of each child, not just children with special needs. The mastery learning model, because of its inherent diagnostic-prescriptive nature, can be a valu-

Individual attention from her teacher encourages Crissy to try again.

able instructional model for children with varying educational needs in both regular and special education classrooms.

Diagnostic-Prescriptive Teaching

Diagnostic-prescriptive teaching is defined as the accurate assessment of learning and behavior problems, followed by systematic intervention evolved from the diagnostic information. Stellern, Vasa, and Little (1976) propose an educational intervention and management model designed to convert the diagnostic-prescriptive philosophy into an operational model for classroom use.

The model includes six interventions or activities integrated to form an instructional process. The first two interventions, Learner Assessment and Task Analysis (in relation to the learner), make up the key diagnostic interventions. Another intervention, Individualization and Success, refers to the "meaningful match of curriculum materials with the instructional needs of the learner" (Stellern, Vasa, & Little, 1976, p. 4). The model closely resembles the mastery learning concept described by Bloom, and the Glaser model of instruction (see pages 8–9). All three systems share these principles:

(a) a systems approach to instruction, (b) a belief in the individuality of learners, (c) assessment as a pivotal component in instruction, (d) specification of precise instructional objectives, and (c) concern for both learner and task analysis.

Gathering Assessment Information: The Significance of Multifactored Assessment

The traditional practice of identifying children as mentally retarded and placing them in a special class on the basis of performance on a single test is no longer permitted by law. In its place, P.L. 94–142 requires a mutlifactored assessment of each individual who will receive special education services. Multifactored assessments are intended to identify skill levels, learning competencies, and additional factors that may affect the handicapped child's learning pattern.

The broad, in-depth assessment mandated by P.L. 94–142 requires that professionals from several fields be involved in assessment and program planning. The multiple factors that make up a broad, in-depth assessment include the following:

1. Information concerning the ability and competencies of the pupil in an instructional context;
2. Information from professionals such as a speech therapist or psychologist in their particular areas;
3. Information regarding the adaptive behavior of the child in both home and school.

Thus, multifactored assessment requires measured levels of intellectual functioning; measurement of the individual's ability to function on a daily basis in the home, school, and community; and determination of additional school-related developmental difficulties.

Sources of Information

A valid, comprehensive, multifactored assessment is the responsibility of several school personnel. The regular and special class teachers and the psychologist, however, have central roles in collecting and analyzing information directly related to instruction. To that end, these professionals have many formal and informal instruments available to use. Formal instruments are generally classified into two categories: norm-referenced standardized tests and criterion-referenced tests. Norm-referenced standardized tests compare an individual's performance to that of others. Criterion-referenced tests compare a child's performance to some established criteria. Red Cross swimming tests are a good example of criterion-referenced tests of performance. Standards or criteria are established for all swimmers taking the test. The objectives established by the teacher are often the criteria to which criterion-referenced tests are related.

Standardized assessment instruments. There are two groups of norm-referenced tests presently in use in public schools: achievement tests and intelligence tests. Achievement tests are designed to determine the individual's present level of knowledge and/or competence; intelligence tests are designed to predict an individual's school success. Norm-referenced tests are most often used in schools to assess academic skills, although there are some norm-referenced adaptive behavior instruments available.

A brief history of norm-referenced testing. The testing movement in the United States matured after the first decade of the 20th century. During World War I the military was faced with the challenge of selecting and training over 1,000,000 draftees. As a result, incentives were provided to psychologists to create aptitude and performance tests to discriminate between those who could be efficiently trained to be successful and those who were unacceptable.

At its core, the testing movement was based on the principle that learner populations perform predictably when tested. Furthermore, their scores are normally distributed, assuming a sufficient number of subjects and an accurate and consistent measurement procedure.* A small number of subjects will score high; most scores will cluster around the mean of the distribution; a small number of scores will be in the low range of the distribution. The goal of normative assessment, as exemplified by the IQ test, was to "sort and sift" learners into their measured placements on score distributions. These scores are then used to imply present learning performance and make predictions about future success. These tests (both aptitude and achievement tests) are called *standardized* or *normed* because they compare an individual's performance against a previously tested sample population whose scoring profile is thought to be similar.

---

* The concepts of validity (accuracy) and reliability (consistency) will be discussed in some depth in Chapter 8.

For example, an individual 12-year-old would be compared to a sample of previously tested 12-year-olds.

The use of norm-referenced testing can be defended on several grounds. It may be quite necessary to know how one group of subjects performs in comparison to previously tested groups. If funds are to be allocated for curriculum innovations, norm-referenced testing results can help decision makers reach rational judgements. Testing information is also useful in determining school or district-wide educational needs. Norm-referenced assessment is valuable in research, for it enables the investigator to apply valid criteria to the subject scores being interpreted. Consequently, any derived results have statistical meaning.

These legitimate advantages have limited application to the individual student in the classroom, however. There are several problems that immediately arise from using norm-referenced data alone in the process of educational planning:

1. Test scores do not denote individual differences in learning characteristics.
2. Test scores do not denote specific levels of individual functioning in classroom-related activities.
3. Test scores have been shown to be inaccurate for minority children due to inherent cultural bias in the tests (Mercer, 1973; Dunn, 1968).
4. Test scores are unstable, especially for young children (Sattler, 1974).
5. Individual learning styles are not taken into account.

The fifth point is especially applicable for mildly handicapped individuals, as their individual learning styles often cause them to be labeled *retarded* according to norm-referenced data.

The intelligence test as a norm-referenced instrument. Intelligence tests, as suggested earlier, were originally designed to sort and select learners. The Stanford-Binet Intelligence Test, which is very commonly used, was developed to predict which children were most likely to fail in school.* Although the tests developed by Binet were not based on any theoretical conception of intelligence, they became synonomous with its measurement.

> The central assumption (of intelligence tests) was that the educational program was and would remain a fixed one in that adapta-

---

* Along with the Stanford-Binet Intelligence Scale (Terman & Merrill, 1973), a second commonly used individual intelligence test is the revised Wechsler Intelligence Scale for Children (WISC-R) (Wechsler, 1974).

tion to individuals was neither possible nor desirable. The school system and its instructional methods were not called into question, only the capacity of children to profit from the standard program offered. (Resnick, 1977, p. 6)

The use and misuse of intelligence tests with minority group children has been the subject of intense scrutiny and debate (Mercer, 1973). Disproportionate numbers of minority children have been identified as mentally retarded as a consequence of low intelligence test scores. The test has been assumed to be valid; the problem was always said to lie within the child. This widespread practice of labeling has resulted in a growing chorus of attacks on the tests themselves.

The most common charge is that intelligence tests are by their nature culturally biased in favor of white, middle- and upper-class youngsters. Some critics are so vehement in their criticism of intelligence testing that they contend that all such tests should be banned from the schools. Yet simply banning intelligence tests will not solve the problem of educating children who learn slowly or differently from the majority.

Doing away with intelligence tests will do little to enlarge the opportunities of children who tend to score poorly on the tests. Their scores are too highly correlated with their school performance for elimination of the tests to make much difference. It is only by changing the school environment so that it accommodates to the social and intellectual differences that we can expect any real opportunity changes. (Resnick, 1977, p. 6)

The achievement test as a norm-referenced instrument.   In contrast to the intelligence test, which tries to assess an individual's aptitude for future learning, achievement tests assess present and past performance. The worst examples of achievement tests suffer from the same flaws as intelligence tests. They may be culturally biased. They do not account for individual learning syles or preferences. In addition, they may not relate directly enough to a school's instructional program to be useful in assessing learning performance. On the other hand, the best standardized achievement tests can provide the teacher with useful information to begin an investigation. In other words, the teacher can find information about a child's present achievement level, but must investigate further to determine the how's and why's.

Suppose the teacher has recognized that John is having difficulty completing some classroom tasks. John, age 10, is unable to complete those tasks that require a certain reading proficiency. The teacher has identified John's area of difficulty informally, and now requires some specific information. She chooses the Peabody Individual Achievement Test (PIAT) (Dunn & Markwardt, 1970), reading comprehension and reading recognition subtests, to determine the grade level of John's reading ability. The test indicates that John is reading at a grade level of 1.2. That information is of obvious limited use. What else would the teacher need to know?

The teacher needs to know what problems John is having that prevent him from reading at higher grade levels. Is the problem word attack skills? Is the problem comprehension? Is there a more subtle problem that is more difficulty to identify? Is it just simply a matter of an unfamiliar word or two in the content presented? Is it the nature of the test itself? Or does John simply not try?

Before the teacher can remediate John's identified reading problem, she must analyze his skill level and reading process to pinpoint the difficulty. Having him read from a basal reader at the 1.2 grade level, and then gradually giving him more difficult material, may shed some light on the problem. The point is that the standardized achievement test is a gross measure of performance and serves only as a guide to the selection of additional assessment procedures. The teacher's task is to identify the source of the difficulty. Standardized achievement tests are one route toward that goal. The information that John reads at 1.2 grade level does not suggest remedial strategies. It merely tells where he's functioning in relation to other children, not why. The answers to these why questions are to found in a more in-depth skill analysis.

Informal Assessment

The limitations of norm-referenced tests in individual assessment have already been explained. To obtain more diagnostic information, teachers can use informal assessment techniques. Teacher-designed tests can be more directly applicable to program development for handicapped individuals. In many cases, teachers place more value on informal assessment information than on standardized assessment data.

There are many types of informal assessment. While it may appear from the discussion thus far that the only way to assess an individual is to give tests, this is not, in fact, the case at all. Observation can provide valuable information in several critical areas. Observations can be informal; the teacher may merely watch a child at play, during a task, in social situations such as lunch, or interacting with peers in the classroom. More systematic observation directed toward specific behaviors in an identified situation can also be fruitful. Behavioral observations can be either descriptive or quantitative. Descriptive observations may entail keeping anecdotal records that focus on specific behaviors. These records can assist the teacher in planning and evaluation. Descriptive behavior observation requires that the teacher record behavior rather than interpret it. Cartwright and Cartwright (1974) have written an excellent guide for developing descriptive observation skills.

A quantitative approach to behavioral observation requires recording the frequency of specific behaviors. Accurate and systematic recording is necessary if this method is to be of value in modifying a particular behavior. Teacher-made checklists are also a valuable aid in quantifying behavioral observations. These checklists can be developed for academic domains, psychomotor areas, or social interaction.

Additional sources of informal assessment data.   The teacher has many opportunities during the course of the day to conduct informal assessments. Observing an individual's response to a new situation (on a field trip, for instance), a student's response to an unusual authority figure in the classroom, or a newly assigned task or a repeated task may prove productive. Questioning techniques can indicate what a child knows and how he solves a problem. Problem-solving games and activities can be used to determine a child's abilities to use inductive reasoning. Class meetings described by William Glasser (1969) can be effective in assessing an individual's ability to listen and respond to his peers in a group. Periodic student interviews can provide useful information and feedback. The child may be asked how she feels about school, her progress, and what she would like to change and learn. She may even be asked to suggest classroom activities or procedures that she would find pleasing. Student interviews can be conducted individually or in groups of three or four. This procedure has been found to be not only informative for the teacher, but quite beneficial for some children who have difficulty expressing their views in a larger group. This approach gives the teacher a much broader range of information than is usually available from "tests." Particularly for children who fear tests, interviews may be less threatening and even enjoyable.

Parents as a source of information.   Parents have a legitimate role in the education of their handicapped children. They know their children best. They live with them, know their likes and dislikes, their interests and their feelings. Parent conferences provide an excellent opportunity for teachers to tap the information parents have regarding their children.

Parents can also help adapt instruction for their children. They can share their unique knowledge, which can help teachers motivate their youngster. For example, when one of the authors was teaching a class of retarded learners, she had a child who was withdrawn and difficult to reach. A conference with the parent revealed that this child loved to sew and had made doll clothes with her mother's assistance. The class was in the process of planning a dramatic presentation for the school. Valerie, the withdrawn child, now had a role. She was asked to take responsibility for making costumes. Although her response was guarded, she was obviously pleased. As the children turned to her frequently for guidance and help with their costume design and selection, she began to be more responsive and out-going. By the time of the performance, she was loudly giving orders regarding the appropriate care of costumes. The information from Valerie's mother was the key to getting Valerie involved in the class project.

Parents can also provide insights into how to affect their child's performance. What interventions are effective? Which approach is most successful? Obviously, certain information regarding family problems can only be obtained from parents. The birth of a sibling, the death of a loved one, or even less traumatic events can affect a child's performance and behavior. All of these factors are significant in individual pupil assessment.

Criterion-Referenced Teacher-Made Assessment Instruments

The most commonly used tests in schools today are "teacher-made" tests. Of all the possible assessment sources, the most important in instructional programming is the teacher-made test. Teacher-made tests must be carefully constructed to provide useful feedback for both the child and the teacher. In contrast to commercially prepared criterion-referenced measures (which accompany some reading programs), teacher-made assessments consist of a series of items that relate directly to the expected learning outcomes as stated in the teacher-developed instructional objectives. We call these *teacher-made* since the teacher determines those items to be included. They are *criterion-referenced* since the teacher assesses an individual student's performance against a standard of success and not in comparison to the performance of others. The performance of each learner is compared only to the specific outcomes expressed in the predetermined objectives established for that learner. These tests are based on a careful analysis of the content to be taught. The teacher must consider both the organization of subject matter and the psychological order of learning tasks.

The El Paso Texas Metropolitan School project to mainstream mildly handicapped and bilingual children into regular classes (Plata, 1977) provides a good example of this kind of analysis. That project involved the development of criterion tests in the management of a program of individualized instruction. According to Plata, such learning hierarchies are necessary in the development of a successful program of criterion testing. To determine what the learner can or cannot do and what needs to be taught, the teacher must first know what steps are involved in the task. Using subtraction as an example, Plata (1977) describes the subtasks involved as follows:

1. Subtraction of single digit numbers.
2. Subtraction with regrouping from ten's to one's place and with two digits on top and one digit on bottom (include problems with zero).
3. Subtraction with regrouping from ten's to one's place with three digits on top and two digits on bottom (include problems with zero).
4. Subtracting with regrouping from hundred's to ten's place with three digits on top and two digits on bottom (include problems with zero).
5. Subtraction with regrouping from hundred's to ten's to one's with variable number of digits on top and bottom (include problems with zero). (pp. 53–54)

It is important when creating teacher-made criterion-referenced measures to consider the following guidelines:

1. Questions must be directly related to the material taught. Plata recommends that items be coded to correspond to particular areas of content analysis hierarchy. (Plata, 1977, p. 54)
2. Questions must be written in language the child can easily understand. Thus the vocabulary must be familiar to the child. The task must be clearly understood.
3. Many assessments of fewer items are preferable to a few assessments of many items.
4. Above all, care should be taken to create a supportive climate during the administration of the test. Phrases such as "I'm going to find out where you might need some help" or "Do the best you can!" are helpful in reducing the level of threat in an assessment situation.

Plata (1977) provides another set of guidelines that relate to the management of a criterion-referenced assessment system:

1. At the beginning of school, allow students to get accustomed to routines in the classroom before tests are administered.
2. Talk to students about forthcoming testing situations to avoid confusion and relieve anxiety.
3. Plan to give a test over a period of several days.
4. Give the minimum number of test items needed to pinpoint the achievement levels of each child.
5. Grade tests within a day or two, since the results are to be used in the appropriate placement of each child in the curriculum.
6. File the test results as baseline data for future use in conferences and for progress reporting.
7. Be open to suggestions on how to improve the tests. (p. 54)

Scoring and reporting test results may also be done humanely. It is necessary to note errors; this can be done by circling the incorrect responses or placing question marks next to them. There is no need to write the total number of errors in large numbers. Remember, these tests are feedback for the teacher, as well as the student.

After the test has been scored and interpreted, good procedure requires that the teacher reteach, focusing on the tasks that were missed by the child. When the child masters the tasks, he can then be retested and receive a 100% correct score.

The Assessment of Adaptive Behavior

For nearly 30 years special educators have pointed out that retarded children's social behavior is often the major reason for their lack of success in the regular classroom. Thus a comprehensive assessment, to fully describe both the child's academic and social behavior, must include data pertinent to adaptive behavior.

Adaptive behavior, or social competence, has long been viewed as an essential element in the determination of mental retardation. Itard and Haslan in 1819, Seguin in 1837, Voisin in 1843, Howe in 1858, and Goodard in 1912 spoke essentially about adaptive behavior, using such terms as *social competency, skills training, social norms,* the power of *fending for onself* in life, *adaptability to environment,* and *efficiency of social value* (Lambert, Windmiller, Cole, & Figueroa, 1974). Although the concept was recognized as early as 1819, at present—nearly 160 years later—there is still no agreed-upon definition. Coulter and Morrow (1977) report at least nine definitions of *adaptive behavior* currently found in the literature. Yet a review of these definitions indicates several "themes" common to nearly all of them. They emphasize adequate development of skills for (a) independent functioning in self-help skills; (b) maintaining responsible social relationships; and (c) personal independence. Mercer (1973) has attempted to clarify the concept by specifying expected behaviors for particular age groups using a social system approach.

Infancy: Birth through 2 years
Measures of adaptive behavior cannot actually evaluate role performances in children this young. However, it is possible to identify certain developmental and maturational abilities and certain embryonic social skills that must be achieved and that are the building blocks from which later social role performance is formed.

Preschool: 3 through 5 years
Assumes more responsibility for his own cleanliness and toileting: for dressing and undressing himself; for being able to distinguish harmful and dirty objects from edible ones; for using tools such as crayons . . . scissors without harming himself and others; . . . performing simple household tasks and running errands . . . expected to be able to move about his house and neighborhood with minimal supervision. . . . This greater independence assumes that he can manage most of his social interactions with minimal adult direction, can relate events that have happened to him, and can communicate his desires to others. . . .

School: 6 through 15 years
Must comprehend a social structure containing unfamiliar roles such as teacher, principal, secretary, custodian . . . must learn the roles and values of his peers and simultaneously meet the ever-increasing demands of the teacher . . . expected to perform more complex family roles and to learn many new roles in the community . . . (e.g., customer in a store, handling his own money and making his own selections) . . . driver of wheeled vehicles, whether they be bikes, or scooters. . . .

The Adult: 16 and over
The primary new role is occupational . . . expected to play a productive occupational role and to be financially self-sufficient. . . . For adults, adaptive behavior is measured both by the number of roles the adult is playing and by his level of performance in those roles. (Mercer, 1973, pp. 134–136)

The degree to which an individual has achieved these behaviors at a given age can only be determined by systematic assessment.

Measurement of Adaptive Behavior

There are many complex variables that must be considered in social adaptation, which makes it difficult to assess. One major effort to quantify adaptive behavior is the AAMD Adaptive Behavior Scale (AMBD). Leland, Nihira, Foster, Shelhaas and Kagin (1968) have identified three basic forms of adaptation which are included in the scales: (a) independent functioning; (b) social responsibility, and (c) personal responsibility, each viewed in relation to the child's age and cultural reference group. The AMBD is, thus, a criterion-referenced standardized test.

The individual's ability to adapt to the demands of school is an obvious consideration in the development of an Individualized Education Plan. If the child is exhibiting maladaptive behavior, specific goals must be established for modifying it. In large measure, the degree to which children can get along socially will determine their success in later life. Informal assessment, using observation, checklists, and parent reports, is an excellent means of determining a child's social skills and deficits.

The Role of the Teacher

The teacher's role in assessment is that of a detective, critically collecting and interpreting clues to solve a mystery. Why does Steven, who is highly motivated and persistent in his efforts to learn to calculate baseball player averages, continue to have difficulty? Where does the teacher begin, in order to fully understand Steven's task-related problem?

Achievement tests are one source of data. These data, however, are merely bits of evidence that have value only as they relate to other evidence. The information must not be misinterpreted. Additional facts are required. Just as the detective gathers all available evidence that has a bearing on the case, the teacher must follow a similar path to make the wisest judgments about instruction.

Determining skill deficits is an inherent part of this fact-finding process. Through observation and the use of informal and formal tests, student interviews and discussions, and review of student work samples, the teacher can determine where Steven's skills falter. Is he able to multiply accurately? Is he able to count decimal places accurately? Does he understand how to add additional times-at-bat and manipulate the average? Is the difficulty a conceptual one or simply one of carelessness? The teacher may have to consult with other professionals to better understand the difficulty.

Collecting assessment data is a complex and often time-consuming task. The teacher often asks, "Where do I find the information?" "What information do I need?" "How shall I get it?"

Figure 2–2 provides a framework of the areas, vehicles, and sources of assessment data. Once the teacher has identified the

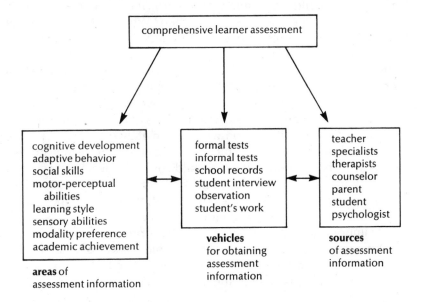

Figure 2–2

areas, sources, and vehicles for assessment, he can begin gathering information. Analysis of the collected data will enable the teacher to zero in on the difficulty and help the child master the task. This process can be used with social behaviors as well as academic skills.

Commercially produced normative and diagnostic instruments (described earlier in this chapter) provide information in many areas crucial to overall human development. These tests can help the teacher understand the learner, but they cannot substitute for the direct assessment of classroom-related objectives. Although it is often said that the primary responsibility of the teacher is "to teach," teaching is more than imparting a steady flow of information to students. Teaching also involves a flow of information from the students to the teacher. This reverse flow, in the form of observations, interactions, and assessment procedures, provides the necessary feedback to let the teacher adjust the instructional process to meet individual needs. Standardized instruments are not generally useful in this regard.

For too long, teachers have abdicated their responsibility in assessment and depended upon others to provide that information. These "others" are usually school psychologists, who are assumed to have unique knowledge about children. There continues to be a mystique surrounding the magical kits and tools of school psychologists. When teachers refer children to the psychologist, the teacher is generally asking, "What is the matter with this child? Why can't he learn what I teach? Give me a quick answer!" The answers which teachers receive rarely satisfy them.

Instead, the teacher must play the central role in the assessment process (Gillespie & Sitko, 1976). The teacher may request information from other professionals such as the psychologist, speech therapist, or physician; any one of these persons can help him interpret the information. Yet the person who is ultimately responsible for the educational progress of the child is the teacher. Of all the professionals who have contact with a child, only the teacher sees him every day in a wide variety of social and academic situations. Consequently, the teacher is in the ideal position to assess the child's physiological, intellectual, and emotional development.

The importance of pupil assessment is primarily in its relationship to the success of the teaching–learning process. That is, the teacher must find out where a child is functioning before instruction begins. That is the first step in the instructional process.

> If the diagnostic process is in situ, it should focus on the teacher. The teacher should be constantly modifying his/her program based on new information—every lesson can be part of the assessment procedure. The teacher should be able to field problems (Hammill, 1971) and to assess the methods and materials used in the educational program. This is a radical departure from traditional diagnostic treatment procedures because it gives the teacher a central role in the diagnostic process. Furthermore, this view considers decision making or problem solving as an integral part of the development of instructional strategies. (Gillespie & Sitko, 1976, p. 401)

The information gained through assessment determines the individual child's entry level skill and knowledge level in relation to the content. It also brings out other characteristics such as motivation, attention span, preferred learning styles, and physical and emotional health. Thus, learner assessment and content analysis are integrated processes.

Supportive personnel serve as consultants to the teacher and assist in assessment and programming. Sarason, Levine, Goldenberg, Cherlin, and Bennett (1977) present an excellent discussion of effective use of the psychologist as consultant to the classroom teacher. The consultant assists the teacher through classroom observation, discussions, and interviews with the child and family if necessary, in an effort to cooperatively assess the child's classroom difficulty. The necessary intervention is then integrated into the educational program as required by an individual child. Instead of the child going out for "therapy," the classroom is the setting for therapeutic intervention.

Learner and Content Analysis

Ysseldyke and Salvia (1974) describe two models of assessment: (a) the *learner* is assessed in the ability training approach; (b) *content* is assessed in the task analysis approach. Each approach has a distinguished group of followers.

The proponents of the ability training model (Bateman, 1967; Kirk, McCarthy, & Kirk, 1968) emphasize the value of using tests to determine individual weaknesses and strengths in a child's learning profile. For example, if a child is having difficulty differentiating among visual stimuli (the letters of the alphabet), these educators would suggest giving a test of visual memory skills. If the test results verify that the child has a visual memory, remediation in the area of visual memory skill would be recommended.

As a complete assessment process this approach has several drawbacks. It assumes that the test used to examine a specific skill is an accurate measure of that skill; it assumes that remedial techniques to enhance, say, visual memory, have a positive effect; and it assumes that visual memory or any other skill is a critical factor in recognizing the alphabet (in this case). Drew, Freston, and Logan (1972) see the ability training approach as a norm-referenced approach, because the individual's level of performance is compared to a reference sample.

The task analysis approach views the learner somewhat differently. The learner is viewed in relation to a specific task and the skills necessary to complete it successfully. There is no attempt to determine causes of skill deficit; the focus is on task-related skills. Gold (1968) and Bijou (1970) are among the strongest supporters of this approach, particularly with the more severely retarded population. The proponents of task analysis claim that at present our ability to identify causes of deficits is so poor that the use of such testing in education programming is highly questionable. Drew, Freston, and Logan (1972) see the task analysis approach as essentially criterion-referenced.

The core disagreement between the two approaches centers on the question of whether causation can be determined accurately and consistently. Given the confusing and conflicting evidence supporting the two approaches, which position should the teacher in the classroom adopt? At present, we believe the most reasonable decision is to use a combination of both ability training and task analysis, depending upon the age and difficulties of the child. To facilitate effective learning for retarded students, the teacher must first analyze curriculum content into its component parts (task analysis). As the child is learning each of the elements of the task and has difficulty, further investigation is needed to develop remedial instruction. Ability training is then used when task-related difficulties become evident. This approach puts the assessment focus in proximity to the task; it is a criterion-referenced approach to assessment and instruction. This view of assessment is supported by a growing number of authorities in educational psychology (Glaser, 1977; Kagan, 1977; Pottinger, 1977). This integrated assessment-instruction model is diagrammed in Figure 2–3. Assessment is used

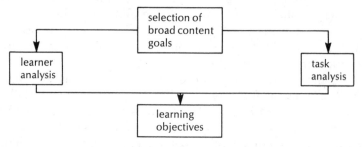

Figure 2–3

as an analytical tool to subdivide broad content goals and relate them to individual learners. The process of analysis not only results in learning objectives that are specific and measurable, but also results in objectives that are appropriate for the learners.

The following procedure is a model for integrating both task and learner information. It requires both an analysis of the task and an analysis of the learner in relation to the task.

   I. Identify instructional content area (broad content goals).
  II. Analyze instructional area into discrete skills (task analysis).
     1. Operationalize through behavioral objectives:
       a. Conditions,
       b. Performance,
       c. Criterion.
     2. Sequence discrete skills to determine order of presentation.

III. Assess child on skill sequence (learner analysis).
    1. Determine specific skill deficit.
IV. Analyze skill to be taught (task analysis).
    1. Identify components of target skill.
    2. Sequence components to determine order of presentation.
 V. Assess child on component sequence (learner analysis).
    1. Determine specific deficits (task analysis).
VI. Identify appropriate instructional activities (individualized instruction).
    1. Active.
    2. Learning styles or preferences.
    3. Reinforcing.
VII. Teach component skills.
VIII. Reassess discrete skill (return to III).

A Task-Learner Analysis Application

We shall now apply the model to a classroom situation. Today, one objective for Susan in the area of "wise buying" is "to identify in the newspaper three furniture stores which are having sales on bean bag chairs, and select the store with the least expensive price." Susan has listed the stores accurately but has not correctly identified the store with the least expensive price. It is necessary to determine why Susan has made this error. Does she understand the concept "least expensive"? Does she know how to determine which is the least expensive? Is she able to discriminate accurately among prices to make this judgment?

The determination of Susan's difficulty is critical if the teacher is to help Susan master the task correctly. Only through further learner analysis can this information be gathered and the instruction be provided to allow Susan to complete the task at the criterion established.

  I. Identify instructional content area: Wise buying–economic education.
 II. Analyze instructional area into discrete skills.
    1. Operationalize through behavioral objectives:
      a. Differentiate among newspaper ads and identify furniture store.
      b. Read ad at 100% level of accuracy.
      c. Read prices in newspaper at 100% level of accuracy.
      d. Compare prices in terms of "more or less."
      e. Subtract prices to determine differences at 100% level of accuracy.
      f. Clearly state meaning of concept "more expensive" at 100% level of accuracy.

       g. Clearly state meaning of concept "less expensive" at 100% level of accuracy.

   2. Sequence discrete skills to determine order of presentation: Same sequence as above.

III. Assess child on skill sequence.

   1. Determine specific skill deficit.

Susan has completed steps (a) through (e) successfully as determined by her response to the objective. She has not successfully completed task (f). Her skill deficit is the concepts of "more" and "less" expensive.

IV. Analyze skill to be taught.

   1. Identify components of target skill.

      a. The difficulty is "more and less expensive." It can be analyzed into the following components.

The student will be able to:

(1) When given two unequal sets of objects, identify the set which has "more" with 100% accuracy.

(2) When given two unequal sets of objects, identify the set which has "less" with 100% accuracy. (This should be repeated with at least three different sets of objects.)

(3) When shown pictures of objects of unequal sets, the student will identify the picture with "more" with 100% accuracy.

(4) When shown pictures of objects of unequal sets, the student will identify the picture with "less" with 100% accuracy.

(5) When shown unequal amounts of real money, the student will identify the set with "more" money with 100% accuracy.

(6) When shown unequal amounts of money, the student will identify the set with "less" money with 100% accuracy.

(7) When shown two newspaper ads for the same item, the student will identify "more" and "less" expensive.

(8) When shown newspaper ads for 8 items, each of which has a more and less expensive price, the student will sort the ads into "more" and "less" expensive groupings with 100% accuracy.

   2. Sequence components to determine order of presentation: See sequence above.

V. Assess child on component sequence.

   1. Determine specific deficit.

Susan was able to successfully complete (1) through (7). She was unable to successfully complete the task in relation to the presentation of the ad.

VI. Identify appropriate instructional activities.
    1. Active.
        a. Susan will role play going to a store (there will be a classroom simulation) and select the item that is "less" expensive.
        b. Susan will state how she made her decision.
        c. Susan will count out the amounts of money required for both "more" and "less" expensive items.
        d. Susan will write the amounts on price tags.
        e. Susan will correctly identify the "less" expensive items from a teacher made ad.
        f. Susan will correctly identify newspaper ad for less expensive item.
    2. Modality considerations.
        The above activities include three sensory-modalities.
    3. Reinforcing.
        The activities listed above are interesting, thus inherently reinforcing, and the teacher provides additional reinforcement as each is successfully completed.

VII. Teach component skills.
    1. After successful completion of the learning activities listed above, return to the skill deficit (7), section IV. In this case, Susan was unable to successfully identify newspaper ads for "more and less expensive" item. This can now be taught directly using the newspaper ad as the classroom material.

VIII. Reassess discrete skill (return to III).
    1. Return to the original objective and again ask Susan to complete it.

This process has led to the identification of Susan's difficulty. Instruction has resulted in her successfully completing the task. She is now ready to move on to other instructional tasks.

Individualized Education Program

A complete curriculum/instruction format that supports and facilitates this concept of assessment (combining both learner and task analysis) is the individualized education program (IEP). As we have seen, the IEP is required as a provision of P.L. 94-142 and is intended to be the vehicle through which education programs can be fashioned to meet each child's learning and related needs. As mandated, the IEP must contain statements of:

1. The child's present level of performance in all areas.
2. Annual student learning goals that are subdivided into short term, measurable objectives against which the student and the school instruction can be assessed.
3. The strategies to be employed in order to help the child achieve these objectives.
4. The specific educational services to be provided for the child (i.e., speech, physical therapy, etc.).
5. The educational placement of the child, including the extent to which the child will participate in regular programs.
6. Specification of schedules and time required for special services.
7. Appropriate objective criteria and evaluation procedures.

Without doubt, the assessment of "the child's present level of performance" as described in the IEP is the crux of an individualized planning process. Without an accurate determination of present performance, short-term objectives and annual goals are of dubious value. The responsibility for gathering all of the information required for an IEP is shared by several professionals. All persons who provide service to a child must have input into the development of that particular child's IEP. Each professional who provides service must ultimately be accountable for the child's progress in his or her special area. The multidisciplinary plan, which includes all necessary services, is then shared with the child's parents. The parent has the opportunity to sign the document, in essence giving "informed consent" to the school to carry out the plan. The IEP, as required by P.L. 94-142, is reviewed annually with the parent.

The role of parents in the development of an IEP can be a significant one. Because mentally retarded students learn slowly, they will not be able to master all the instructional objectives established for their peers. Parents, then, should be involved in selecting the skills and concepts they believe are most important for their children. In this way, parents have an opportunity to provide input regarding what their children learn. The law also requires that, when appropriate, the student be a part of the planning process and the selection of specific educational goals.

The IEP requirement has made professional educators uneasy. Three reasons for this unrest have been identified. First, the IEP process requires the cooperation of the classroom teacher, special teacher, supportive personnel, building principal and the parents or guardian of the child to develop, monitor, and evaluate the student's program. Consequently, a substantial investment of time and coordination among professionals is demanded. Second, the process holds all concerned "accountable" for student achievement. Accountability is undeniably tied to teacher reward. Third, professional educators are aware of the problems associated with the central issue inherent in the IEP concept, namely assessment. The IEP requirement for "appropriate and objective criteria and evaluation procedures" cannot be "appropriate" if the initial assessment is faulty.

We have come full circle from the implementation of the individualized education program to the central issue it involves. Can the teacher, working with other professions, parents, and the child himself, accurately assess a pupil's knowledge and level of competency on any given tasks? Indeed, if the classroom teacher is capable of successfully performing instructional assessment, then concepts such as the IEP, or Bloom's mastery learning or diagnostic-prescriptive instruction can truly revolutionize education in all classrooms in America.

Conclusion

We have suggested in this chapter an assessment program that is diagnostic in purpose (as opposed to normative). Students should be encouraged to succeed in learning appropriate school tasks. Given the individualized, performance-based curriculum/instruction model (IEP) mandated by P.L. 94-142, teachers will need to become assessment-minded. They will have to be aware of the nature of assessment and its problems. They will need to be aware of the limitations of norm-referenced testing and thus use information derived from such tests wisely and only for appropriate purposes. To institute a classroom assessment program, teachers must use many measures, including observation, and must learn to develop and administer criterion-referenced tests to individual students. For their accuracy and usefulness, these tests depend upon a careful analysis of the subject matter content to be learned. In fact, this analysis is the heart of the assessment process. Because of its importance, we have devoted a significant portion of Chapter 5 to explaining the process of analysis which undergirds the development of criterion-referenced assessment.

REFERENCES

Bateman, B. Three approaches to diagnosis and educational planning for children with learning disabilities. *Academic Therapy Quarterly*, 1967, *3*, 11–16.

Bijou, S. What psychology has to offer education—now. *Journal of Applied Behavior Analysis*, 1970, *3*, 65–71.

Bloom, B. S. *Human characteristics and school learning*. New York: McGraw-Hill, 1976.

Cartwright, C. A., & Cartwright, G. P. *Developing observation skills*. New York: McGraw-Hill, 1974.

Coulter, W. A., & Morrow, H. W. (Eds.). *The concept and measurement of adoptive behavior within the scope of psychological assessment*. Austin: Texas Regional Resource Center, 1977.

Drew C., Freston, C., & Logan, D. Criteria and reference in evaluation. *Focus on Exceptional Children*, 1972, *4*, 1–10.

Dunn, L. M. Special education for the mildly retarded—Is much of it justified? *Exceptional Children*, 1968, *35*, 5–24.

Dunn, L. M., & Markwardt, F. C. Peabody Individual Achievement Test. Circle Pines, Minn.: American Guidance Service, 1970.

Gillespie, P., & Sitko, M. Training preservice teachers in diagnostic teaching. *Exceptional Children*, 1976, *42*, 401–402.

Glaser, R. Adapting to individual differences. *Social Policy*, 1977, *8* (2), 27–33.

Glasser, W. *Schools without failure*. New York: Harper & Row, 1969.

Gold, M. The acquisition of a complex assembly task by retarded adolescents. Urbana: University of Illinois, Children's Research Center, 1968.

Hammill, D. Evaluating children for instructional purposes. *Academic Therapy*, 1971, *4*, 341–353.

Harvey, K., & Horton, L. Bloom's human characteristics and school learning. KAPPAN, 1977, *59* (3), 190.

Kagan, J. Testing skills, not intelligence. *Social Policy*, 1977, *8* (2), 18–19.

Kirk, S., McCarthy, J., & Kirk, W. *Illinois Test of Psycholinguistic Abilities* (rev. ed.). Urbana: University of Illinois Press, 1968.

Lambert, N. M., Windmiller, M., Cole, L., & Figueroa, R. *AAMD Adaptive Behavior Scale: Public School Version* (1974 Revision). Washington, D.C.: American Association on Mental Deficiency, 1974.

Leland, H., Nihira, K., Foster, R., Shelhaas, M., & Kagin, E. *Conference on measurement of adaptive behavior*, III. Parsons, Kans.: Parsons State Hospital and Training Center, 1968.

Mercer, J. *Labeling the mentally retarded*. Berkeley: University of California Press, 1973.

Plata, M. Criterion-referenced assessment for individual learning. *Social Policy*, 1977, *8* (2), 53–54.

Pottinger, P. S. *Competency assessment at school and work. Social Policy*, 1977, *8* (2), 35–40.

President's Committee on Mental Retardation. *The six-hour retarded child.* Washington, D.C.: Department of Health, Education and Welfare, 1970.

Resnick, L. Matching tests with goals. *Social Policy*, 1977, *8* (2), 6.

Sarason, S., Levine, M., Goldenberg, I., Cherlin, D., & Bennett, E. Translating psychological concepts into action. In B. Blatt, D. Biklen, & R. Bogdon (Eds.), *An alternative textbook in special education.* Denver: Love Publishing, 1977.

Sattler, J. M. *Assessment of children's intelligence.* Philadelphia: Saunders, 1974.

Stellern, J., Vasa, S., & Little, J. *Introduction to diagnostic-prescriptive teaching and programming.* Glen-Ridge, N.J.: Exceptional Press, 1976.

Terman, L. M., & Merrill, M. A. The Stanford-Binet Intelligence Scale (3rd ed.). Boston: Houghton Mifflin, 1973.

Wechsler, D. Wechsler Intelligence Scale for Children. New York: The Psychological Corporation, 1949; rev. ed., 1974.

Ysseldyke, J., & Salvia, J. Diagnostic prescriptive teaching: Two models. *Exceptional Children*, 1974, *41*, 181–185.

Educational settings for retarded students

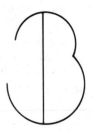

Incidental learning occurs as each of us reacts to the stimuli received from our environment. Learning occurs as we proceed through our daily activities; it occurs as we dress at home, plan our meals, travel, work, and relax. In almost any kind of environment, much learning is unplanned and haphazard.

Because of the uncertainty of incidental learning, all societies provide varying amounts of "instruction"—planned encounters designed to achieve predetermined learning goals. In Chapter 1, the learning characteristics of retarded learners were described. In each case, these characteristics have implications for the design and implementation of instruction. However, an examination of learning characteristics would not be complete without focusing on the special environments where instruction occurs. These environments or settings are often important factors in explaining and predicting instructional success or failure, particularly when applied to the education of retarded learners.

History of Retarded Individuals in Educational Settings

Creation of Institutions in the United States

Historically, mentally retarded persons were treated only in public institutions.

Guggenbuhl (1816–1863), a Swiss physician, created the first treatment facilities for the care of mentally retarded persons, in Switzerland. His pioneering work led to the establishment of institutions throughout Europe and the United States. By 1920, all but four states in America had some type of institution for the mentally retarded. Although there were isolated efforts to establish instructional classes for retarded pupils in the community, other treatment alternatives available to the parents of retarded children were very limited.

During the 1800s, many institutions for the retarded were established. These early institutions, though segregated, were designed to make deviant people less deviant (Wolfensberger, 1975). This was to be accomplished primarily through education. According to Wolfensberger (1975), only some retarded children were candidates for institutional education. Thus the more severely retarded individuals, who showed limited potential to benefit from education, were not to be included in these settings.

This rehabilitative and optimistic view of institutions was altered by changing social attitudes during the late 19th century. By 1915, such experts as Goddard (1912) and Fernald (1912) were advocating segregation of the "feebleminded" because they felt the condition was hereditary. They further held that all of society was in jeopardy due to the excessively high reproductive rate of retarded adults.

Thus, institutions that were originally designed for education quickly were transformed into "warehouses" designed to segregate. Furthermore, not only were those retarded people with the potential to benefit from education admitted, but a much broader range of individuals judged to be a possible menace to society were admitted too.

As a result of these changing practices, more institutions were built far from metropolitan areas, to further segregate the residents from the larger society. This distance from the social mainstream created many problems. It was difficult to attract qualified staff. Politicians and decision makers were isolated from the realities of life in the institutions. Medical, technological, and social advances in the outside world rarely found their way into these facilities. For most families, accessibility to these settings was difficult or the distance was used as an excuse; thus, residents were rarely visited and often forgotten. More often, the social stigma of acknowledging a retarded relative, let alone visiting this person, was a much greater deterrent than the actual distance to the institution.

Characteristics of institutions. These early facilities were overcrowded, understaffed, and lacked good programs. As more of the lay and professional community became aware of these conditions, a cry for change was sounded. In the early 1950s, some states began to upgrade living conditions within their institutions. Residents were grouped according to their ages. Most lived and slept in large wards or dormitories; selected children were placed in unlocked cottages. In general, humane, supportive environments were few and far between.

As professionals, parents, and policy makers directed their attention to these intolerable conditions, new programs were initiated on a highly selective basis. Educational programs were again offered to those residents "most likely to succeed." While the more competent residents attended school classes for a small portion of the day, the others were confined to their wards for 24 hours. Less competent residents were left to fend for themselves in the wards.

Frequently, higher functioning individuals were assigned jobs commensurate with their abilities, but they received no renumeration for these tasks. As a captive labor supply, their exploitation became a way of life. But for many, work without pay was more desirable than doing nothing. This practice became known as "institutional peonage."

Changing Practices

Because institutions were inadequately staffed and insufficiently funded, they were unable to provide adequate programs to meet the complex needs of the populations they were established to serve. Until successful judicial intervention occurred, these conditions persisted. In *Wyatt* v. *Stickney* (1971), the litigation brought about specific standards that could be enforced by the courts for the adequate treatment of mentally ill and mentally retarded persons. Similar lawsuits have been filed in nearly every state since then.

Public institutions are, by their very nature, restrictive environments. Their residents are isolated from the larger society and, in many institutions, residents are isolated from each other. The issue of restrictiveness included in the *Wyatt* v. *Stickney* decision states:

> Residents shall have a right to the least restrictive conditions necessary to achieve the purposes of habitation. To this end, the institution shall make every attempt to move residents from (1) more to less structured living; (2) larger to smaller facilities; (3) larger to smaller living units; (4) group to individual residence; (5) segregated from the community to integrated into the community; (6) dependent to independent living.

Since the early 1970s, a national effort has been underway to release mentally retarded individuals from large state facilities and return them to their own communities. This process, *deinstitutionalization,* has significantly decreased the populations in formerly massive state institutions. Merely discharging people from undesirable living conditions, however, is not sufficient to meet their needs. Alternative community living facilities, appropriate educational programs, and a network of community services are essential to meet the goals of deinstitutionalization. Policy making, sufficient personnel preparation, financial resources, and community education must accompany this process if the goal of community reintegration is to be realized.

Community Residential Facilities

As an alternative to public institutions, the concept of community residential facilities (CRF) has gained wide acceptance during the last 10 years. Often called *group homes,* CRF's provide an appropriate living environment for retarded individuals, especially retarded adults. O'Connor (1976) reports that, although CRF residents range in age from the very young to the very old, the majority of the population is between 17 and 34 years of age. Group homes are preferred placements for people of all ages who need specialized residential care.

The CRF's serve retarded adults in many ways previously not available in large public institutions. Most residents are employed in the community, exposed to the larger society, and free to interact socially with their peers and family. The residents are taught life survival skills, and it is expected that about 40% of them will be able to live independently in the community sometime in the future.

Each CRF has a staff of trained personnel responsible for aiding in the social, employment and growth experiences of the residents. O'Connor (1976) reports two primary staffing patterns, which fall into the following groups:

1. Full-time administrators and direct case staff, principally in large facilities and those serving children;
2. Houseparents, most common in small facilities and those serving older residents. (p. 66)

Group homes have primarily served moderately and severely retarded individuals. Mildly handicapped persons usually live at home and, in most cases, are able to live independently in the community. However, in many cases, these individuals could also benefit from such group settings.

Public Schools

In public schools, the history of retarded learners reveals constant struggle. However, there were sporadic examples of educational day classes for retarded pupils. Despite the concerted effort to expand public school programs begun after World War II, these programs, almost invariably established in major urban centers, provided segregated education to selected handicapped children. These children were isolated from other students; their teachers were separated from the rest of the staff. In fact, a specialized system for delivery of special education services was established. Essentially, regular educators and influential lay persons were apathetic towards special education.

The social and political turmoil of the 1960s resulted in heightened public awareness of the need for change in many of our institutions —among them the schools. With advances in civil rights, penetrating questions probed the procedures used for identifying and educating retarded learners, many of whom were from minority and ethnic groups. During these years, the term *mainstreaming* first appeared. *Mainstreaming* is the process of returning the retarded learner back to the regular classroom for most of the school day. This movement frightened most educators because the drive for equality would force the educational establishment to provide an appropriate education for *all* children, regardless of the nature and severity of their handicap. Much fear centered around the unfounded suspicion that retarded children would be "dumped" into regular classrooms where the teachers would not have the skills to teach them.

Judicial and Legislative Actions

As recently as the early 1970s, many state and local boards of education provided educational access only to mildly handicapped learners, continuing the practice of excluding more severely retarded youngsters from public education.* In 1971, the Pennsylvania Association for Retarded Children (PARC) filed a class-action suit against the Commonwealth of Pennsylvania for alleged failure to provide all retarded school-age children with access to a free public education. Abeson and Zettel (1977) summarize the outcomes of the suit:

> The court supervised agreement which resolved that phase of the suit decreed the state could not apply any policy that would postpone, terminate, or deny children who were mentally retarded access to a publicly supported education. Further, it stated that all retarded children in the State of Pennsylvania between the ages of six and twenty-one were to be provided with publicly supported education by September, 1972. (p. 117)

In a similar case in 1972, *Mills* v. *Board of Education of the District of Columbia*, the court decided that all school-age children, regardless of the severity of their handicap, were entitled to an appropriate, free public education. Most states have since responded by proposing legislation to provide, at the minimum, a free public education to retarded individuals.

However, we must look to federal legislation to find the greatest impetus for change in the education of handicapped youngsters. Setting the stage for change were Section 504 of P.L. 93–112, the Vocational Rehabilitation Act Amendment of 1973, and P.L. 93–380, the Education for all Handicapped Children Act, and its 1975 amendments, known as P.L. 94–142.

Federal Legislation—P.L. 94–142

The legislation responsible for producing successive waves of change in the education of handicapped children was Public Law 94–142, the Education for All Handicapped Children Act of 1975.

---

*This was most marked in rural states and communities. Even in urban areas, where emphasis on the education of the handicapped is traditionally greater, children with severe or profound retardation have been granted the right to a free public education only in the last 5 years.

This law assures each handicapped person that education is a right, not a privilege that may be bestowed by a state or local board of education at will.

If a local board of education is to qualify for federal funds, it must provide the following characteristics in its education for handicapped children: (a) zero reject, which means the inclusion of all handicapped children in a free, appropriate public education; (b) nondiscriminatory evaluation and classification; (c) procedural due process; (d) parent and consumer participation in school decision making; and (e) placement in the least restrictive, appropriate educational setting (Klein, 1978).

If a local board does *not* comply with these criteria, it does not simply forfeit the special education funds. The potential penalty for noncompliance is the forfeiture of *all* federal funds. Compliance is made possible through monitoring by the Office of Civil Rights, under the Department of Health, Education and Welfare.

Specifically, P.L. 94–142 is concerned with the identification and placement of handicapped individuals in public schools. Its major provision, the *least restrictive alternative,* will be discussed later in this chapter, along with labeling and nondiscriminatory testing, due process, and the individualized educational programs (IEP).

Labeling and nondiscriminatory testing. Traditionally, children with developmental difficulties are assessed by psychologists who administer a battery of standardized tests and intelligence tests. Based on these test results, children are labeled and identified for classroom placement or other necessary services. However, the current practice of classifying children in labeled categories was found to produce major problems (Abeson, Bolick, & Hass, 1975). Inappropriate labeling affects children adversely:

> Labeled children are often victimized by stigma associated with the label. This may be manifested by isolation from usual school opportunities and taunting and rejection by both children and school personnel. In the latter instance, it may be overt or unconscious.

> Assigning labels to children often suggests to those working with them that the children's behavior should conform to stereotyped behavioral expectations associated with the labels. This often contributes to a self-fulfilling prophecy in that a child, once labeled, is expected to conform with the stereotyped behavior associated with the label and ultimately does so. When a child is labeled

and placement is made on the basis of that label, there is often no opportunity to escape from either the label or the placement

Children who are labeled and placed in educational programs on the basis of that label may often not need special education programs. This is obviously true for children who are incorrectly labeled, but it also applies to children with certain handicaps, often of a physical nature. The fact that a child is physically handicapped does not mean that a special education is required. (p. 5)

To guard against misclassifying children, P.L. 94–142 guarantees that each child be administered nondiscriminatory evaluations. The individual must be tested in his or her native tongue or mode of communication; the tests must be selected and administered so that they are not culturally biased; and no single procedure or test can be the sole criterion in determining the labeling or the appropriate school program. This provides protection for both the child and the parents or guardians of the handicapped individual. They are also protected by procedural due process safeguards guaranteed under the Act.

Due process. The right to due process, one of the most important provisions of the act, is included so that all parties involved in the process of placement are guaranteed their constitutional rights. Handicapped children, their parents or guardians, and the public schools are guaranteed equal protection so that an appropriate education can be determined for each individual in harmony with the wishes of the parents. Consequently, parents have a role in placement decisions. Abeson and Zettel (1977) summarize the major points of due process:

The specific elements of due process the Congress included in the law follow:
1. Written notification before evaluation. In addition, the right to an interpreter/translator if the family's native language is not English (unless it is clearly not feasible to do so).
2. Written notification when initiating or refusing to initiate a change in educational element.
3. Opportunity to present complaints regarding the identification, evaluation, placement, or the provision of a free appropriate education.
4. Opportunity to obtain an independent educational evaluation of the child.
5. Access to all relevant records.

6. Opportunity for an impartial due process hearing including the right to:
   a. Receive timely and specific notice of the hearing.
   b. Be accompanied and advised by counsel and by individuals with special knowledge or training with respect to the problems of children with handicaps.
   c. Confront, cross examine, and compel the attendance of witnesses.
   d. Present evidence:
      1. Written or electronic verbatim record of the hearing.
      2. Written findings of fact and decisions.
7. The right to appeal the findings and decisions of the hearing. (pp. 125–126)

Decisions for placing a handicapped child in the most appropriate educational program are made in conjunction with the development of an individualized education program (IEP). The placement decision, which is part of the IEP process, includes both parents and professionals from several disciplines.

Individualized Education Programs.   Special education is conceived to be "special" in that instruction is designed to meet the unique needs of handicapped learners. Special education has not always lived up to this expectation however. There are some who contend that special education is neither special nor education. To control the lack of individualized instructional modifications that have characterized many special educational classes, the federal government included a requirement for IEP. Weintraub (1977) describes this requirement as follows:

> The term "individualized education program" itself conveys important concepts that need to be specified. First "individualized" means that the IEP must be addressed to the educational needs of a single child rather than a class or group of children. Second, "education" means that the IEP is limited to those elements of the child's education and related services as defined by the act. Third, "program" means that the IEP is a statement of what will actually be provided to the child, as distinct from a plan, which provides guidelines from which a program must subsequently be developed. (p. 27)

The Act states that the IEP is not to be written by the teacher alone. Rather, it is to be developed by parents, the child where possible, and a team of professionals who are intimately involved in the child's education. The specific components of the IEP are further illuminated in this definition included in P.L. 94–142:

A written statement for each handicapped child developed in any meeting by a representative of the local educational agency or an intermediate educational unit who shall be qualified to provide, or supervise the provision of, specially designed instruction to meet the unique needs of handicapped children, the teacher, the parents or guardians of such child, and, whenever appropriate, such child, which statement shall include (a) a statement of the present levels of educational performance of such child, (b) a statement of annual goals, including short-term instructional objectives, (c) a statement of the specific educational services to be provided to such child, and the extent to which such child will be able to participate in regular educational programs, (d) the projected date for initiation and anticipated duration of such services, and appropriate objective criteria and evaluation procedures and schedules for determining, on at least an annual basis, whether instructional objectives are being achieved. (Sec. 4.a,19)

Each child has a responsibility in this small-group activity.

Today many school systems involve teachers, psychologists, principals, counselors, remedial reading and math specialists, physical educators, special therapists, and parents in the formulation of each handicapped child's IEP. Although this multidisciplinary approach requires time and effort, it builds accountability in education. Finally, this process assures that each child receives an individually prescribed, appropriate education, one that has clearly defined objectives and measurable outcomes.

We discussed the assessment features of the IEP in Chapter 2. Although the IEP is indeed an individualized, accountable instructional system, it will require substantial changes in the way children's learning strengths and weaknesses are assessed. This implies that changes will be required on the part of the entire school system if the spirit as well as the letter of the IEP is to be realized. Such changes are much greater than merely individually planning for children with special needs.

Least restrictive alternatives.   The integration of handicapped children into the mainstream of regular education has been one of the most widely discussed issues among professional educators in recent years. The terms *normalization* and *appropriate education* provide the principle upon which the definition of the least restrictive alternative is built.

The normalization principle requires that educational experiences for handicapped children closely resemble those of their nonhandicapped peers. Normalization implies integration; nonnormalization or restricted implies segregation. Hence, P.L. 94–142 mandates the least restrictive setting, one that will insure the most interaction between handicapped children and their peers in the regular classroom.

Maximizing interactions among diverse populations requires more than merely placing children with different learning, physical, or behavioral characteristics in the same classroom. It includes at least four dimensions: (a) social integration, (b) status characteristics, (c) physical proximity, and (d) instructional participation.

Social integration involves teachers who play an important role in facilitating the social integration of children with differing characteristics. Through the purposeful design of experiences and activities, children of varying levels of competency can be brought together. For example, pairing children for field trips, lunch, and games helps children (who may otherwise not do so) interact socially. Structured, socially integrated experiences let students become acquainted and develop relationships that can lead to assimilation and acceptance among peers.

Through the use of wise instructional groupings in the classroom, the teacher can also affect social interactions that will be beneficial for both on handicapped and nonhandicapped children. Individual strengths and weaknesses can be discussed openly, and helping relationships can be fostered by teachers and students in a variety of cooperative efforts. The incidental learning of the handicapped children, especially in the social realm, may increase, and non-handicapped pupils can learn patience from handicapped pupils. All can learn to respect individual differences.

Status characteristics identified by the teacher affect the degree of social and instructional integration. Sociological and socio-psychological researchers have observed that classrooms contain several status systems and that the teacher is intimately involved in constructing and maintaining some of these systems. Furthermore, under certain conditions, these status systems have important effects on peer attitudes, social integration, and learning. Rist (1970) studied a group of black youngsters from kindergarten through the second grade. In kindergarten, the lower social-class children were more likely to be placed in the back of the room, regardless of their reading scores. They had less interaction with the teacher and often appeared to be unable to see or hear her instructions. By the second grade, the initial division had become a true performance differential, so that those at the back table were now poorer readers.

Physical proximity refers to the actual distance between children in a classroom. The status of particular children in a classroom is affected by the distance between them or between particular groupings of selected children (see Rist, 1970). The climate of a classroom is affected by the proximity of the children to each other as well as the varying distance of the teacher relative to the children. Thus, this dimension has important implications for a child's classroom social integration; the teacher is the organizer and the modifier of the physical environment.

Instructional participation refers to the degree to which handicapped children share instructional experiences with their non-handicapped peers. The teacher needs to develop instructional activities that require varying levels of participation from the students in a class. Some handicapped children can participate with the class in all activities, with special support in certain skill areas from the regular teacher or an itinerant aide. Others will only be able to participate in nonsequential skill activities such as gym, social studies, music, and art. The degree of instructional participation depends upon two factors: (a) the teacher's willingness and ability to modify instruction to include tasks of varying levels of difficulty, and (b) the handicapped child's ability to accommodate the demands of the instructor.

Assuming that a school board wished to examine existing instructional environments for the purpose of selecting a least restrictive environment for its handicapped students, what alternatives would be available? Which alternatives take into account such factors as status characteristics and social, physical, and instructional integration? We shall now turn our attention to these questions.

Instructional Alternatives: Deno's Cascade System

Deno (1970) proposed a cascade system of special education services that can clarify the program models available as the least restrictive alternatives. The cascade system (Figure 3–1) includes eight levels, ranging from the least restrictive settings (regular classrooms) to the most restrictive settings (institutions). This model reminds us that not all handicapped children will be placed in the regular school class-

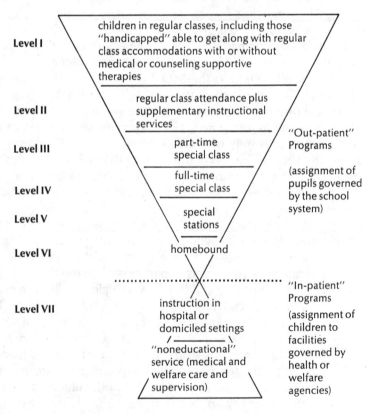

Figure 3–1   *The cascade system of special education service*

Reprinted from *Exceptional Children*, "Special education as developmental capital," by Evelen Deno by permission of The Council for Exceptional Children. Copyright © 1970 by The Council for Exceptional Children.

room. For many severely or profoundly impaired individuals, a self-contained classroom is the least restrictive setting. In all cases, the cascade model must be viewed in reference to meeting individual needs, which is the primary consideration in the placement decision.

Since the primary focus of this book is on mildly and moderately retarded children and youth, we will look at the cascade system in terms of these children's educational needs. The cascade "region" we shall refer to include Levels I through IV. We will look at four available placement options.

1. Self-contained classroom
2. Resource room
3. Engineered classroom
4. Learning centers

The Self-Contained Classroom

The largest group of the mildly mentally retarded (MMR) population, those whose IQ scores generally range from 50 to 70, have traditionally been assigned to self-contained classrooms in public schools. These so-called special classes are obviously unable to meet the criteria of integrated education. On other dimensions, however, the quality of education has improved somewhat over the past two decades.

During the 1950s, these classes were low-priority concerns for public school systems. The sad, true facts are that retarded learners (pre-1960) were the second-class citizens of the educational society. The classrooms were either in the basement or on the top floor, and the regular classroom pupils had no contact with these "special kids" or "retards." Due to the inadequate budget allocated to special education, these students used books and desks and other equipment from the regular classrooms that had been discarded. A self-fulfilling prophecy accompanied the label; the students frequently performed accordingly. The kind and quality of treatment many pupils received led them to believe that they were unimportant and not highly valued by the system, and many teachers felt the same way. Their teachers were told, overtly and covertly, that their task was hopeless. Many gave up at the outset. They had little, if any, interaction with either the administration or the regular class teachers. Special education teachers were often peripheral to the running of the school. Their students, likewise, were outside the mainstream of school life. The lack of specialized training in special education was another major contributing factor to the failures in these earliest classes.

Placement practices for the mildly retarded differed widely among states, cities, and schools within a district. Most school systems relied upon individual intelligence test scores derived from the Wechsler Intelligence Test for Children (Wechsler, 1974) or the Stanford-Binet Intelligence Scale (Terman & Merrill, 1973) to determine placement. During the early 1960s, if the child scored below 80 or in some cases 85, then he was labeled "retarded." Often, though, children who had problems in social behavior in the regular class were put into a special class, regardless of test scores. Such students were so placed for several reasons: to decrease class size, to relieve a regular classroom teacher, or to punish an individual. These procedures have been altered considerably by the requirement of multifactored evaluation in P.L. 94–142, discussed in detail in Chapter 2.

In many schools, little attention was given to breadth of age ranges among the retarded learners in the special classes. Special classes for retarded students were known to have as many as 15 to 20 students who ranged from 8 to 17 years of age. Even a casual consideration of the social results of a situation like that portends disaster.

The curricula were as diverse and numerous as the placement patterns of the various school systems. Some major school systems had an outline of a curriculum, which contained watered-down elementary school activities. There were no assessment and evaluation criteria. The teacher almost always planned his own curriculum; the learning of the students was rarely scrutinized by the school principal. Usually the school principal was uncomfortable with a special class in the building and was satisfied to let it and its inhabitants remain in quiet neglect.

Recent changes. With the advent of better training programs for teachers, parent advocacy, and increased societal awareness, self-contained classrooms have improved during the last 10 years. Although class sizes have remained the same, more emphasis has been placed on grouping children of similar ages. Most school systems presently have four age groups for the mildly retarded. The classifications are generally: (a) primary, grades 1–3; (b) intermediate, grades 4–6; (c) junior high, grades 7–9; and (d) secondary, grades 10–12, with some pupils to the age of 21.

Although many school systems still have vague curricula, elementary classrooms focus on basic skills and work-study experiences. The addition of diagnostic-prescriptive teaching has also improved the level of instruction. It has enabled the teachers to better assess, plan, teach, and evaluate learning in more precise and accountable ways.

However, for many retarded children, the self-contained classroom certainly does not provide the least restrictive environment. Its use with mildly retarded learners has been questioned since the early 1960s. Johnson (1962) struck one of the earliest blows with this statement:

> It is indeed paradoxical that mentally handicapped children having teachers especially trained, having more money (per capita) spent on their education, and being designed to provide for their unique needs, should be accomplishing the objectives of their education at the same or at a lower level than similar mentally handicapped children who have not had these advantages and have been forced to remain in the regular grades. (p. 66)

Much of the research on the efficacy of the self-contained class has been criticized on methodological grounds. Although there are conflicting data, several studies have concluded that retarded pupils make as much progress in regular classes as they do in self-contained, special education classes (Huelke, 1966, Kirk, 1964; Smith & Kennedy, 1967). Yet even in the light of this evidence, public schools have increased the number of self-contained special education classrooms. Against a standard of the least restrictive alternative, a self-contained classroom falls short in all dimensions. Consequently, many schools have attempted to provide for greater integration through a *resource room*.

Resource Room

Dunn (1968) reviewed the research highlighting the failures of special education for mildly retarded learners. As an alternative, he recommended that retarded learners be integrated as much as possible into regular classrooms. To provide additional supportive services, he suggested that a specialized supplementary area and teacher be available to enrich the educational program of special education youngsters. This supportive environment became known as a *resource room*. The cascade model places the resource room concept in both Levels II and III.

The resource room concept places all learners in regular classrooms for most periods during the school day. The special needs learner leaves the regular classroom only for designated periods each day, for special assistance in identified academic areas. The resource room is under the direction of a trained special education teacher who tailors specialized instruction for children who require it. Cooperation and coordination of efforts between regular and special educators are essential.

Many educators felt that the resource room would provide the support needed to allow retarded pupils to be integrated into the regular classroom. In some cases, this did occur. But several problems have emerged, among them social acceptance among peers. One sociometric study focused on 40 former special class educable mentally retarded children, in an effort to determine the degree of interactions among children. These children all participated in a resource room program in a large urban area. Results indicated that the EMR children receiving resource room services were no more likely to be accepted by their regular classroom peers than were EMR children, reported in previous studies, for whom no such supportive services were available (Iano, Ayers, Heller, McGettigan, & Walker, 1974). Other approaches are obviously needed.

More recently, social skills of mildly retarded learners have been the focus of several investigators. Stephens (1977) and Goldstein (1974) address the importance of teaching social skills to individuals with special needs in order for them to be more readily accepted by their peers. The procedures they suggest can be taught and reinforced by the classroom and resource teacher in cooperation with parents.

There are several other problems in successful implementation of the resource room. One problem is that the regular classroom teacher has not been trained or accustomed to individualizing instruction. Some teachers have been unable to provide careful instruction to follow-up the work of the resource room teacher. At the same time, the resource teacher, who must assist the classroom teacher with instructional modifications and adaptations, is often too busy to provide adequate classroom consultation. This consultation is essential, because regular education practices are characterized by group-oriented classroom instruction that may run counter to the needs of special children. Clearly, much time, thought, and cooperation are required if the potential benefits of resource consultation are to be realized.

Classroom Models

We have described the characteristics of some self-contained classrooms. Our discussion may lead you to conclude that all special classrooms are alike. Such a conclusion is no more valid than the statement that all regular classrooms are alike. That is just not so. Classrooms vary in size, curriculum, routines, and organization.

Several models for classroom organization have been touted during the past several years. These include teacher-centered, traditional classes with desks in neat rows facing the front of the room; modified open classrooms with desks in groups of four or five children or larger tables that seat six or eight children in a group; highly individualized classrooms completed with isolated carrols; and open classrooms with content-oriented learning centers. There are some classrooms that combine several of these models. The organization of a classroom is closely related to the philosophy and goals of the teacher. Traditional classrooms tend to provide less freedom of movement and choice for the students; open classrooms afford the students a great deal of freedom and choice of activities, and many opportunities for movement within the class.

Some classroom organization models are more easily modified to include children of differing needs than others. The ease with which a retarded child can be integrated into a classroom depends not only on the skills, knowledge, and attitudes of the teacher, but also on the organization of the classroom as well.

In the following section we will describe several classroom organization models that hold the most promise for successful integration of handicapped and nonhandicapped students. Some models are quite open, and others are inherently more structured. One example of a highly structured classroom was developed by Hewett (1967).

Engineered classroom. One of the most clearly defined instructional settings for exceptional children is the engineered classroom described by Hewett (1967). Although Hewett's classroom was designed primarily for emotionally disturbed youngsters, it could be easily modified as a practical setting for both regular and special classes. The engineered classroom focuses on relating the instruction to the child's individual needs. To make an engineered classroom functional requires individualized assessment, strategy setting, and evaluation. As conceived by Hewett, the engineered classroom (see Figure 3–2) has predetermined activity centers:

1. *Exploratory center* (child pursues puzzles and problems involving a multisensory exploration of his environment);
2. *Order center* (child works on clearly defined tasks to practice attending to and completing educational tasks, thus gaining success and further confidence);
3. *Mastery center* (child attends to basic skill activities intended to remediate deficiencies.)

The engineered classroom concept is not only a classroom organizational scheme, it is also an attempt to match organization with

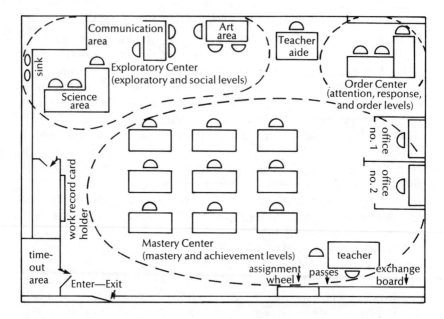

Figure 3–2   *Floorplan of an engineered classroom*

Reprinted from *Exceptional Children,* "Education engineering with emotionally disturbed children," by Frank M. Hewett by permission of The Council for Exceptional Children. Copyright © 1967 by The Council for Exceptional Children.

appropriate tasks. In Hewett's model, educational tasks such as attention are accomplished in the order center; basic skills, the mastery center; and social skills, the exploratory center.

Although the concept of the engineered classroom is designed for controlling social behavior problems, the concept and the physical environment contain many useful elements that would enhance individual teaching and learning for retarded students. Often, retarded children have emotional problems that interfere with their academic learning, and a classroom structure similar to the engineered classroom could be helpful in providing the least restrictive *and most productive* environment for them.

Learning center.   The idea of using the physical environment to alter teaching practices has been reflected in the development of *learning centers, activity areas* and *interest areas* in classrooms. The engineered classroom is one example of a learning center. Open classrooms are another. Both models share the common idea that *centers* designate specific areas for specific kinds of activities. The hierarchy of learning guides the content for specific centers in

Hewett's model. Subject-matter content usually serves as a guide to the selection of activities in learning-center classrooms.

Learning the rules helps students use the learning center more effectively.

Flexibility for instructional presentations and classroom organization is one positive aspect of learning-centered education. Freedom of movement and choices afforded students is another. Finally, the more flexible models lend themselves to student diversity. Because various activities can occur simultaneously, students can choose their activities and the people they work with. The teacher can facilitate interactions, both socially and academically, for all the students.

The learning-center approach deemphasizes teacher-directed instruction. In its place are peers, materials, and an environment that provides choices for students. These settings afford more freedom for pupils than is usually found in traditional classrooms. This model lends itself most readily to the integration of children with diverse learning characteristics. The materials available in each specific area can be tailored to the needs of each student.

Dell (1972) presented several plans for classroom organization incorporating the learning-center approach. Plan 1 (Figure 3–3) is more complex and more expensive than Hewett's model, but it does provide individualized space for all areas of the established curriculum. Because of the way the classroom is sectioned, a single

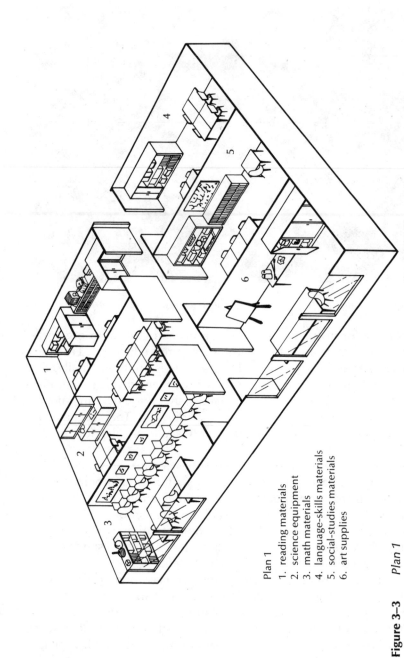

Plan 1

1. reading materials
2. science equipment
3. math materials
4. language-skills materials
5. social-studies materials
6. art supplies

Figure 3–3   *Plan 1*

From *Individualizing Instruction: Materials and Classroom Procedures* by Helen Davis Dell. © 1972, Science Research Associates, Inc. Reproduced by permission of the publisher.

teacher may find management and supervision difficult. This setting may be more amenable to team teaching. Teaming regular and special education teachers could provide integrated education. Placement in this model would be determined by the learning characteristics, needs, and interests of the children.

Plan 2 (Figure 3–4) is similar to the first, but includes a discussion area. This addition could be used for small group activities, class meetings, or group project planning.

Plan 3 (Figure 3–5) presents a model that could be managed by a teacher and an aide. There are fewer barriers in this plan, although there are work partitions. This plan lends itself to groupings for quiet study and partner study, two essentials for integrating retarded children with their peers. The size and space available in this plan is more appropriate for classrooms rather than for resource rooms.

An assumption underlying all of these learning-center models is the importance of students developing self-direction and social and academic responsibility. The development of positive social skills would of necessity be included as educational goals. Both social and academic independence can be fostered by the more open classroom settings.

These goals can be justified by the normalization principle. All educational experiences should be directed toward the development of independence. Learning-center classrooms by their very nature foster decision making, responsibility, and independence.

The openness of learning-centered classes is valued by those who espouse freedom for children. These classrooms are not problem-free, however. Noise and management are problems frequently cited; fortunately, there are strategies teachers can employ to accommodate these problems.

The management of children and their learning can be assisted by the use of anecdotal records, individual performance profiles, or a combination. The nature of these settings necessitates teacher-made monitoring systems for student progress. There are several possibilities from which to choose; however, some system must be implemented and communicated to the students. In fact, students can take responsibility for part of the recordkeeping.

Successful implementation of learning-center classes will require some modification of existing classes. Large classrooms are obviously more easily modified for these arrangements. But space alone is not the real issue. Using all the space in the school would not assure an appropriately integrated education. What is required is the recognition of the individuality of each learner. Diverse educational

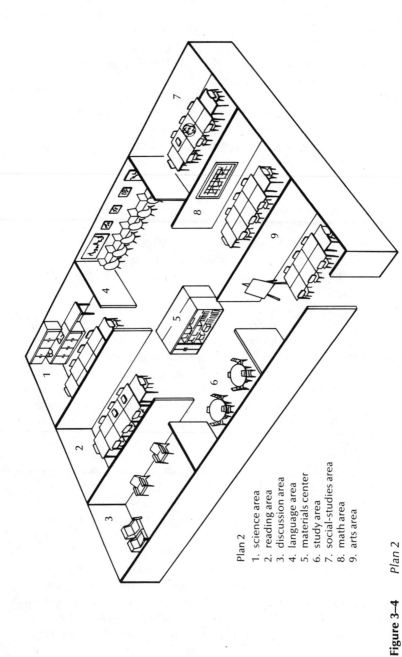

Plan 2

1. science area
2. reading area
3. discussion area
4. language area
5. materials center
6. study area
7. social-studies area
8. math area
9. arts area

Figure 3–4 *Plan 2*

From *Individualizing Instruction: Materials and Classroom Procedures* by Helen Davis Dell. © 1972, Science Research Associates, Inc. Reproduced by permission of the publisher.

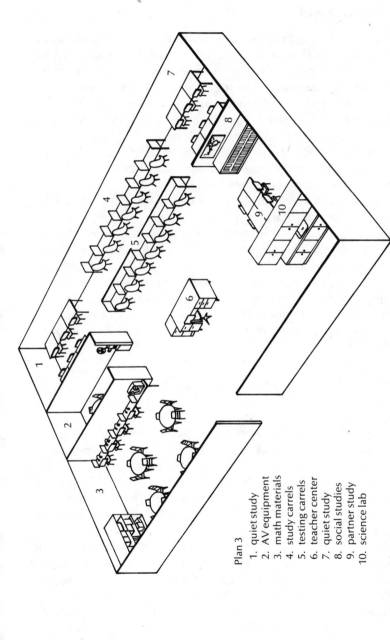

Plan 3

1. quiet study
2. AV equipment
3. math materials
4. study carrels
5. testing carrels
6. teacher center
7. quiet study
8. social studies
9. partner study
10. science lab

Figure 3–5 *Plan 3*

From *Individualizing Instruction: Materials and Classroom Procedures* by Helen Davis Dell. © 1972, Science Research Associates, Inc. Reproduced by permission of the publisher.

experiences tailored to meet varying needs are essential elements of appropriate education in least restrictive settings.

Indirect Service Model

One of the most rapidly growing service models in public school systems is the special education consulting teacher. This individual provides no direct pupil services to handicapped students; rather, the consulting teacher assists the regular classroom teacher in meeting the needs of mildly handicapped pupils in the regular classroom. The special education consultant aids the regular classroom teacher by observing classroom and individual pupil situations, advising teachers on appropriate curriculum decisions, devising instructional strategies and evaluation measures, and suggesting or selecting materials for handicapped learners.

The consulting teacher provides valuable instructional services indirectly. This person is also in a nonthreatening position to teachers. By being neither an evaluating supervisor nor a principal to the teacher, the consulting teacher can offer suggestions and discuss difficult situations within a helping relationship. Also, the consulting teacher can effect many social changes by providing information concerning retarded individuals that is realistic, objective, and based on solid teaching experience. The consulting teacher can assure the regular classroom teacher that he or she has the skills to teach retarded chldren.

Conclusion

Mentally retarded children, who in the past were relegated to isolated institutions, are now assured the right to a free, appropriate public education in the least restrictive environment possible. This legislative mandate requires the development of alternatives to self-contained classrooms in the public schools. The resource room, engineered classroom, and learning-centered classrooms are alternative integrated settings.

It must be stressed, and not forgotten, that the separation of handicapped children from the regular school program created and perpetuated the myth that only special educators could teach retarded learners. The myth also discriminated between curriculum and instructional concepts and processes, those which were for children in regular classes and those which could be used with children with special needs. It is apparent that any learning or teaching deficiency affects the selection of educational goals and the implementation of instruction. Still, special educators have readily observed that regular educators have suitable approaches to reach both nonretarded and retarded learners. The task at hand is to convince regular and special educators that they have similar goals for children and that with cooperation they can design and implement least restrictive environments for all children.

REFERENCES

Abeson, A., Bolick, N., & Hass, J. *A primer on due process: Education decisions for handicapped children.* Reston, Va.: The Council for Exceptional Children, 1975.

Abeson, A., & Zettel, J. The end of the quiet revolution: The Education of all Handicapped Children Act of 1975. *Exceptional Children,* 1977, *44,* 2.

Baldwin, W. K. The social position of the educable mentally retarded child in the regular grades in the public schools. *Exceptional Children,* 1958, *25,* 106–108; 112.

Dell, H. D. *Individualizing instruction: Materials and classroom procedures.* Chicago, Ill.: Science Research Associates, 1972.

Deno, E. Special education as developmental capital. *Exceptional Children,* 1970, *37* (3), 229–237.

Dunn, L. Special education for the mildly retarded—Is much of it justifiable? *Exceptional Children,* 1968, *35* (1), 5–22.

Fernald, W. E. The burden of feeblemindedness. *Journal of Psycho-Aesthetics,* 1912, *17,* 87–111.

Goddard, H. H. *The Kollikak family.* New York: Macmillan, 1912.

Goldstein, H. *The social learning curriculum.* Columbus, Ohio: Charles E. Merrill, 1974.

Hewett, F. M. Educational engineering with emotionally disturbed children. *Exceptional Children,* 1967, *33,* 459–467.

Huelke, G. M. *Effectiveness of special class placement for educable mentally retarded children.* Lincoln: University of Nebraska, 1966.

Iano, R., Ayers, D., Heller, H., McGettigan, J., & Walker, V. Sociometric status of retarded children in an integrative program. *Exceptional Children,* 1974, *40* (4), 267–271.

Johnson, G. O. Special education for mentally handicapped—A paradox. *Exceptional Children,* 1962, *19,* 62–69.

Johnson, G. O. A study of the social position of mentally retarded children in the regular grades. *American Journal of Mental Deficiency,* 1950, *55,* 60–89.

Kirk, S. A. Research in education. In H. A. Stevens & R. Heber (Eds.), *Mental retardation*. Chicago: University of Chicago Press, 1964.

Klein, N. Special education: Implication of new rules. *Citizen's Guide to Quality Education*. Cleveland: Citizen's Council for Ohio Schools, 1978.

O'Connor, G. *Home is a good place: A national perspective of community residential facilities for developmentally disabled persons*. Mimeograph of the American Association of Mental Deficiency, Washington, D.C., 1967, (No. 2).

Rist, R. The self-fulfilling prophecy of the ghetto school. *Harvard Educational Review, 1970, 40* (3), 411–451.

Smith, H. W., & Kennedy, W. A. Effects of three educational programs on mentally retarded children. *Perceptual and Motor Skills, 1967, 24,* 1974.

Stephens, T. M. *Teaching skills to children with learning and behavior disorder*. Columbus, Ohio: Charles E. Merrill, 1977.

Terman, L. M., & Merrill, M. A. The Stanford-Binet Intelligence Scale. Boston: Houghton Mifflin, 1973.

Wechsler, D. Wechsler Intelligence Scale for Children. New York: The Psychological Corporation, 1949; rev. ed., 1974.

Weintraub, F. Understanding the individualized education program (IEP). *Amicus, 1977, 2* (3), 23–27.

Wolfensberger, W. *The nature and origins of our institutional models*. Syracuse, N.Y.: Human Policy Press, 1975.

Educational goals for
the retarded learner

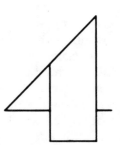

The Purpose of Education

You have been chosen to chair the "Task Force on Curriculum Development for the Mildly Retarded Learner." An awesome task you realize, and one that requires careful study. There are so many factors to be considered: the learners themselves, the skills to be learned in school subjects such as math and language arts, questions of independence and responsibility and rights. The basic problem can be expressed in different ways: What knowledge and skills are of most value to a mentally retarded learner? How do you decide what to teach? What are the essentials in a curriculum for the mentally retarded? Should a curriculum for the mildly retarded learner be similar or different than one implemented for other children?

These questions are of intense interest to professionals in the field of mental retardation. Their answers cannot be found in simplistic phrases or cliches, because the curriculum decisions teachers make each day affect children's lives. What is required is an organized process of curriculum analysis.

Special educators today agree that learning experiences for mentally retarded persons should prepare them to be productive, independent members of society. What is not clear is how that goal is to be achieved. What is the role of the school? Tradition and law say that schools are the agents to which society delegates the responsibility for educating its children and youth. Boards of Education, elected by the citizens of the community, are charged with the responsibility for setting policy, establishing curriculum, and in general, determining what is to be taught to their children.

In practice, the school's professional staff is often assigned the responsibility of developing educational goals. Too often, lay people and professionals who establish educational goals seem to use a "supermarket" approach to goal setting—randomly picking from a limited supply. This haphazard selection process results in curriculum decisions that have no foundation in theory and are subject to fads and pressure from special interest groups. Others maintain an inflexible belief that certain bits of knowledge are essential for all young people to learn. Both approaches are unsuitable. Haphazard education is antithetical to a systems approach to instruction. To base an educational program only upon standard academic disciplines—math, science, history, language arts—assumes that all learners have the same needs. Moreover, this essentialist view of education is too narrow a perspective from which to develop educational goals for a widely varying group of learners.

We believe that the purpose of education is to prepare each child to participate (to the maximum extent possible) in all arenas of society: social, political, economic, and intellectual. To meet the varying needs of the children for whom they are responsible, schools need a strong philosophy of education. This philosophy rests on several principles: (a) needs and interests of learners vary; (b) integrating children of varying physical, intellectual, and behavioral characteristics enhances the benefits of schooling for all children; (c) human diversity is valuable and educationally relevant; (d) each child is unique and as important as every other child; (e) each child can benefit from an appropriate educational program; (f) educational experiences tailored to the needs of individual children promote growth and learning.

One approach to education is that it is intended to provide children with the requisite skills, values, and attitudes necessary to cope with and maintain the status quo. People who support this idea argue that children should be taught appropriate coping skills. But this position would lead to a static society of people who cannot identify and solve the problems that accompany modern technological progress. As an alternative, we support a problem-solving approach. Education must equip children with the skills to solve problems of everyday life. Educational experiences, then, must come from a broad spectrum of sources.

Tyler's Rationale

Tyler (1949) has developed a systematic framework for setting educational goals. According to Tyler (see Figure 4–1), there are three primary sources from which educational goals may be derived: the needs of contemporary society, the needs and interests of the learner, and subject matter content. Each source is a rich depository of ideas; each must be considered when selecting educational goals.

To determine all relevant information contained in each source, Tyler suggests that each be intensively analyzed. The information derived from this analysis is translated into a series of goals. These goals are then filtered though an underlying educational philosophy and a psychology of learning. The final products are instructional objectives, precisely stated, yet developed from a broadly based perspective that includes the learner, the social context, and subject matter.

The Needs of Contemporary Society: The First Source

A learner's society provides the context for the goals of his education. That is, the goals set for a student in an agricultural society would be different from those for a technological society. Let's look at several aspects of American contemporary society to see how they affect the educational goals set for retarded learners.

Attitudes toward education. The need to educate mentally retarded children in schools was first identified at the turn of the 20th century. Although mentally retarded children were to be educated, they

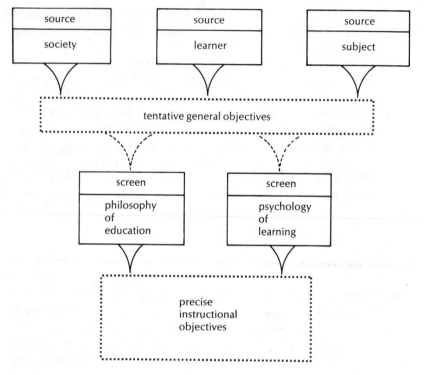

Figure 4–1 *Tyler's curricular rationale*

From W. James Popham and Eva L. Baker, *Establishing Instructional Goals,* Englewood Cliffs, N.J.: Prentice-Hall, 1970. Copyright © by Prentice-Hall. Based on material from various chapters in Ralph Tyler, *Basic Principles of Curriculum and Instruction,* Chicago, Ill.: University of Chicago Press, 1969. Copyright © by University of Chicago Press. Reprinted by permission of publishers.

were to be separated from their nonretarded peers. Curriculum guides used during this period were "watered down" versions of the standard curriculum. Consequently, the curriculum goals established for retarded learners were generally amorphous. There is little evidence that assessment, systematic goal setting, or accountability were included in the curriculum development process. As we consider the values and attitudes of our society during that period, this is not surprising; the schools had other issues—response to new technology—which preempted their attention.

During the 1970s new forces began to change public attitudes toward education of retarded learners. Advocates of the retarded—including their parents—created pressure which led to judicial and legislative actions. The *PARC* and *Mills* cases resulted in judicial decisions upholding the right to education for all children, regardless of their handicapping condition. An example of federal legislation that has had far-reaching educational implications is Section 504 of the Rehabilitation Act of 1973. The 504 Statute reads as follows:

> No otherwise qualified handicapped individual in the United States shall, solely by reason of his handicap, be excluded from participation in, be denied the benefits of, or be subjected to discrimination under any program or activity receiving Federal financial assistance.

Thus, Section 504 is essentially a civil rights provision designed to end discrimination in the employment of handicapped citizens in the United States. It applies to all handicapped persons, including mentally retarded individuals. This mandate places direct responsibility on the schools to see that all handicapped children acquire the skills, attitudes, and knowledge they need to be "otherwise qualified." The Education for All Handicapped Children Act (P.L. 94-142), as well as legislation requiring that all federally funded preschool programs include 10% handicapped childern, are new laws affecting the handicapped. These federal mandates have assured the handicapped access to education; they include provisions for school accountability and integration of handicapped and nonhandicapped students. So even if attitudes toward retarded persons are slow to change, the schools must take action.

Industrial America.   Present-day America is a land of industry and technology. Rural American society has been replaced by a highly complex, machine-powered civilization. As a result of new technological advances, the American economy has changed. Machines are now available that can do the work of many people efficiently and at low cost. New industries—plastics, electronics, and aeronautics—have been developed, all of which owe their growth to technology. Along with the technology, the nature of employment has shifted. There are fewer manual labor jobs; service activities and new technical occupations have been created. People no longer work 12 hours; the working day lasts 8 or in some cases 6 hours. Paid vacations and holidays are now accepted.

Industrial America has also altered the demands of homemaking. Modern home appliances have diminished the number of hours required to maintain a home. Most homes have automatic clothes washers and dryers. Dishwashers, garbage disposals, and microwave ovens have become widely accepted. Prepackaged convenience foods are readily available.

Thus, people have more leisure time. This places a burden on the schools to design a curriculum that supports continuing education, life-long learning, adult education, and the stimulation for hobbies and recreation.

Industrialization has also affected life in American society in potentially harmful ways. Pollution and industrial wastes irresponsibly deposited in rivers are new problems. The technology of food processing has resulted in artificially derived foods with little nutritional value; some may actually prove to be harmful. The possibly harmful effects of food coloring and other chemical additives have been the subject of several research studies. The effects on behavior from these chemicals, frequently contained in foods consumed in large quantity by young children, are suspect. Education has an obvious role here. It may choose to divert its attention from these problems, but to do so risks serious consequences for many of our nation's learners.

Family life.   Recent economic and social changes have had an impact on the structure of the family. Historically, families worked together, lived in close physical proximity, and shared many recreational and leisure activities as well. Today, we are a transient society. The closely knit family patterns of the past have been replaced by a new dependency on the community and its resources.

More mothers are employed outside the home than ever before, either to supplement the family income or for personal satisfaction. In millions of homes, children get their own lunches, come in alone after school, and are required to assume responsibility and be independent at an early age. In urban areas, there is a new demand for day care centers so that mothers can work with the knowledge that their children are receiving good care in the hands of responsible adults.

The family is also being affected by the increasingly high divorce rate. Many children from "broken" homes are insecure or tense and anxious. Certainly these tensions affect a child's ability to benefit from the learning experiences provided by the school. The impact of this increasing divorce rate has yet to be fully understood.

While the decision to marry and have children is a personal issue, the responsibility for transmitting the information needed to make the decision is a public issue. The schools have long neglected sex education. Children picked up whatever information they could from parents, peers, and siblings. Thus, many people got married with little or no factual information about sex. Schools are now beginning to accept their educational responsibility for sex education, including sex education for the retarded. Early efforts consisted of teaching personal hygiene, menstruation, and social decorum. These efforts reflected concern over the prevention of parenthood for retarded couples. Today, as the concern for individual rights increases, laws that allow mentally retarded persons to be sterilized without their consent are beginning to disappear (Krisshef, 1972).

There has been a national impetus to normalize sexual relations among the retarded. The President's Committee on Mental Retardation (1975) reported that 60% of the respondents in a nationwide survey favored the concept of marriage for retarded adults. Many people believed mildly retarded persons to be capable of maintaining a stable marriage. There was a significantly smaller positive response to the issue of parenthood, however. In fact, many respondents advocated sterilization.

As the courts, parents, and advocacy groups extend the rights of mentally retarded individuals, family living information and sex education will have to be provided for them. It has become increasingly important that school curricula reflect these changing attitudes toward marriage, parenthood, and the sexuality of mentally retarded persons.

Citizenship responsibility.   The rights and responsibilities derived from the U.S. constitution are additional guideposts for the development of curriculum goals. Recent changes in the legal status of mentally retarded persons have political as well as economic and social ramifications. An obvious example is the exercise of each individual's rights as a citizen through the political process. In many states, mildly retarded persons now have the right to vote for local, state, and national candidates and issues. Few retarded persons exercise this right, however. An unpublished survey of voter participation of mildly retarded adults living in licensed residential facilities in Ohio found that only 2% of those who were eligible did in fact vote. But in residential facilities with voter education programs, the frequency of voting increased to 80% of those eligible.

Having rights is one thing; having the skills and knowledge to fully exercise them is quite another matter. The schools need to provide educational experiences that enable all citizens to exercise their rights.

Societal diversity.   The lure of religious freedom brought many persons to the American colonies and states from foreign lands. More recently, the lure of economic opportunity has brought immigrants from Ireland, Italy, Puerto Rico, and Mexico. Each of these groups— and others—brought with them a rich culture, in many cases different from that known to most Americans. Today we are a pluralistic country, with many different viable subcultures. Spurred by the civil rights movement of the 1960s, we have come to recognize the richness of the African cultures from which American blacks are descended. Recent court decisions highlight the importance of racial diversity in public schools. Diversity in American society is also seen in the many religious groups who freely worship here.

Our schools must deal with cultural, religious, racial, ethnic and language diversity. This diversity influences children in several ways: (a) it shapes values; (b) it influences opportunities; (c) it may limit experiences; and (d) it influences motivation and attitudes toward schooling. The needs created by these diverse elements in our society must be woven into the fabric of public school curriculum if all students are to fully benefit from education.

The Needs and Interests of the Learner: The Second Source

Learning characteristics. Any attempt to design curriculum systematically must take into account the capabilities, interests, needs, experiences, learning styles, cutural background, and personality of

Teachers come in all sizes.

each learner. Ignoring this source of information risks failure or, at the very least, wastes valuable time teaching inappropriately. Unfortunately, present practice rarely begins with these considerations.

Let's examine the ordinary third grade class in a public school. The teacher may have several sets of third grade material, all of which have been developed from normative assumptions about children's performance. That is, these materials assume that most children will perform around the mean, some children will learn quickly, and others won't learn. The teacher directs his or her efforts toward the average; by definition, some children will succeed, some children will be bored, and others will fail. The variations in children's abilities beg for alternative curricular approaches. These alternatives are needed for "ordinary" children as well as for children with special needs.

There is a great deal of available information about each learner. It can be gathered from formal and informal instruction-related tests, from observation, from reports from other professionals, from parents, and from existing records. Much of this information is useful in resolving issues as to "how" curriculum is implemented.

Teachers of retarded learners can also use results of research conducted using mentally retarded children as subjects (see Chapter 1). For instance, research shows that mentally retarded children frequently have difficulty generalizing from one situation to the next. Jose may be able to solve worksheet money problems, but when he handles the milk money he makes many errors. Or the converse may be true. Marie sells newspapers at a newsstand and each day quickly and accurately makes change for her customers. However, when she is asked to solve money problems on a worksheet in the classroom, she has great difficulty. Given that we know that mentally retarded learners have difficulty with the transfer and generalization of knowledge, it is important that their curricula provide the opportunity to apply new knowledge in a variety of situations. This does not mean that a classroom store or a simulated classroom post office will suffice. All people learn by *doing*, and mentally retarded children are no exception. Generalization and transfer of information occur through repeated experience in a variety of settings. The classroom simulations are fine for initial practice, but are no substitute for the actual experience itself when possible. Helping mentally retarded children make connections and associations among similar experiences, repeated over time, will assist their learning.

Research also shows that the mentally retarded child is an active organism who seeks to grow and learn. Thus the learning experiences provided for the retarded person should take this natural state into account. For example, the use of manipulative materials for seriation and number concepts allows the learner to begin focusing on relationships. A child is able to learn more about magnets by experimenting with the different magnetic materials than by listening to a lecture about magnets; "playing" with magnets is inherently more interesting and more fun than a passive listening experience.

Mentally retarded children need to overlearn in order to internalize what is taught them. The ability to retain information depends upon how well it was learned in the first place and how often the learner uses the information. If a learner sees a lesson as meaningful, he is more likely to use the information and, thus, remember it later.

Background and experiences. Mildly mentally retarded learners make up 89% of the retarded population. Most of those who are mildly retarded come from families with low socioeconomic status. Crowded conditions, poor heating and plumbing, inadequate clothing for changing seasons, high noise levels, inadequate nutrition, inadequate attention, and little educational stimulation characterize many of their homes. Many of these children also come from single parent families. In many cases, no routine for meal times, bed times, or family life has been established.

A disproportionate number of children labeled *mildly retarded* are members of minority groups. Their experiences, cultural values, and expectations may differ from those of the predominant culture in our public schools. For many of these children, English is a second language, learned after they begin formal schooling.

Some children come to school having never seen a book or had one read to them. Some children have never had to assume responsibility; some have never been an integral member of a group such as a "family." Some children have never been outside the three- or four-block area surrounding their own house and have had limited personal interactions. Other children, of course, have broader, more diverse experiences. All these variables must be considered when designing curriculum goals. For example, if a child has never been to a department store, to assume that she can understand its various departments is to risk failure. The usual way a child learns about "downtown," or "the factory," or "the mill," or "the mine," or "the circus" is to experience these things first hand. The fact that in the same class some children have had these experiences and others have not will affect the way lessons about them are received.

Traditional approaches to curriculum have resulted in content that is "poured" into the child. Subject matter, textbooks, and bodies of information are forced upon the child, who is expected to accept the choices willingly, docilely, and obediently. The child is expected to ingest what such methods offer—whether or not it is useful or appropriate.

This practice of imposing knowledge and subject matter upon a child presents significant problems for some learners. It imposes normative methods and expectations upon children whose growth may be erratic or slow. For children from minority cultures, the gap between the culture of the school, with its implied expectations, and their own culture, with its methods of learning and behaving, is so great that school is beyond them from the start. Traditional curricula assume the use of the predominant culture, and pour in information to fill the gap. But this is contrary to the naturally developing curiosity and motives of young children. These practices make learning difficult. When all the information presented in the classroom is outside the child's own experience and not relevant to his home life, the child will feel a disturbing dissonance (Dewey, 1938) and will have extra trouble absorbing the new knowledge. Curriculum design must take into account the child's background and previous experience; it should expand his world, not replace it.

Developmental tasks.   Patterns of growth and development also vary. A small child may be nearly one year older than a larger child in the same class. Children develop motor skills at different rates as well. Boys, for example, develop motor skills somewhat later than girls. Individual children may have idiosyncratic development. For instance, a 7-year-old may be very bright and able to spell his name, even recognize the letters. But if he has not achieved the motor proficiency required to hold and direct a pencil, he will have difficulty writing it. These varying rates of growth must be considered in curriculum development.

Although the rate of growth will vary, development for almost all children follows a predictable sequence; retarded children are no exception. Some of these children may reach developmental milestones later than their nonretarded peers, but the sequence of development is the same.

Children hold up their heads before they sit, sit before they walk. They understand the concrete before the abstract, the present before the future. Specific behaviors and skills have been organized by psychologists into "stages." Each new stage of development (see Chapter 1) is accompanied by characteristic developmental tasks. Havighurst (1973) has identified these as "developmental tasks of life." According to Havighurst (1952), a developmental task arises at or about a certain period in the life of the individual. Successful achievement of tasks leads to happiness and success with later tasks, while failure leads to unhappiness and disapproval by the society (Havighurst, 1973). These developmental tasks, whether physical, intellectual, or emotional in nature, are especially important elements around which to construct curriculum goals. Havighurst proposed the following list of *Developmental Tasks*

Developmental Tasks of Infancy and Early Childhood
1. Learning to walk
2. Learning to take solid food
3. Learning to talk
4. Learning to control elimination of body wastes
5. Learning sexual differences and sexual modesty
6. Achieving physiological stability
7. Forming simple concepts of social and physical reality
8. Learning to relate oneself emotionally to parents, siblings, and other people
9. Learning to distinguish right and wrong and developing a conscience

Developmental Tasks of Middle Childhood
1. Learning physical skills necessary for ordinary games
2. Building wholesome attitudes toward oneself as a growing organism
3. Learning to get along with age mates
4. Learning an important masculine or feminine social role
5. Developing fundamental skills in reading, writing, and calculating
6. Developing concepts for everyday living
7. Developing conscience, morality, and a scale of values
8. Achieving personal independence
9. Developing attitudes toward social groups and institutions

Developmental Tasks of Adolescence
1. Achieving new and more mature relations with age mates of both sexes
2. Achieving a masculine or feminine social role
3. Accepting one's physique and using the body effectively
4. Achieving emotional independence from parents and other adults
5. Achieving assurance of economic independence
6. Selecting and preparing for an occupation

7. Preparing for marriage and family life
8. Developing intellectual skills and concepts necessary for civic competence
9. Desiring and achieving socially responsible behavior
10. Acquiring a set of values and an ethical system as a guide to behavior

Developmental Tasks of Early Adulthood
1. Selecting a mate
2. Learning to live with a marriage partner
3. Starting a family
4. Rearing children
5. Managing a home
6. Getting started in an occupation
7. Taking on civic responsibility
8. Finding a congenial social group

These tasks are influenced by physiological growth patterns. All tasks are experienced by all learners, regardless of their disability, although the extent of the disability will affect the timing and composition of these developmental tasks. The adolescent with an IQ between 55 and 70 has the same needs as his more capable peers. He will be striving toward these shared goals, but with the added burden imposed by his retardation. Classroom instruction can assist his development, however, through the selection of goals focused on decision making and through opportunities designed to lead to insight and understanding.

Subject Matter Mastery: The Third Source

The third source of educational goals for the curriculum is the traditional content subsumed within the school subjects each of us studied in our youth. Mathematics, language arts, history and social sciences, biological and physical science, physical education, the fine arts, and the other subjects are in the school curriculum because they have been judged to be valuable. It would be foolish, for example, to argue that an individual should not learn to use his native language with as much facility as possible. By the same token, mathematics is the key to grouping and subdividing, to measurement and prediction. Explanations and concepts in the social sciences help an individual to understand the complex, confusing world around us. What pleasure art, music, and literature provide to those who have learned to appreciate them! Only a simpleton or a charlatan wants a curriculum which denies a central place for subject matter content, but this content need not be taught in isolated subject categories. We believe that a curriculum for the mentally retarded learner should not be based on separate subjects, taught separately and often unrelated to each other. A separate subject approach fails to help the child generalize knowledge from one situation to another, nor does it help him deal with his own problems of daily living.

We believe that curriculum design for the mentally retarded learner should be directed toward helping him deal effectively with problems of everyday living. This can be done most efficiently through an integrated approach to subject matter. The product of such integration must reflect the needs and interests of the individual students as well as the role of the individual in society, both at present and in the future. This belief rests on four assumptions. First, the educational needs of mentally retarded children are best served by "integrated content" approach to learning. Second, a curriculum that prepares children to meet the challenges of everyday living is a promising approach to instruction in basic subject matter knowledge and skills. For example, if a child needs practice in reading, the newspaper provides a number of possibilities—sports, classified ads, comics, news articles. Third, this approach places the teacher in the role of an educational designer rather than a technician, since it elevates instruction from a stimulus-response, analytical approach to a broadly based theoretical conception. Last, the selection of curriculum goals is based on both relevance to the individual student and the need to assist the youngster to become a contributing member of society.

Our concept of an integrated curriculum is an attempt to focus instruction on selected problem areas relating to personal, academic, and social concerns. These problem areas should be reasonably distributed among the major areas of human activity—social—cultural, economic, political, and personal (intellectual, emotional, and moral) development.

This integrative approach to instruction for retarded learners can be defended on several grounds

1. It focuses on the development of ideas related to a large body of knowledge.
2. It is efficient in that basic skills (reading and math) are practiced and used in pursuit of new knowledge and content in real-life situations.
3. The content is oriented toward the problems experienced by learners.

4. It assumes that "normalized" educational experiences aid the learner's growth toward independence.
5. It places discrete subject matter into a larger context, directly related to learner needs.
6. It enables the learner to generalize knowledge and skills to his own experience.
7. It lets teachers observe student responses immediately and give them feedback on their efforts to deal with problems and solutions.
8. The content is broad enough to encourage creative approaches to instructional goals.
9. The content is broad based so that cognitive, social, and task-related goals can easily be related to the same activity.
10. The nature of the content commits educators to accountable instructional experiences for retarded learners.

Experienced teachers can generate many examples of an integrated, socially relevant curriculum. As starters, consider each of the following activities. Notice that the content is significant for all learners. The content area studied would be the same; there would be differences in depth of investigation and speed of accomplishment.

A primary class visits a work site where members' mothers and fathers earn a living.

A second grade classroom is divided up into teams of three. Each team spends an afternoon in a different home, assisting an adult in preparing food for a class party.

A fourth grade group is re-formed into a "Feelings Group" to discuss personal, class, school or community concerns.

A sixth grade class establishes an economic unit to earn money to back a community project.

Eighth graders simulate marriage and child care, using dolls to represent actual children.

Tenth graders gain work experience in a special work-study project that involves school and community.

Twelfth graders are required to complete an individualized community action project before graduation.

Psychological and Philosophical Screens

Learner and Content Analysis: The Psychological Screen

In Chapter 2, the process of assessment was introduced and discussed in depth. Assessment is the psychological screen through which one views the learner in relation to the task. Assume an instructor has generated a set of broad goals, some of which were derived from subject matter, others from societal needs, others from the needs and interests of particular learners. Assessment assures that when the goals are translated into precise learning objectives, the objectives will be both appropriate and accountable. From our perspective, appropriateness refers to the match between instruction and the learner; accountability implies confidence that the child is progressing satisfactorily or is not.

Normalization: The Philosophical Screen

The philosophical screen we use to sort goals—to accept some, revise others, and reject still others—is the principle of normalization. Normalization, as we discussed in Chapter 1, refers to providing mentally retarded persons with experiences and opportunities that resemble those of their nonhandicapped peers as much as possible. The principle applies to both the process and goals of services. Although there has been some disagreement about it (Zipperlen, 1975), this philosophy has many enthusiastic adherents. We believe that a commitment to normalization provides the best guide to the question of what knowledge is most important for mentally retarded learners as well as to integrating educational experiences. Normalization implies a curriculum that blends cognitive and affective learning to enable retarded persons to share in the world of work; to learn to become independent, responsible citizens alongside their nonretarded peers.

Since the 1930s, the schools have increasingly accepted the task of preparing young people for the world of work, citizenship, and social adjustment. Because they were segregated into their own schools and classes, handicapped learners were excluded from these opportunities. Vocational education, home economics, and citizenship education have been offered to them only on a piecemeal basis, if at all. These practices are changing. Normalization requires that retarded children learn with all children when possible, and that special instructional adaptations be employed for them. These instructional modifications must be designed to prepare the learner to fully participate in the mainstream of society.

Toward "normalizing" education. How can education for mentally retarded children be modified to provide them with the skills, knowledge, and attitudes necessary for full participation in society? This goal can be accomplished through a process of analysis and curriculum development that is learner and problem oriented. This approach requires changes in attitudes, expectations, and practices by teachers, supervisors, principals, curriculum designers, specialists, therapists, parents, and members of the community. This multilevel educational process cuts across traditional lines of professional versus nonprofessional. Instead, all persons who share interests, concerns, and responsibility for the education of retarded learners must be helped to realize that: (a) successful implementation of curriculum reform is a shared responsibility among special education, regular education, parents, administrators, and members of the community; (b) haphazard approaches to the construction of curriculum result in mere tinkering; (c) schools are just one of many systems of which the child is a part; (d) problems experienced by retarded learners do not differ significantly from those experienced by all children (it is a matter of degree rather than kind); and (e) "appropriate education" as mandated in P.L. 94-142 requires schools to educate handicapped students so that they are qualified for the jobs now available to them. A new curriculum design is needed to help the retarded learner develop skills, knowledge, and attitudes necessary to fully partake of normal life experiences.

The class constitution puts democratic principles into action.

The Functional Life Curriculum

We propose an integrated approach to curriculum development known as the *Functional Life Curriculum*. The overall purpose is to prepare retarded learners to function optimally in the mainstream of society. A similar approach has been suggested by Stratemeyer, Forkner, McKim, and Passow (1947) for all school children. The content is appropriate for all children. Therefore, it can be implemented in resource rooms, self-contained classes, or regular education classrooms.

The following principles are the rationale for our proposed curriculum. Full understanding of the concept depends upon the individual's readiness and ability to:

1. View retarded learners as an integral part of the mainstream of school life, not as "different" children to be isolated and treated separately;

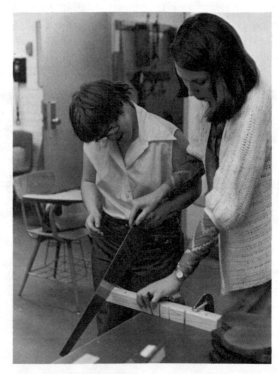

The Functional Life Curriculum provides a full range of learning experiences.

2. Provide educational experiences that are not imposed upon the child, but rather evolve from the needs, interests, and problems of the learner;
3. Organize educational content to foster the development of ideas;
4. Organize classroom experiences so that they parallel children's patterns of growth;
5. Realize that, for children of school age, school is more than preparation for life, school *is* life;
6. Implement basic principles of democracy in the classroom;
7. Adopt a view of education which encompasses social, moral, aesthetic, intellectual, and personal growth and independence;
8. View teachers as facilitators of learning as opposed to guardians of knowledge;
9. Acknowledge the importance of the role of parents in the education of their children and welcome and include them in the educational process;
10. Broaden their vision of what education might be;
11. Provide educational experiences that foster the development of innovative solutions to personal, social, and technological problems;
12. Create and fashion classroom experiences which are self-rewarding and not dependent on external reward and punishment;
13. Value the process as well as the product of education;
14. Value each learner and his or her contribution to life in the classroom and the school;
15. Demonstrate a commitment to the belief that education must enable each learner to be the best he or she can be, starting with the young child's earliest school experience;
16. Commit schools to a path which leads the child to see himself as important, worthy, and valued for what he is, rather than for what he is not; and
17. Integrate subject matter content into functional life categories.

These 17 issues provide a framework for this proposed curriculum. Each is important; each is related to providing educational equality for all children.

Four Curriculum Centers

The focus of the Functional Life Curriculum must be the learners and their needs to become full participants in school and social life. Consequently, learners must confront content that involves the

Students can bring in posters that have special meaning for them.
Here Jennifer explains why she likes this poster best.

application of knowledge to daily living, to the problems faced by citizens in our democratic, pluralistic society. We believe that this approach is the most promising curriculum response to the "motivation crisis" that faces both special education and regular education teachers each day, as they attempt to encourage students to become enthusiastic about learning.

Specifically, we recommend that the Functional Life Curriculum be organized within four curriculum centers.

1. *Gaining insight into contemporary life:* Examination of humanity's past and present through the persistent themes that affect contemporary life—science and technology, morals and values, aesthetics, exploitation and coexistence with the environment, appreciating human experience, communication;
2. *Understanding oneself and others:* Building a positive self-concept, understanding human growth and development, establishing social relationships, appreciating cultural differences;
3. *Becoming a responsible adult:* Economic and career education, political socialization, family living;

4. *Education for independence:* Mastering basic skills, applying problem-solving skills, using leisure time, maintaining home activity, expressing one's individuality.

Each curriculum center category is subdivided into elements which specify content topics. These elements are designed to spiral. An element may be introduced in the primary grades, extended through study in junior high, and completed in high school. For example, in the curriculum center *Education for independence,* an element "Mastering the Basic Skills" would be a continuous program with content allocated to each grade level. A different approach would be used with the element "Homemaking/Home Maintenance." Homemaking content would be introduced during the elementary years and expanded through junior high school, with extensive application in the last years of secondary schooling. Thus, all four curriculum centers are represented through particular elements in each level of formal schooling but with varying emphases.

Table 4–1 is a schematic of the Functional Life Curriculum. It shows how the curriculum centers, elements, and subjects are related.

While she varnishes her bookends with help from a classmate, Evelyn gets a chance to make friends.

Table 4–1 *Functional Life Curriculum: Categories, elements, and sources of content*

Curriculum center	Elements	Subjects
Gaining insight into contemporary life	Applications of science and technology to everyday life	Science art, music, literature, theatre
	Appreciating aesthetics	Science, social studies
	Ecology/environmental education	Science
	Scientific method	Philosophy, religious studies
	Morals and values	Linguistics, mathematics
	Symbolic language	Communication, language
	Mass media communication	History
	Appreciating the human experience	
Understanding oneself and others	Understanding oneself	Psychology
	Establishing social relationships	Sociology, psychology
	Working succesfully in groups	Sociology, psychology
	Multicultural awareness	Sociology, anthropology
	Broadening understanding through travel	Geography
	Family living	Psychology, value education
	Human sexuality	
Becoming a responsible adult	Participating in a democratic society	Political science
	Career choice	Economics
	Production and consumption of goods and services	Economics
	Managing money	Economics
		Sociology, health science
Education for independence	Fostering thinking and problem-solving skills	Social studies, science, mathematics
	Mastering the basic skills (Reading, written and oral communication, mathematical computation)	Language arts, communication, mathematics

Table 4–1 (cont.)

Curriculum center	Elements	Subjects
Education and independence cont.	Using leisure time productively Homemaking/home maintenance Expressing one's individuality and self-expression	Music, art, dance, physical education, literature Home economics, industrial arts Art, music, dance, psychology

Scope, Sequence, and Continuity

The proposed curriculum is all-encompassing. All needs, interests, and problems of the learner are valued content and thus included within the scope of the curriculum. School is life for a growing child; all of his difficulties, joys, growth, pleasures, and concerns are an integral part; they *are* the curriculum. Helping a child find solutions to pressing problems is as important as helping her master basic arithmetic. For example, the scope of the study of family life for elementary age children would include learning how the human body works and learning to work and play with both sexes. This content in the Functional Life Curriculum is included within the curriculum center *Understanding oneself and others.*

People don't exist in a vacuum—they are part of several social systems. Children, as part of a cultural system, are products of their culture. They internalize hopes, values, and goals that affect their attitudes and productivity in school. This curriculum helps children articulate their hopes and values, helps them understand themselves and reach goals they have set for themselves, both in the present and for the future.

Children are developing all the time, with or without assistance from school. The stages of development come from within; they are either fostered or hindered by home, school, and social environments. The sequence and continuity of the Functional Life Curriculum are determined by needs of each developmental stage as children strive toward independence and mastery.

This view of sequence implies several assumptions: (a) individual assessment, including criterion-referenced assessment, is essential; (b) the age of the child is an indication of his social needs; (c) developmental tasks are the focus of instructional presentation; (d) repetition and practice are determined by individual need;

Dominic
I have two brothers. My name
is Dominic. My favorite food
Easter food is HAM. My best
friend is ... I like to
play ball.

Suzanne ...
My hobbies is art. My favorite foods
is ice cream. My favorite sport is
... My pet is a cat. My best
friend is Kathy.

My Name is Douglas
I have a bruthr

Mike H.
I have 1 sister, she is 13.
I have a dog his name is Sherlock.
I have a guinea pig, his name is Peckie.
My mom works at McKee.
My dad works at the Book shop.
I collect beer cans.

146

(e) assessment and instruction are intimately intertwined; (f) tasks are continued until mastery; (g) successful performance is expected, fostered, and self-rewarding; (h) failure is avoided through carefully planned assessment; and (i) sequence comes from the child in relation to the task and not vice versa.

For example, let's return to the study of family life. At the elementary level, the concepts stressed are concrete (how the human body works) and relate to work and play. Sequence implies that for children at the junior high school level, content should be adjusted to include more abstract concepts and ideas. At the junior high school level, goals for the study of human life would include understanding the social implications of a maturing body, understanding sexual feelings which accompany puberty, and adjusting to one's physical changes and those of the opposite sex. At the high school level, the sequence would include marriage and choosing a mate.

The sequence is developmental in nature and related to the growing needs and abilities of each learner. Student questions, answers, and logic are all clues the teacher can use for the best choice of content for instruction.

Another example of sequence is found in studies related to *Becoming a responsible adult*. "Production and consumption of goods and services" and "Managing money" are elements related to economic independence. The development of relevant skills begins in the earliest years of schooling. During the elementary years, the focus of instruction will be the identification of items to purchase and their prices (toys, candy, presents for parents), price comparison, and the determination of the ability to engage in a transaction. The next phase in the sequence, during the junior high school years, includes the identification of factors that regulate price, factors of production and responsible consumption of goods and services, market research, and the individual in a free market economy.

In our view, economic independence is demonstrated by "wise buying"; sound financial management cannot be accomplished without a fundamental understanding of economics and the ability to perform everyday mathematics. You will notice as we progress through the steps of curriculum development, as organized in this text, that we keep returning to the curriculum centers in the Functional Life Curriculum. We will use the "wise shopping" example to illustrate the process of content goal analysis and the design of criterion-referenced testing in Chapter 5. We will return to it again as we consider the selection and implementation of learning activities in Chapter 7 and the evaluation of curriculum materials in Chapter 9.

Elaine Yates

How do you deal with your
parents on an adult level?

OK for one all teenagers and
parents have the ups and
downs about different things

I'll sit down and talk to them
both about whatever there
problem is with for instance
my mother don't want
me to get married but my
mother, father, boyfriend and I
still come up with a solution
that all of us is willing
to try for the time being.

but basic we get along
fine as long as I let her know
where I am going and be in the
house when I suppose to

3ᵃ Am Hist 3ok
May 12 '78

1) Try to Talk with them
   if you can.

2) Dont get Bosses with them.

3) Help my Mom out the Best
   I can

4) I will Be home on time
   when she said to do so.

dear mom I love you and
I hapey you have a nice day
and I like wine you help me
and howe you itsplan to me
and you look buteflul
and you are nice to me
and r te nice even wine
and
you are mad so I love you
so have a nice day

Love
Dominic

148

Two concerns about a Functional Life Curriculum require discussion. First, how can the teacher take an integrated approach to learning before the children have mastered basic skills, especially reading and math computation? Initially, it will be necessary to teach and practice these basics in isolation as well as apply them to more general context. The immediacy of their application to the needs of the learner motivates learning. Even very young children can be introduced to real world problems translated to their level of competence, through activities which require drawing conclusions, making choices, and determining causes.

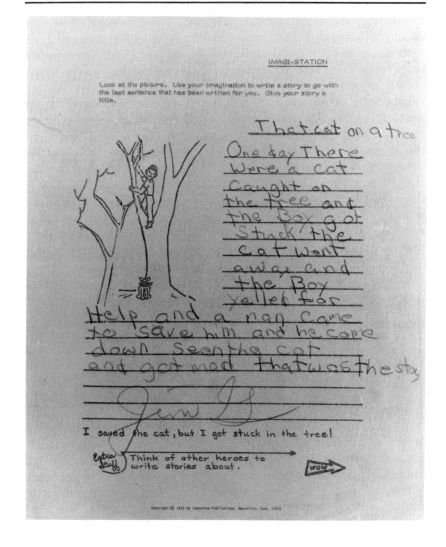

A second concern relates to what content must be sacrificed if the Functional Life Curriculum is adopted. As seen by Stratemeyer, the problem is that "A curriculum growing out of the needs and concerns of learners, by the very nature of the values it stresses, cannot give equal weight to other values. This is the design least likely to guarantee that extended acquaintance with subject matter bodies of knowledge will be part of all learners' experiences" (Stratemeyer, et. al., 1947, p. 104). One must of necessity give up some things in order to achieve others. Mental retardation by definition imposes limits on the amount of subject matter that can be internalized by the learner. Research into all facets of learning has demonstrated that mentally retarded children have deficits to make up in many performance variables, i.e., concept learning, retention, transfer, etc. In addition, we have to examine present practice to determine what depth of subject matter is actually required to achieve a productive life in today's complex society. What does a citizen need to know about the role of Congress in the structure of the U.S. government in order to be an informed, productive citizen? Do you need to know that there are 535 members of Congress? Probably not. Should a retarded student know that his vote may help to determine which candidate is elected to Congress? Certainly he should! To a large extent, these are value decisions, in terms of what information is of such import as to be included in the curriculum. It is our position that the curriculum emphasis should be placed where it has the potential to most benefit the learner and the society, with the understanding that learning should not end when formal schooling terminates.

Conclusion

We have presented a rationale for an integrated approach to curriculum design. To build the design which we have called a Functional Life Curriculum requires an amalgam of three sources of curriculum goals—the needs and interests of individual learners, the needs of contemporary society, and the knowledge and skills inherent in subject matter mastery. Given the principle of normalization, which mandates that mentally retarded learners be prepared to live independent productive lives, the Functional Life approach is the "right" curriculum response. Figure 4–2 describes the curriculum development process, as it appears in this chapter.

The following generalizations are recommended as guides to curriculum development and the selection of educational goals for retarded learners.

1. The needs of contemporary society related to employment, values and attitudes, housing, transportation, schooling and other institutions as they effect mentally retarded individuals and their families is a source of curriculum goals.
2. An understanding of the needs and interests of retarded learners is a source of content.
3. Repetition of concepts in a variety of situations can both assist the learner to generalize a concept and to internalize its meaning.
4. Varying rates of growth must be considered in curriculum development.
5. The child must be taught in terms of his own culture and experiences as well as the culture of the school.

Mike woke up one morning and the Sun was gone He got out of bed and went to the window He ran to look at the clock to make sure it was 7:00 It was 7.00 A trap door opened up underneath him and sucked him in fell down down down until he hit the He opened his eyes saw a 7 foot Ape man half man and fish mike so scared that he Toped up against the wall and said please don't hurt me what ever you are Ape man said I wont hurt you I want to be your friend Mike said I'll be your friend but did you take the Sun Ape man said yes I was hungery So I ate it gave me heart burns so I'll put back last Mike heard his mother calling him for school mike said what a scary dream

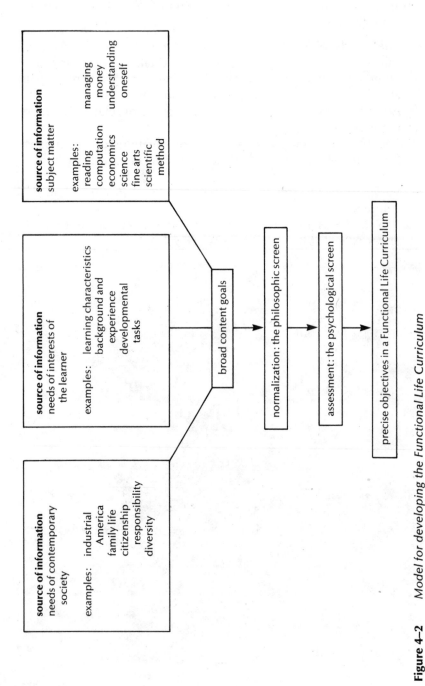

source of information
needs of contemporary society

examples: industrial America
family life
citizenship
responsibility
diversity

source of information
needs of interests of the learner

examples: learning characteristics
background and experience
developmental tasks

source of information
subject matter

examples:
reading   managing money
computation   understanding
economics   oneself
science
fine arts
scientific
method

broad content goals

normalization: the philosophic screen

assessment: the psychological screen

precise objectives in a *Functional Life Curriculum*

Figure 4–2   *Model for developing the Functional Life Curriculum*

6. Developmental tasks are relevant to curriculum planning for retarded learners.
7. As an alternative to discrete subject matter emphasis, subject matter should be integrated or synthesized for the learner.
8. Normalization as both a process and a goal of education for retarded learners provides a philosophical screen for including or rejecting educational content.
9. Educational assessment is the psychological screen which assists the teacher to match the curriculum goal to the individual child.
10. The Functional Life Curriculum contains four major categories:
    (1) Gaining insight into contemporary life,
    (2) Understanding oneself and others,
    (3) Becoming a responsible citizen,
    (4) Education for independence.
11. The sequence and scope of the curriculum are based upon principles of human growth and development as they relate to educating the retarded student to be a productive, integral member of society.

REFERENCES

Havighurst, R. *Developmental tasks in education.* 2nd ed. New York: David McKay, 1952.

Havighurst, R. *Developmental tasks in education.* 3rd ed. New York: David McKay, 1973.

Krisshef, C. H. State laws on marriage and sterilization. *Mental Retardation,* 1972, *10,* 36–38.

Presidents Committee on Mental Retardation. *Mental Retardation: The Known and the Unknown.* Washington, D.C.: Department of Health, Education and Welfare, 1975.

Stratemeyer, F., Forkner, H., McKim, M. & Passow, A. H. *Developing a curriculum for modern living.* New York: Teachers College Press, 1947.

Tyler, R. *Basic principles of curriculum and instruction.* Chicago: University of Chicago Press, 1949.

Zipperlen, H. Normalization. In J. Wortis (Ed.), *Mental retardation and developmental disabilities* (Vol. VII). New York: Bruner/Mazel, 1975.

Analyzing curriculum content

part 1 *Curriculum analysis in education*

The Jack Stevens Quandary

Riverside High School is a progressive secondary school—progressive because of the attention given to young people who do not always learn as quickly as normally expected. There are no isolated special education classrooms at Riverside. The special education students are integrated into the mainstream of education with supportive resource personnel available to retarded learners.

Jack Stevens, a teacher of mentally retarded learners, recalled the faculty meeting held in the school library 2 months ago. He could actually visualize the principal, Martha Hutchins, announcing to the group that, as a response to the assessment of school needs, a curriculum writing team would be formed to create a new economics unit for senior students. The unit would carry a title such as *Economic Understanding for Daily Living.* All students, terminal and college bound, would be required to study the unit as a component of their senior social studies class. Stevens was pleased that he had been selected to chair the writing team. He felt especially honored because his selection as chairman implied that he was accepted as an integral member of the faculty. It also showed that the support of the administration for special education was deeper than even he realized. He wondered if the barriers between regular and special education were being torn down.

His selection also meant 6 weeks of summer curriculum development salary, as well as an opportunity to make an important contribution to the school curriculum. Still, Stevens was noticeably uneasy because of a lingering uncertainty as to what the group was expected to produce when the writing was completed. How could he offer strong leadership to a writing team when he saw no clear path to proceed? Also, as a teacher of special education, could he convince this committee that he had some useful curriculum ideas for all learners?

After a period of unproductively arguing with himself, Stevens decided to review the needs assessment information that had been synthesized from faculty, student, and parent committees. Along with the suggested title for the economics unit, the groups submitted a list of their ideas of basic economic principles that should be learned by all high school graduates. Stevens reread the list:

A U.S. high school graduate should be familiar with:
1. Basic economic concepts,
2. Responsible money management,
3. Credit and contracts,
4. Banking and bank services,
5. How to be a successful and efficient consumer (elements of wise shopping),
6. Economic problems, i.e., inflation and unemployment.

Reading the goals proved to be useful. Stevens decided that the curriculum team would respond directly to the goals. For the first time the task became clear. The writing team would translate the broad goals into a set of specific objectives. The objectives would need to be written clearly enough to guide the development of learning activities and the selection of learning materials. Fine, thought Stevens, that insight was important, but how can I translate broad goals into specific objectives? He thought back to his teaching methods courses, although a 5-year gap dimmed the recall. Nevertheless, he needed only a few moments to realize that his teaching preparation courses had only alluded to the problem that faced him and the other curriculum writers. He had vague recollection of ideas such as "taxonomies," "task analysis," "learning processes," but he had never consciously applied them in his teaching; he now wished that he had!

The Process of Analysis

The translation of complex physical or abstract material into its set of essential elements and their interrelationships is referred to as *analysis*. The resulting product of analysis may be represented as a pyramid (Figure 5–1) where the apex of the triangle is the complex material supported by a large network of the elementary materials at the base of the pyramid. Three kinds of analysis are commonly used. *Physical analysis* can be used when the material or action whose elements are to be identified can be observed. For example, when a car breaks down, the mechanic examines the parts in order to analyze the problem. In political or legal debate, *logical analysis*

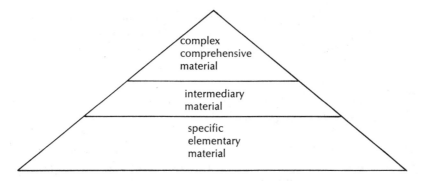

Figure 5–1   *The pyramid as a representation of the process of analysis*

is used to break arguments down into supporting facts and asser-
tions. Learning theorists who study human and lower animal behavior use *psychological analysis* to determine the basic elements of
a given behavior. Teachers, because of the synthetic nature of instruction, are required to use both logical and psychological analysis.
Teachers of physical education, industrial arts, and the fine arts also
must be able to analyze physical behavior. For example, in order to
teach accurate basket shooting, one must be able to analyze the
skill into its basic subparts—holding the basketball, positioning the
body, etc. The same process is required for all physical activities that
have targeted skills as elements to be learned.

The analysis of subject matter content, whether physical, logical,
or psychological is a tall order, particularly for teachers, who often
do not have enough time for thoughtful analysis of the subjects
and learners they teach. In all too many instances, the products
of analysis—the teaching episodes in the classroom—reflect this
inadequacy. Consequently, students are taught misinformation,
recently conceived instructional ideas are ignored, or students confront poorly sequenced learning tasks. Because most teachers receive
inadequate supportive supervision and feedback from colleagues,
supervisors, and parents, the teaching processes and instructional
activities used in the classroom are normally not observed and not
evaluated. One exception to this generalization is the kind of situation Jack Stevens found himself in. The curriculum products developed by his writing team would be viewed and scrutinized by his
colleagues and supervisors. Thus, he could not be content with a
perfunctory or poorly conceived analysis.

Fortunately for Stevens and other curriculum writers, much has
been done in the broad field of subject matter analysis during the
last 2 decades. The remainder of this chapter is directed toward

psychologists' and instructors' investigation into the structure of school-taught subject matter. We will use Jack Stevens and his new economics course as an illustration throughout the chapter.

The Logic of Subject Matter: A Structure of Knowledge

The concept of "structure of knowledge" is a productive one to consider. We have seen that analysis implies an understanding of the elements of a given material or abstraction together with the relationships that organize it. As a result of the analysis, a *structure* of the given material or idea is generated. The structure then is a product of analysis (the pyramid) and can be used as a framework to describe and explain the way the material or idea being investigated is put together. Specifically, we can define the structure of a school subject such as mathematics, history, or physical education as a *framework that describes and explains the relationships* among *the elements inherent in the subject*. With the school subjects that are derived from long-established academic disciplines, teachers can employ the analytical structures investigated by generations of scholars. The structure of mathematics, for instance, has long been accepted as "a series of logically validated and interrelated hypotheses (propositions) which are discussed through a precise language of symbols" (Phenix, 1964). The so-called "hard sciences" also have structures whose utility has remained more or less fixed from one generation to the next.* In contrast, school subjects that are amalgam versions of many disciplines (for instance, home economics, physical education, social studies, general science) appear to be ever-changing. Teachers must maintain close contact with subject journals in fields marked by alternative structures competing for attention and influence.

The Building of Logical Structure

Although there is no universal agreement on the one valid structure of most subjects, the general components of structure are clear. Using our pyramid analogy again, we see a logical structure of a discipline as composed of the various explanations, concepts, and specific facts that describe how and why the elements of a subject are related in a particular fashion. Let's look at the three parts of the

---

* However, Thomas S. Kuhn in *The Structure of Scientific Revolutions* (1962) argues that even the physical sciences have been marked by changing structural designs.

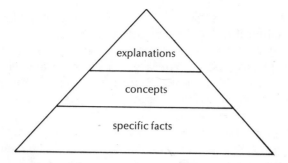

pyramid. Considering the discipline of economics, here is one *explanation* that accounts for one reason why responsible money management is essential to successful independent living.

> Responsible money management involves both planning for one's expenses as well as specifying one's needs, goals, and values. In order to determine how one will spend one's financial resources it is necessary to specify the necessary wants which must be satisfied. One then determines how to spend the money that is left. Each person has a set of goals, values, and preferences which differ from others. Thus each must make the decisions based on an individually determined basis.

This is an intellectual tool that helps educated people understand the complexities of modern life. Consider for a moment the effects on our lives if we could not satisfactorily explain why objects fall and rise in price, why we must set priorities for spending money, and that there are numerous valid value systems for satisfying our wants. Explanations like this help us make decisions and solve problems in response to puzzling, sometimes frightening, phenomena. Youngsters who have no experience in developing explanations are severely crippled in meeting the complex challenges of everyday life.

But explanations do not simply emerge spontaneously in school classrooms. They are learned as a result of careful, systematic preparation by knowledgeable, dedicated teachers. They are learned after students have previously learned the concepts that are integral elements of the explanation. (See Figure 5–1, page 157.)

A *concept* is a category comprising individual "somethings"—objects, people, abstractions. For instance, "table" is a concept. It represents all the individual tables one encounters. As a result of these encounters, a person creates a mental category, a concept of "table." In order for the child to internalize the concept of a table, he must understand that all the sizes and shapes of tables comprise this same concept. He must be able to hold the concept of table constant, even when the size, shape, and color vary.

Concepts enable people to immediately classify new experiences. Our minds quickly discriminate a given example and label it as a "table" or a "chair" or a "desk." Referring to the economic explanation of money management, "expenses," "wants," and "financial resources" are all concepts.

Learning and mastering concepts is especially difficult for the retarded learner. "Money and its management" is an example of a concept that is difficult to master. While money is an essential tool for survival in our society, the concept of "money" is difficult to teach and to learn because money takes many different forms. There are several sizes and colors of coins, and there is paper currency in which the size and color are the same, but the value of each bill is different. There are also less visible forms of money, such as checking and savings accounts. The seemingly simple concept of "money" is actually a very complex one that must be carefully analyzed in terms of its elements, and then systematically taught.

In addition to the elements contained in the concept of "money," there are additional concepts learners must acquire in order to meet their own financial responsibilities. To spend money wisely, learners need to discriminate between two additional concepts—"luxuries" and "necessities." These are prerequisite concepts that the learners must understand before they can effectively and efficiently plan personal finances. Learners must also conceptualize the term "budget," another concept directly related to personal finances. These concepts, although difficult to master for some retarded students, can be broken down into their subparts to facilitate learning.

To return to the pyramid, the lowest level, *specific facts,* comprises the most elementary level of material to be learned. This level is the foundation upon which more complex thought processes are built. In other words, mastery at the concept level depends upon knowledge gained at the lower level. This aspect of the structure of knowledge is an important guideline when developing planned, systematic, sequential instruction for retarded learners.

To summarize, the knowledge of any discipline can be analyzed into specific facts, which are combined into concepts; these are then interrelated as explanations. The specific-facts level of knowledge must be analyzed, selected, and carefully taught by the teacher as the first step in the presentation of information.

Facts may be thought of as statements that describe what we

believe is true as a result of an experiment, an observation, or what we accept from authority. In the context of a logical structure, specific facts describe individual instances, the subsets around which concepts and explanations are constructed. Before students can understand the role of money in a personal economy, they must know some basic facts about money—for example, how an individual acquires money, what coins and paper constitute money, one's own money versus that of another. These facts are usually broken down into discrete parts so that each step leading to an application of the concept is carefully analyzed. All the memorized rote facts are necessary elements upon which a student can build the concept of "money" as the medium of exchange the individual uses in the market place.

The classroom dialogue below illustrates how explanations, concepts, and facts are organically related in a well-designed high school lesson for retarded learners. The class has just completed a unit on concepts related to money. The students have dealt specifically with differences between necessities and luxuries and their relationships to money management.

Mr. Stevens: (teacher prompts students to recall appropriate facts learned during a personal planning simulation)	Class, let's think about the money we earned during one week. What types of things should we use the money for?
Bill:	We should use the money to pay for our necessities.
Mr. Stevens: (teacher reviews the definition of the concept, "necessities")	Good! Bill, you used the word "necessities." As you will recall, necessities are those areas such as food, clothing, rent, and transportation that are necessary for us to live in society.
Mr. Stevens:	Now, class. Let's say you have $30.00 cash in your pocket on Monday. This is all the money you have until payday, which is Friday. What question do you ask yourselves about how to spend it?
Bill:	I would see how much money I needed for lunches and for buses.

Mr. Stevens:	Those are necessities. Very good. What next?
Bill:	I would put that money in my necessities box and see if I had any left over.
Sam:	I could go to a movie or buy a new shirt or just save it.
Mr. Stevens:	Right! And what do we call movies or things that aren't really necessary?
Hilda:	We call them "luxuries."
Mr. Stevens: (teacher distinguishes between the two concepts)	Yes, luxuries are those items which are usually very nice, but not necessary. Our money should be used for those things after we have carefully paid for our necessities. Now, can anybody tell me the difference between necessities and luxuries?
Bill:	Necessities are things we need to keep our jobs and to live freely in this city. Luxuries are things that are fun, but we must buy them after we have paid for the necessities.
Mr. Stevens: (states explanation)	Fine, Bill. In the world of working, you have things that you really need to buy in order to survive. You have to make these decisions yourselves as adults. However, I feel you all have a good idea of what the necessities for living are. The luxuries will be different for all of you. Will each of you make a list of luxuries you would like to have? If you can't spell it, ask me for help. We will share our lists with each other.

This classroom discussion is an analysis of the differences between necessities and luxuries in daily living. We can display the pattern of relationships surfaced by our analysis using our pyramid display (Figure 5–2). A more common diagram used to display relationships is the flowchart pattern shown in Figure 5–3. Whether in pyramid or flowchart form, the logical structure includes the elements of the explanation (concepts and related facts) and also describes their relationships.

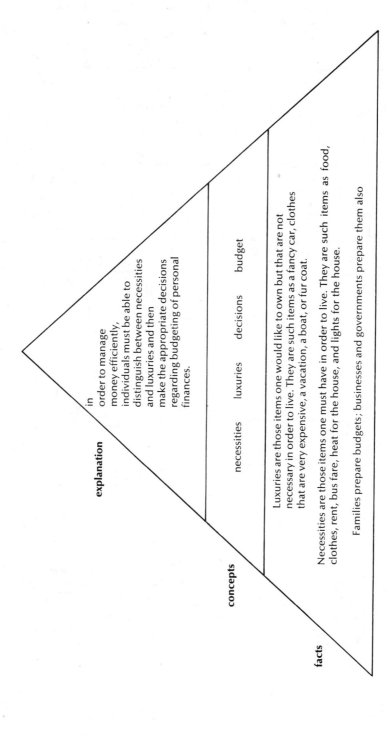

explanation

in order to manage money efficiently, individuals must be able to distinguish between necessities and luxuries and then make the appropriate decisions regarding budgeting of personal finances.

concepts

necessities   luxuries   decisions   budget

facts

Luxuries are those items one would like to own but that are not necessary in order to live. They are such items as a fancy car, clothes that are very expensive, a vacation, a boat, or fur coat.

Necessities are those items one must have in order to live. They are such items as food, clothes, rent, bus fare, heat for the house, and lights for the house.

Families prepare budgets; businesses and governments prepare them also

Figure 5–2   *A pyramid view of a structural analysis in economics*

163

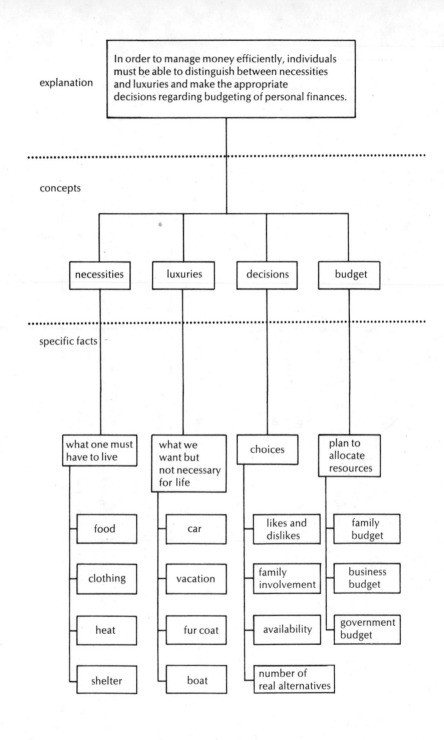

Figure 5–3   *A flowchart view of a structural analysis in economics*

Psychological Analysis:
A Structure of Learning Process

As with logical analysis, teachers are necessarily involved in the psychological analysis of the processes that produce learning. When learning is defined as *an increased capability to exhibit knowledge of certain physical, emotional, or intellectual subject matter,* two areas of investigation become apparent.

1. What are the elements of the subject matter to be taught and how are the elements interrelated? (logical analysis)
2. At what level of complexity or difficulty is the subject matter to be presented? (psychological analysis)

Where in logical analysis we were concerned with the conceptual breakdown of subject matter, in psychological analysis the focus is on "what happens inside the learner's head" when presented with the content to be learned. Or, to express it another way, how is knowledge acquired by the learner? Are we satisfied with the recall of information we taught in class? Or is our goal beyond the mere recall of facts?

The ability to function independently in society and compete as a worker in the job market requires more than just learning facts. Developing facts into concepts and applying those concepts to real-life situations is clearly a more useful goal. School experiences must have as a goal the understanding of ideas (concepts) so that students can learn more efficiently outside the classroom. We can only be satisfied when what students learn in the classroom can help them solve real-world problems. This is an educational goal for all students, including mentally retarded learners. Since any content area can be taught at many different levels of difficulty, the question remains: how do curriculum developers analyze psychological learner processes in such a way as to create a useful organizational scheme? We shall describe and examine two common approaches to this problem and use our economics example to illustrate their application in instruction.

The Objective-Taxonomic Approach

A number of years ago, a group of educational measurement experts attempting to determine the relative success of given objectives realized that an organizational scheme for classifying objectives was needed (Bloom, 1956). They were hopeful that their conceptual scheme would clarify and sharpen the language of educational objectives. As a result of their continuing efforts, Benjamin Bloom and his colleagues conceived a taxonomy of educational objectives subdivided into three learning areas or domains. Bloom (1956) and his associates placed intellectual processes such as memorizing and thinking into the *cognitive* domain. The *affective* domain contains emotional responses such as feeling, demonstrating interest, and valuing. The *psychomotor* domain includes sensory attention to stimuli and physical responses of a simple and complex nature.

The cognitive domain.   The educational objectives involving intellectual processes are classified into a design comprising six major categories and numerous subcategories. The six categories are knowledge, comprehension, application, analysis, synthesis, and evaluation. The categories reflect a hierarchial conception of learning; increased cognitive skills are required at the higher levels. This process assumes mastery of each category before moving onto the next higher level. The cognitive domain, with a suggested modification and examples, is presented in Table 5–1. Although some teachers argue that it is useful to target learning objectives within each of the six categories as conceived by the taxonomy developers, it is unrealistic to expect most of us to do so. It appears to us that the four-category modification (recall, lower level thought, higher level thought and evaluation) retains the principles of Bloom's original conception while reducing its complexity. The same taxonomy can be applied to educational objectives developed for retarded learners. The following classroom example highlights Bloom's conception of the cognitive domain.

Sarah Johnson is a teacher in a resource room in an elementary school. Bill is a 7-year-old boy who is assigned to the resource room for 90 minutes every day. He has identified learning problems in the area of mathematics. Johnson wishes to teach Bill the value of money. She knows that Bill will need to know some of the complexities of our monetary system in order to survive in today's society. Bill can count rationally to 30 and has seen coins. He is unable to state the value of coins, however, or use coins independently.

Johnson sets the following objectives so that she can assist Bill to reach a higher level of functioning concerning the value of money.

Recall: Bill will identify and match a penny, nickel, and dime with their corresponding numerals.

Lower Level Thought: Given a nickel and a dime, Bill will be able to demonstrate that five pennies make a nickel,

Table 5-1 The cognitive area of Bloom's taxonomy, a suggested modification and examples

Categories as conceived by developers	Suggested modification	Examples
Knowledge—The ability to memorize previously learned facts, concepts, and explanations	Recall	Students can list six life necessities for money management.
Comprehension—The ability to interpret information and filter out what has already been learned	Lower level thought (understanding)	After reading about the problems Jim Jones had managing his budget, students will recognize the necessities from the luxuries in Jim's money management scheme.
Application—Using previously learned concepts and explanations in unfamiliar situations to examine the particulars in the situation	Higher level thought (understanding plus manipulation of information—applying, analyzing, synthesizing)	After constructing a composite of the various budget forms found in books and magazines, the class will develop a personalized budget based on the individual ideas of what a budget ought to be.
Analysis—The ability to break down given information into its essential parts		
Synthesis—Combining pieces or parts to construct a whole which was not previously obvious		
Evaluation—Making judgments in comparison of practices or procedures to a given set of criteria	Evaluation	After comparison shopping in which several stores charge the same price for the product a student wishes to purchase, the student will make other interstore comparisons before deciding where to purchase the product.

Column 1 from Benjamin S. Bloom et al., *Taxonomy of Educational Objectives: The Classification of Educational Goals: Handbook 1: Cognitive Domain*. Copyright © 1956 by Longman Inc. Reprinted by permission of Longman.

	ten pennies make a dime, and two nickels make a dime.
Higher Level Thought:	Bill will demonstrate the value of the coins by selecting articles from a toy store and producing the appropriate coins for the articles to be purchased, with any combination of coins.
Evaluation:	Given an apple, a candy bar, and a packet of gum each priced at 10¢, Bill will buy the item that will be the most beneficial to him and will explain to Johnson his reason for purchasing this item.

The ordering of cognitive content into a taxonomy arranged from simple to complex has several benefits for both teacher and learner. First of all, the task can be presented from simple to complex, which is the most productive method for teaching retarded learners. Second, this step-by-step procedure provides the teacher with the increments in the instructional process out of which criterion-referenced assessment can occur. Third, the teacher can guide the student in the instructional process through systematic monitoring of learning. Fourth, this approach allows teachers to "teach from success" by beginning at a level at which the child has success, reviewing, and then building toward a more complex achievement level.

To illustrate, let's return to the hierarchy presented to Bill involving money management. Bill has demonstrated that he has mastered the objectives at the *recall* level. He is unable, however, to demonstrate mastery of the objectives at lower level thought. These objectives must be used to guide his instruction until he has demonstrated mastery, before going to higher thought processes—application, analysis, and synthesis.

The affective domain.   The area of learning that deals with emotional content is contained in the affective domain of the taxonomy (Krathwohl, Bloom, & Masia, 1964). As such, it includes such non-cognitive behaviors as feelings, interests, appreciations, and values and classifies them according to the depth and strength of the behavior.

The major categories are

1. *Receiving*—A willingness to attend to a given phenomenon; for example, reading an article that presents a particular viewpoint toward abortion.
2. *Responding*—Acting in response to some belief; for instance, agreeing to sign a petition supporting or attacking a public policy.

3. *Valuing*—A conscious acceptance of a position, becoming an advocate for a particular position or cause.
4. *Organization*—Moving toward a hierarchical system of values, recognizing conflicting values, and determining their relative place in a complex of values.
5. *Characterization*—Developing a hierarchical integrated "philosophy of life" that guides a person's life. For example, someone who espouses a total world view of life such as a religious or economic theorist or the developer of an alternative life style might qualify.

Although the affective domain contains five categories, teachers who include affective objectives in their teaching and are conscious of the need to move students from simple awareness to more advanced stages probably fulfill the goals of the hierarchy's developers.

Many retarded learners are confused by their feelings. They may find themselves in difficult circumstances because of their inability to identify and control their feelings. Consider this classroom problem.

An adolescent retarded learner, Jim, has been placed in a regular junior high school classroom. Several students in the classroom verbally identify him as a "retard." The only way that Jim knows to respond is to strike the person who makes this offensive remark. He has responded this way many times and has frequently gotten into trouble. Jim does not *feel* retarded, so he gets very angry when others call him something he neither likes nor understands. Today, Jim chooses to ignore the verbal insult because he knows that fighting will be grounds for expulsion from school.

Instead, Jim says to the other student, "I may not be so smart but at least I try to do my work. I feel real bad when you call me 'retard.' I wish you'd call me 'Jim.' " Some of the students laugh, but the laughter is more of a nervous release than a taunt. One student sits down next to Jim, smiles, and says nothing. However, this nonverbal approval of Jim's behavior is very rewarding to him. It is also an integral part of the affective domain. Notice that Jim has learned to respond in an effective, honest manner that modifies the reaction of his classmates.

As in this example, the processes involved in the affective domain do not always follow a set, logical order. Our feelings and emotions cannot be broken down into sequential parts like a mathematical equation.

The affective taxonomy can be applied to Jim's situation.

1. *Receiving*—Jim received negative comments from a classmate about a label that has involuntarily been placed on him.

2. *Responding*—Jim acts in response to his own hurt feelings, and to his belief that trying is important.
3. *Valuing*—One classmate demonstrates his acceptance of Jim's response by moving closer to him. (The teacher can serve as facilitator for a class discussion regarding values and value clarification.)
4. *Organization*—A more formal series of activities can follow which deal with negative aspects of labels, individual worth, and so on.
5. *Characterization*—The teacher can then facilitate a discussion regarding personal philosophy, the congruence of words and actions, and how to identify one's own belief system as an individual and a part of a group.

In large measure, this example is a question of values in terms of whether some individuals are more important than others. Mentally retarded persons have long been devalued by American society; societal values do not change easily. Mentally retarded people themselves can help to change those attitudes by developing appropriate behaviors and the skills needed to compete in society.

The attitudes of students and teachers toward the retarded are especially critical in light of the mandates of P.L. 94–142, the new Education for all Handicapped Children Act. The success of "mainstreaming" depends upon the actions and attitudes of each individual involved in the process—parents, teachers, administrators, and children. To whit, regular classrooms, according to P.L. 94–142, are termed "least restrictive environments." The degree of restrictiveness, however, is in large measure determined by the values and attitudes of those who reside there. The affective characteristics of the classroom contribute to the degree of its restrictiveness.

The taxonomy of the affective domain provides a sound hierarchical framework for dealing with this content in the classroom, school, or school system. Helping children value themselves and others through well-planned classroom activities is an essential part of the educational process. There are long-term benefits for all the individuals involved and for the larger society through these educational endeavors. Both behaviorists and psychoanalysts, even though they use different words, agree that positive relationships must be established among teachers, students, parents, and the community. And children can be helped to be in touch with their feelings, to identify and clarify their attitudes and values, and to understand the elements of a personal philosophy. These concerns, after all, are the foundation upon which one becomes a responsible citizen.

Retarded persons need this instructional focus as well. As more and more retarded persons are placed in regular classrooms, they must be armed with coping skills that let them effectively deal with new teachers, peers, responsibilities, and experiences. Their non-retarded peers will also require assistance in examining their attitudes and values toward people who may be different from themselves. The affective development of the child will not be fully realized if left to chance. Planned and well-organized classroom activities that focus on the content in the affective domain can be a source of valuable learning for all children.

The psychomotor domain. Only recently have educational re-searchers directed much attention to the psychomotor area of learn-ing. The work of Piaget and other developmental psychologists has identified the importance of the role of motor development to later learning. Several special educators, particularly Kephart (1960) and Cratty (1969), have demonstrated the importance of motor-percep-tual training for certain learners. The increased research into the relationship of motor development and overall development has resulted in the expansion of efforts to analyze psychomotor develop-ment. Harrow (1972) has tried to organize the psychomotor domain into a hierarchical set of categories. The Harrow taxonomy is divided into six categories organized along a continuum from less complex to more complex skills. The categories include

1. *Reflex movements*—Movements that involve a single spinal seg-ment as compared to more sophisticated behaviors that require participation of the brain centers and lead to observable behaviors such as grasping toward objects and righting one's position.
2. *Basic fundamental movements*—Basic movement patterns—push-ing, pulling, twisting, walking, running; movements that form the basis for complex, skilled movements.
3. *Perceptual abilities*—Judgments of one's body in relation to surrounding objects in space; visual, auditory and tactile discrimi-nation and their coordination.

The following categories are more complex skills.

4. *Physical abilities*—Endurance, strength, flexibility, and agility.
5. *Skilled movement*—Progression from beginner to expert in activities from dancing to gymnastics.
6. *Nondiscursive communication*—Aesthetic and creative message routines involving facial expressions, postures, and gestures to dance and gymnastic choreographies.

These categories provide a framework for developing motor activities on a developmental basis. Teachers can use the approach to guide decisions regarding appropriate motor activities. Such activities, when integrated into the instructional program, can reinforce learning as well as stimulate motor development.

Since the advent of the President's Council on Physical Fitness reports, urging that all school-age children have considerable physical activity, there has been a greater emphasis placed on psychomotor development. Learning experiences in the psychomotor domain, until recently, have focused on progression from gross to fine motor skill performance. The work of Harrow is a refinement of past efforts. The concept of "body image" has recently become widely accepted as an important construct in special education. Many teachers have found that, as children become more aware of their bodies and learn to move and control their bodies through gross motor activities, they develop a more positive self-image. And physical prowess is highly valued in our society, as evidenced by the large number of people who attend sports events or watch them on television. Children value competent physical performance as well. A visit to an elementary school playground before the afternoon bell reveals children engaged in many motor activities, often competing intensely. There are many reasons, including health, for our schools to concentrate on developing psychomotor classroom activities.

Mentally retarded learners can often successfully compete with their nonretarded peers in the motor domain. Thus, these activities should integrate all learners. In fact, many retarded learners can be outstanding in motor tasks and such successes can serve to enhance the view of retarded students in the eyes of their peers.

The Task Description Approach

A second analysis of the structure of learning process was developed by psychologist Robert Gagné. The explanation that guides his classification system, as written by Gagné, is:

> In theory, one can reconstruct conceptually the entire set of operations to be carried out by any system, without errors or misconceptions, by reading a properly prepared description which is given in terms of tasks listed in the correct order. (1971, p. 87)

In other words, any task can be described in a step-by-step progression that identifies the elements of the task.

The process of obtaining valid task descriptions is called *task analysis*. Gagné describes the relationship of task analysis to learning as follows:

> When a task to be learned is analyzed into simpler capabilities that need to be learned as prerequisites, and when such an

analysis is continued progressively to the point of delineating an entire set of capabilities having an ordered relation to each other (in the sense that in each case prerequisite capabilities are represented as subordinate in position, indicating that they need to be previously learned), one has a learning hierarchy. (1970, p. 238)

Gagné (1962) has suggested that learning hierarchies exist within all broad subject-matter fields. The important contribution made by his work to the field of teaching and learning rests in the fact that it has provided a useful method for combining subject matter and learning process analysis. The learning hierarchies that result from data obtained from task analysis have the potential to maximize success at various stages of learning.* This analysis and synthesis (to use Bloom's terminology) give the teacher a vehicle for examining the elements of a task in relation to the acquisition of those elements by the learner. For mentally retarded students, this approach can be very helpful. In the broadest sense, it allows the learner to proceed through the task elements; errors or nonlearning can be quickly identified by the teacher.

The task analysis process is closely allied with the training programs used in the military during and after World War II. There the development of validated task descriptions reduced training time and errors in job areas from pilot training to electronic and mechanical repair. As a simplified training example, consider the task of teaching someone to disassemble an ordinary flashlight. A task analysis expert might first separate and list the parts:

1. Flashlight body,
2. Batteries (2),
3. Bulb protector,
4. Bulb,
5. Bulb retainer,
6. Lens,
7. Lens hood.

A display of the parts as they properly align together would be the next step in the process (see page 174). It is followed by a verbal description of the disassembly tasks. (Notice the instructions contain "item identification" and directions for manipulating items.)

1. Holding flashlight in your left hand, unscrew the lens using a counterclockwise motion.

---

* Strictly speaking, Gagné suggests that learning hierarchies are most appropriate for the development of intellectual skills—concepts and principles, but they can also be helpful in displaying the hierarchical relationships in motor skills and memorized information.

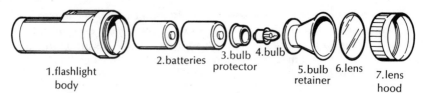

1.flashlight body   2.batteries   3.bulb protector   4.bulb   5.bulb retainer   6.lens   7.lens hood

2. Place lens hood on the table.
3. Tip flashlight body downward and catch the two batteries in your right hand as they fall out.
4. Place both the batteries and the flashlight body on the table.
5. Pick up the lens hood in your left hand so that the white bulb protector is facing upward.
6. Holding the lens hood firm, use your right hand to pry the bulb protector from the bulb retainer. Place the bulb protector on the table.
7. With your right hand, remove the bulb and place it on the table.
8. Again with your right hand, pry the bulb retainer from the lens hood. Place it on the table.
9. Now turn the lens hood over on the table, and the lens will drop out.
10. Move the lens hood to the right and place it on the table.

With sufficient practice following these sequential steps, a student can learn to disassemble a flashlight.

Instructional developers have attempted to translate the task analysis paradigm used in practical job training in business, industry, and the military to the much more complex world of the school classroom. A fairly comfortable translation to a school-related problem would be in handwriting instruction. Here is an illustration of this application to the task of handwriting.

Task: Writing the Upper Case Letter A (Manuscript)
Utensils
    1. Blank paper with a 2-inch square,
    2. Pencil.
Assumption: Child has mastered the prerequisite skill of holding a pencil in proper writing position.

On a blank piece of paper, a 2-inch square is drawn.

1. The student identifies the middle of the top line of the square.
2. The student identifies the left-hand lower corner and the right-hand lower corner.

The student is then given the following verbal direction:

3. Pick up your pencil.
4. Place the pencil in the middle of the top line.
5. Draw a line from the middle of the top line to the left-hand corner of the square.

6. Place your pencil in the middle of the top line.
7. Draw a line from the middle of the top line to the right-hand corner of the square.

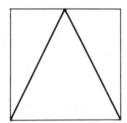

8. Put your pencil in the middle of the left line.
9. Draw a line only from the left line to the right line.

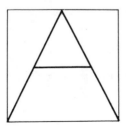

10. You have now successfully written an upper case letter A.

The next task is to make the letter A without assistance. The procedures would entail fading the square and having the student write the letter A without the aid of the square.

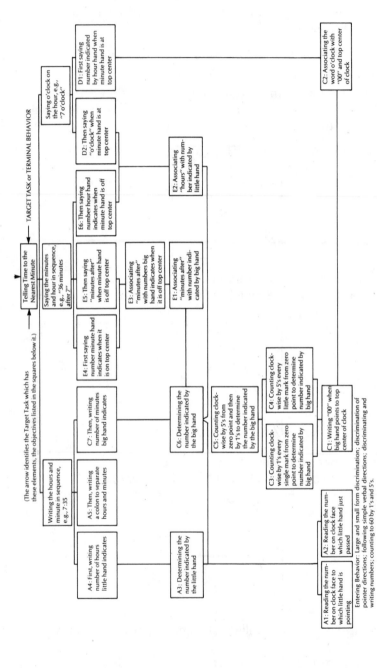

Figure 5–4 *Sequence of subbehaviors in the Time-Telling Program*

Reprinted from DEFINING EDUCATIONAL OBJECTIVES edited by C. M. Lindvall by permission of the University of Pittsburgh Press. © 1964 by the University of Pittsburgh Press.

Table 5-2 *Gagné's classification of learning task skills*

Categories as conceived by Gagné	Suggested modification	Examples
Signal learning—Emotional reaction to a given stimulus	*Emotional learning*	Showing anxiety over tests, excitement at the knowledge of danger, pleasure at the sound of another's voice.
Stimulus response learning—Precise muscular responses to given stimuli	*Simple psychomotor skills*	Repeating sounds, basic movement patterns —grasping, taking a step.
Chaining—Complex physical movements when S-R responses are strung together	*Complex psychomotor skills*	Writing, running, swimming, playing ball.
Verbal association—Verbal chain which consists of attaching names or syllables to given stimuli	*Memorization*—Recall of previously learned material	Memorizing the names for letters of the alphabet, recognizing various letters in a written word.
Multiple discrimination—Selecting the correct verbal response from previously learned alternatives		Identifying one's name, reading, correctly answering a question.
Concept learning—Classifying new stimuli into previously learned general categories	*Complex cognitive*—Classifying unfamiliar information into previously taught categories, explaining relationships, and problem solving	Identifying objects that are round.
Principle learning—Statement of relationships		
Problem solving—Combining concepts and principles to solve complex problems		

Column 1 from R. Gagné, *The Conditions of Learning*. New York: *Holt, Rinehart and Winston*, 1970.

177

Task analysis has also been used to describe more difficult cognitive processes. The task description shown in Figure 5–4 was used as a guide to teach first grade children to tell time (see page 173). The program begins at "A," where children are asked to "read the number on the clock face to which the little hand is pointing," progresses to the discrimination between minutes and hours at "E^1" and "E^2," and concludes at the apex of the program with the ability to tell time to the minute.

The task description taxonomy: An ordering of task descriptions. The outcome generated by a task analysis process is a series of task descriptions that follow the progress of a given task through its various component operations. Where Bloom and his co-workers conceived of three distinct learning domains—cognitive, affective and psychomotor—Gagné combines them in a unified design.

Gagné (1970) argues that there are eight varieties of learning that can be differentiated, and these can be ordered hierarchically. These eight include (from simple to complex) signal learning, stimulus response learning, chaining, verbal association, multiple discrimination, concept learning, principle learning, and problem solving. Table 5–2 defines each category, with suggested modifications.

Gagné has conceived of an arrangement of eight generalized task skills that he believes subsumes all learning types. He implies, as does

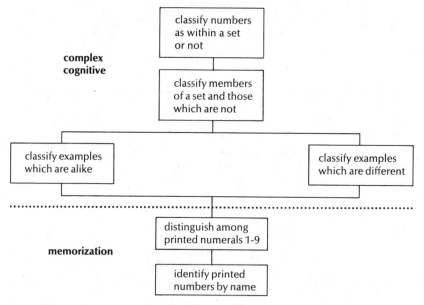

Figure 5–5   *Hierarchy of number set in mathematics*

Bloom, that the categories are hierarchical in nature and that mastery at any particular category level assumes mastery at the lower levels. The hierarchical nature of Gagné's scheme implies that each lower level is a prerequisite for the more advanced levels. In other words, concept learning would of necessity precede the ability to discover the relationships among concepts in order to describe a principle. Gagne's focus is on the learner and the learning process, as it applies to the acquisition of skills and knowledge.

The Learning Hierarchy: A Synthesis

A useful instructional tool that combines logical and psychological analysis is the learning hierarchy. It presents the anatomy of instruction from the most complex subject content and learning process to the specific information to the memorized by the students. Learning hierarchies can be generated for all school subjects and all grade and ability levels. A well-conceived hierarchy has two essential characteristics.

1. It contains the thoughtful analysis of the logical elements of the subject structure. Consequently, the pattern of facts, concepts, and explanations displayed in the hierarchy have content validity as verified by authorities in the subject area.
2. It combines the logical structure with a psychological analysis of the learning processes to be demonstrated by the students.

An example of a learning hierarchy for subject matter that might be taught to retarded learners is the teaching of the concept "set" in mathematics, Figure 5–5.* In constructing the hierarchy we will use the modified task description approach described in Table 5–2.

Specifically, in this hierarchy the concept "set" is analyzed through subordinate concepts "one-group" and "like-different." At the base of the hierarchy are the specific memorization tasks (the simplest level of cognitive tasks) to distinguish the various numerals and state their names. The tasks increase in difficulty as you move up from one level to the next. The elements of the concept "set" are included in order of difficulty from concrete to abstract. The hierarchy represents the pattern of relationships of the sequential development of the concept, thus serving as a guide from which the teacher can select instructional objectives. In addition, it serves as a visible reminder of the pathway for instruction, detailing all prerequisite facts

---

* Adapted from R. M. Gagné, *The Conditions of Learning.* New York: Holt, Rinehart & Winston, 1970. Used with permission.

and necessary concepts. In addition, the hierarchy specifies those elements that must be memorized as facts.

A summary and comparison of the work of Bloom and Gagné will perhaps make this presentation clearer. Table 5–3 shows the relationship between the two schemes. In the left column, Bloom's categories show the level reached when, in the corresponding right column, Gagné's categories are present. Signal learning, stimulus response learning, and chaining are all precursors of the knowledge level; the ability to make verbal associations and multiple discriminations enables the learner to acquire knowledge.

Table 5–3

Bloom →	Level reached when →	Gagné
I. *Knowledge*—Memorize facts, concepts, and explanations	*Verbal association* (attaching names or symbols to stimuli), and *multiple discrimination* (select the correct response from those previously learned) have been acquired	
II. *Comprehension*—The ability to interpret information and filter out what has already been learned	*Verbal association/multiple discrimination* have been acquired	
III. *Application*—Using previously learned concepts and explanations in unfamiliar situations to examine the particulars in a situation	*Concept learning* or the ability to classify new stimuli in previously learned general categories has been acquired	
IV. *Analysis*—The ability to break down information into its essential parts and *Synthesis*—Combining pieces or parts to construct a whole which was not previously obvious	*Principle learning,* which explains when relationships occur among elements or concepts, is reached	
V. *Evaluation*—Making judgments in comparison of practices or procedures to a given set of criteria	*Problem solving,* the ability to combine concepts and principles to solve complex problems, is reached	

The model represented in Table 5–3 is a comparison and analysis of the relationship of the ordering of task analysis to the analysis of cognitive learning. The work done by both Bloom and Gagné relates to the analysis of learning, and the acquisition of knowledge can be applied to any instructional experience in the school. While neither worked with mentally retarded persons per se, their work has direct application to special education.

Table 5–4 shows how subject matter content can be integrated into the two classification schemes.

Table 5–4

I. *Knowledge*—The student can identify coins; count money to $1,000; identify items that are luxuries and necessities; and explain their selections in terms of a personal economy

Verbal association—The student can name each coin when presented by the teacher.

II. *Comprehension*—The student can determine what the teacher wishes him to identify in the context of questions or stories.

Multiple discrimination—The student can discriminate among coins by correctly identifying each; can verbally describe similarities and differences among coins.

III. *Application*—When presented items with varying prices, the student can identify the coin combination needed to purchase each item.

Concept learning—From a group of five items, the student can select those which cost more and those which cost less.

IV. *Analysis*–The student can complete the following exercise: "Johnny has $1.20 to spend. He wants to go to the movies, buy a candy bar, and ride the bus. If the movie costs $.75 and the candy costs $.25, how much does he have for bus fare?"
and
Synthesis—The student can write a personal budget, when given a hypothetical situation (a job which pays $120/week and a particular identity and life style).

Principle learning—The student can explain why the size of a coin is not an accurate indicator of a coin's value.

V. *Evaluation*—The student will judge whether two particular individuals with varying life styles are leading productive or unproductive lives.

Problem solving—Given prepared case studies, the student will make recommendations for improvement in productive use of money resources.

part 2   *Curriculum analysis for the retarded learner*

Gagné's learning hierarchy assumes a continuum of normal growth and development on the part of the learner. We feel that the development of retarded learners with no organic impairment (by far the largest number of retarded persons attending public schools) parallels that of their nonretarded peers. This "developmental" position, more fully explained by Zigler (1969, 1973), assumes that retarded and non-retarded individuals proceed along the same developmental continuum. Thus, the assumptions that underlie Gagné's learning hierarchy for non-retarded learners apply to retarded learners too.

This position is challenged by the "defect" interpretations of researchers such as Ellis (1969). The research data have shown, however, that when retarded and normal subjects are matched for mental age, there are differences in their performances on several kinds of tasks. Zigler (1966, 1969, 1973) suggests that the unique experiential history of the retarded learner may explain the differences in performance, particularly regarding motivation.

As a leading spokesman for the developmental position, Zigler (1966) differentiates between "organic" and "familial" mental retardation. The wide differences within the group of people called "mentally retarded" has led to much of the confusion regarding the impact of cognitive deficits. Zigler has attempted to clarify the issue by proposing a two-group approach: those who have organic impairment and those whose low intelligence is the result of normal intellectual variation.

The largest number of retarded persons are those who fall into the second group, the mildly mentally retarded. Their performance is best understood in terms of the expected variability of human characteristics. This text is directed toward that population.

The developmental orientation assumes that the individual who is classified as mildly mentally retarded progresses through the same stages of cognitive development as the normal individual, although at a slower rate. Furthermore, this position assumes that the order of the developmental stages will be the same for both groups, although the mentally retarded person will reach each level of cognitive competence at a later age than his normal peers. Some retarded individuals may not reach the more advanced stages of cognitive development or abstract reasoning at all. This position implies that when retarded and nonretarded individuals are at the same point in cognitive development, they should perform equally well on learning tasks. Thus, they can use the same curricula, albeit modified to meet individual needs.

The beliefs educators hold regarding retarded students and their development influences the way in which they conceptualize educational experiences for these students and select tasks and subject matter content. For example, if a teacher believes that mildly retarded learners are more *like* their nonretarded peers than different, then their instruction is planned accordingly. That is, standard curricular and instructional theory will provide the basis for developmental activities. This has not, however, been true of special education. There has been a hit-and-miss sort of approach to curriculum for the retarded learner, with the basic decision making done by the teacher. In most cases, teachers have had limited resources and lack the requisite skills. The basic assumption was that retarded students need different curricula than regular students.

Curriculum development in special education has only recently drawn the attention of psychologists, social scientists, and measurement and evaluation specialists (McNeil, 1969). Their interest and activity has resulted in an increased demand to use sound theoretical approaches in systematic curriculum development. The need to integrate the growing body of knowledge from both psychology and education into new curriculum models has been articulated by several authors (Heinz & Blackman, 1977). Appropriate and meaningful curricula for retarded learners can no longer be left to chance if we are to be held accountable in special education. These curricula must follow the patterns used by regular educators if retarded students are to function in regular classrooms.

Early Attempts at Curriculum Development for Retarded Learners

Using a "watered-down" general education curriculum has been the most pervasive practice in the area of curriculum for the retarded learner. No guiding philosophy has been used. In 1951, Kirk and Johnson suggested two principles that should guide the presentation of subject matter content to retarded learners: "concrete level" and "gradual rate." Along with others, they expressed a somewhat paternalistic attitude toward retarded learners; for instance, they stressed teaching these learners to read "to the best of their ability" (Kirk & Johnson, 1951, p. 183). Specific content and objectives were avoided; the uncertainty of achievement was the excuse.

During the late 1950s, the emphasis in educating mildly retarded learners was on "preparation for life." Goldstein and Siegle (1958) wrote a curriculum that included specific knowledge in areas such as arithmetic, science, and language arts. These writers stressed, however, that achievement in academic endeavors was only important in terms of its application to the problems of daily living. Thus, successful application of basic knowledge was viewed as the primary goal of education for the retarded learner. Goldstein's Social Learning Curriculum (1975) is an excellent example of a specialized curriculum tailored to the social needs of retarded learners.

Even today, there is no agreement among educators and educational psychologists in the field of mental retardation as to the appropriate level of academic skills to be included in a curriculum for retarded learners. The "defect" vs. "developmental" question contributes to the disagreement. The argument is also fired by the lack of consistent data on expected or actual achievement levels of these students.

To illustrate the confusion, we need only look at studies reported between 1929 and 1958 (from Bennett, 1929, to Blatt, 1958). Those writers found that mentally retarded individuals can achieve in academic skills when their success is viewed relative to their mental age rather than chronological age. Other studies have reported conflicting data, however. Studies were more concerned with placement than with "what to teach" retarded learners. The time has come for a systematic approach to instruction to take center stage in the education of mentally retarded persons. The adoption of the "normalization" principle by many professionals provides a philosophic basis for curriculum and instructional planning. The work of curriculum workers and educational psychologists such as Bloom, Gagné, and Bruner provide a theoretical framework from which to view curriculum planning.

The old excuse that we are unsure of the overall potential for achievement will no longer work. The time has come to determine what to teach systematically and to continue instructional sequences as long as the student is learning. As far back as 1963, Dunn described educable mentally retarded persons with an IQ of 75 as able to perform at the early seventh grade level. Since there still is little agreement on overall achievement potential for these learners, it is time to stop predicting and begin curriculum development designed to teach effectively.

Curriculum and Development: An Integrated Approach

Among the most significant work regarding the integration of new knowledge into curricula was the proceedings of a conference on curricular reform (Bruner, 1960). The essence of Bruner's work is the importance of organizing curricula around the structure of knowledge. He emphasized the potential benefits of this approach to the slower learning child when he stated that "any subject matter can be taught effectively in some intellectually honest form to any child at any stage of development" (p. 33). He further added that "good teaching that emphasizes the structure of a subject is probably more valuable for the less able student than for the gifted one, for it is former rather than the latter who is more easily thrown off track by poor teaching" (Bruner, 1960, p. 9).

Bruner says simply that the structure of knowledge should be the basis upon which curricula are built. Fields of knowledge such as history, language, physical geography, and mathematics are rich sources for creating curricula. Furthermore, Bruner believes that these rich resources can make academic subjects more comprehensible. The difference between Bruner's approach and more traditional modes is the emphasis on the comprehension of basic elements or fundamentals of knowledge, rather than learning and memorizing rote facts. For example, in a geography lesson that has as its target objective the knowledge of river ports in America, the traditional method might entail memorizing the ports along major rivers. Bruner's approach would focus on why rivers are important to the life of a society and the role that rivers have had in the development of population centers.

Research has shown that mentally retarded persons have difficulty memorizing facts. Using fundamental knowledge as the basis for teaching retarded learners should enable them to grasp ideas, separate from the memory of isolated elements. For example, some retarded students have difficulty remembering the names of coins. They are, however, able to understand the use of money as a medium of exchange, supply and demand, and other fundamental elements related to economic understanding. By devising classroom simulations and activities, the teacher can present fundamental economic principles, even if some students are unable to name the coins.

Bruner believes in immersing the student in meaningful activities designed to facilitate the learning of the basic structure of knowledge.

> To understand something as a specific instance of a more general case—which is what understanding a more fundamental structure or principle means—is to have learned not only a specific thing but also a model for understanding other things like it that one may encounter. (Bruner, 1960, p. 25)

Improvement of transfer of learning is thus implied.

Piaget's work supports Bruner's view of the way to optimize learning. The core of Piaget's theory is that cognitive development is a dynamic process that results from interactions with the environment. His work describes the process rather than the product of intellectual development. His concern is not with right or wrong answers, but with the process of arriving at them. For Piaget, living is learning; learning is an active process. This work has many implications for classroom practice. Research by Klein and Safford (1976, 1977) has explored the significance of his work with retarded children, and found it to hold promise as a means by which to better understand how retarded children learn.

The theories of both Bruner and Piaget regarding how children learn and acquire information can be applied to the classroom and the instructional process. There are several useful principles that can be derived from their work. These principles can be used as guidelines in deciding the appropriateness of certain experiences for the developing learner.

The following principles, based upon the work of Bruner and Piaget, can be used as a guide in analyzing curriculum and instruction for mentally retarded learners.

1. Materials for young children should be manipulative and have multisensory dimensions.
2. Content should be organized so that students have an opportunity to employ already learned knowledge to build new knowledge.
3. Content should include experiences which enable students to discover cause-and-effect relationships.
4. Content and materials should be selected in terms of relevance and degree of meaningfulness to the student's age level.
5. Learning experiences, which allow children to act upon ideas as well as materials, should be active.
6. Problem-solving activities should be related to learner's interests, concerns, and experiences.

7. Students need opportunities to develop the internal structures of language, with teacher or peers as language facilitators.
8. Opportunities to act upon and explore the dimensions and attributes of objects in order to "know" them enhances the development of concepts.
9. Sorting and classification activities help children define an attribute of the group; they need extensive practice.
10. Manipulative seriation tasks are prerequisite to math skill development.
11. Activities that lead to the development of conservation skills help the child move from perceptual to conceptual thought.
12. Reasoning tasks at many levels provide practice.
13. The teacher acts as *facilitator* for the learning process.

An analysis of curriculum for retarded learners begins on these principles. They can be applied to any subject matter area—the selection of materials is determined by the content. To demonstrate the applicability of these principles to content areas, they have been cross-referenced by number to activities in three tables on content areas. These tables have lettered cross–references to figures of learning hierarchy goals. Tables and corresponding figures are Table 5–4, page 187, and Figure 5–6, page 199; Table 5–5, page 191, and Figure 5–7, page 200; Table 5–6, page 195, and Figure 5–8, page 201.

Table 5–4 *Money and budgeting*

	Activities	Objectives	Principles
I.	Class Discussion		
	1. The student participates in a class discussion examining the two quotes "Advertising is the best thing to happen to the consumer" and "Advertising has ruined the consumer's budget."	A, C, D, E	2, 5, 12
	2. The student will discuss the conflict between a limited income and unlimited desires. As a group develop a chart, divided into two columns, one "necessities" and the other "luxuries."	A, D, E	2, 5, 9, 12
	3. After clipping magazine and newspaper advertisements, the student will participate in a discussion of how a wise consumer	C, D, E	2, 5, 9, 12

	Activities	Objectives	Principles
	evaluates and views typical advertising techniques.		
4.	Students discuss the steps taken in setting up a personal budget. These steps would include listing reasons for budgeting, items included in a budget, an assessment of one's income, discriminations between luxuries and necessities, fixed and variable expenses, and the relative priorities of family and individual needs.	C, D, E	2, 3, 6, 9, 12
5.	As a group discuss the various ways which one may increase personal income. Include possibilities such as working overtime, obtaining part-time employment, saving more to earn interest.	A, B, C, D	2, 3, 4, 9, 12
6.	The student will take part in a class discussion on why trust and confidence are necessary for anything to be accepted as money.	A	5, 12
7.	Discuss the advantages of using checks for buying and selling instead of cash. Include good record keeping and balancing a budget.	A, D, E	2, 12
8.	The student will take part in a class discussion concerning the following hypothetical situation: "After comparison shopping, you find that several stores charge the same price for the product you wish to purchase. What other interstore comparisons can a shopper make?	C, D, E	2, 9, 12
9.	After constructing a composite of the various budget forms found in books and magazines, the class will develop a personalized budget based on individual ideas of what a budget ought to be.	D, E	2, 5, 8, 9, 12

	Activities	Objectives	Principles
10.	The student will take part in a class discussion on how budgeting involves consideration of use and misuse of credit, hidden costs, balancing one's saving and spending habits, and lifestyles.	D, E	2, 5, 9, 12
11.	With reference to the various budget forms available, the students will select the best features of these budgets and develop a class budget model.	E	2, 5, 9, 12
12.	The student will participate in a group discussion describing the effect of spending more than in the budget. Follow discussion by field experience in store (spending more than you have).	A	2, 3, 5, 12

II. Role Play

13.	Set up a classroom "store" where the entire purchasing process may be reinforced. This may be tied into a token economy. The students are to exchange various roles (e.g., shopper, clerk, manager).	A, C	1, 3, 4, 5, 9

III. Worksheet

14.	The student will complete a crossword puzzle consisting of concepts and vocabulary words pertaining to the role of money in and fluctuations of our economy.	A, B	6, 12
15.	Students will complete worksheets reinforcing arithmetic and recognition skills related to handling and management of money.	A, E	6, 11, 12
16.	The student will complete various matching, fill-in, and short-answer worksheets pertaining to the vocabulary and concepts related to the making of money (e.g., indications of	A, B	6, 12

Activities	Objectives	Principles
counterfeit bills, silver certificates, Federal Reserve, Bureau of Engraving and Printing, Minting, U.S. Treasury, etc.).		

IV. Class Speaker
17. Invite a bank representative to visit and discuss the information and assistance on budget planning that banks offer. Role play the information with him. — D, E — 2, 3, 6

V. Field Trips
18. Field trip to a fast food restaurant where the student is to note various aspects of the purchasing process (e.g., items bought and the cost of individual items, as well as total cost, amount of money given to the clerk, and the amount of change received). — A, C — 2, 3, 5, 12
19. If possible, visit a Federal Reserve Bank. — A — 4, 5
20. The students will take a trip to a grocery store to purchase various items for a special class event (e.g., class picnic). Follow by analyzing the sales receipt itemization. — A, B, C, D — 1, 2, 3, 4, 5, 12

VI. Panel Discussion
21. The student will take part in panel or committee discussions concerning the planning of budgets for classroom activities. — B, C, D — 2, 6, 12
22. After being given different cards indicating a hypothetical family's income and fixed expenses, the student will take part in preparing a monthly budget for the family assigned to his budget. Subsequently, a panel discussion will be conducted allowing each group to respond to the other budgets. — D, E — 2, 3, 5, 6, 12

	Activities	Objectives	Principles
VII.	**Miscellaneous**		
23.	The students will construct a bulletin board display of the different forms of money (e.g., currency, coins, checks, bonds, credit cards, savings, etc.).	A	1, 4, 9
24.	When shown flashcards of various amounts of money, the student will identify the amounts shown.	A	5
25.	When shown flashcards of various amounts of money, the student will replicate the amount with real money.	A	1, 2, 4
26.	The student will develop a "luxury" book that contains his most desired wishes and explain them to his classmates.	D	2, 4, 5, 7
27.	The student will classify items or pictures of items along the dimension of luxury—nonluxury.	D	1, 2, 4, 9
28.	The student will select six items from the classroom store and put them in order from most to least expensive.	A	1, 2, 4, 10
29.	The student will go to a store and identify six items and their costs, and then come back to the classroom and order them from least to most expensive.	A	2, 4, 5, 10
30.	The student will sort 30 items according to the areas of planned spending, i.e., food, clothing, etc.	D	2, 4, 5, 9

Table 5–5 *Credit and contracts*

	Activities	Objectives
I.	**Class Discussion**	
1.	The student will take part in a class discussion on the advantages and disadvantages of credit buying.	A, H, I
2.	Students will discuss which credit cards might be most helpful	A, B, C, D, H, I

Activities	Objectives
to take on an out of town trip and why (e.g., gasoline credit cards, local department store credit cards, bank credit cards). Also, discuss the security precautions which one should take when traveling with credit cards, and actions which should be taken if one loses a credit card.	
3. As a group, the students will construct a list of possible reasons for the misuse of credit. Include poor planning and managing of expenditures, striving for status, misunderstanding of the differences between necessities and luxuries.	A, C, D, E, F, I
4. The student will participate in a class discussion on the establishment of a good credit rating. This list should include making as large down payment as possible, repaying as quickly as one can, having a steady employment record, using credit to buy needed items.	A, H
5. The student will take part in a discussion concerning important rules to follow before signing a contract (e.g., read before signing, do not sign if there are blank spaces, get a signed copy.)	A, E, F, G, I
6. After examining several contract forms the students will discuss and list contractual obligations on both the buyers, as well as the sellers part. Include the concepts of mutual consent, ownership status of goods, legal age.	B, C, G
7. The student will participate in a class discussion distinguishing between character, co–signer, and collateral loans.	B, C, D, E, F, G
8. After clipping magazine and newspaper advertisements and articles for various lending institutions, the student will take part in a class	A, B, C, D, H

Activities	Objectives

discussion concerning the future
role that credit may take in our
society (e.g., the decreased use of
cash for making purchases and
the possibility of a cashless future
society).

9. The students will participate in a   B, C, E, G
   class discussion comparing the
   various interest rates offered by
   different lending institutions.

10. Students will take part in a class   A, H
    discussion of the characteristics
    associated with good and poor
    credit risks.

11. The student will take part in a   A, B, D, I
    class discussion on the things a
    consumer may do if one is in
    serious financial trouble resulting
    from debts.

II. Role Play

12. Students will role play the   A, B, C, E, F, G, H
    following situation: An individual
    applying for a loan first completes
    a credit application and then is
    interviewed by a representative
    of the loaning institution. Students
    are to take turns alternating the
    roles of interviewer and potential
    loan customer. Questions and
    answers are to pertain to the credit
    application and the ability of the
    potential customer to repay the
    loan (focusing on income,
    expenses, and contract terms).

III. Worksheet

13. Following a class discussion on the   A, B, E
    manner in which interest rates
    vary, the student will complete
    several worksheets determining the
    interests costs of hypothetical
    purchases.

14. The student will complete various   A, B, D, C, E, F, G, H, I
    worksheets pertaining to the
    vocabulary and concepts associated

Activities	Objectives

with credit (e.g., installment contract account, revolving account, down payment, interest, case price).

15. Students will fill-out teacher pre-pared credit applications. — B, D, H

16. Students will complete a work-sheet reviewing the concepts relating to what a consumer may do if one has serious debt problems. Include such concepts as cash reserve, filing bankruptcy, Better Business Bureau, the court system. — A, G, I

17. The student will complete various worksheets computing the interest charge made on hypothetical credit transactions. These work-sheets will require the student to find the interest cost by subtracting the cash price from the total cost (including interest), as well as by multiplying by decimals (percents). — B, C, E

IV. Class Speakers

18. Invite a representative from a local finance company to discuss the reasons that finance companies charge higher interest rates than most other lending institutions of a similar nature (e.g., banks, saving and loans, credit unions). — B, C, E, I

19. Invite a representative from a credit bureau to discuss credit records and the importance of having a good credit rating. — A, H

20. Invite a representative from a local lending institution to visit and discuss different ways to borrow for different purposes. — A, B, C

V. Field Trips

21. Visit a local credit bureau and tour the facilities. Have the bureau's policies regarding the kind of information which is included and — A, H, I

Activities	Objectives
excluded in its files and the manner in which the bureau is used by businesses explained.	
VI. Panel Discussions	
22. The students will take part in a panel type discussion whereby conflicting positions will be taken to the statement that "credit is a consumer privilege, not a right."	A, C, D
23. Students will participate in a panel discussion examining the pros and cons to the statement "The merchant is not to blame for credit problems, rather it is the consumer who is at fault."	A, B, C, D, H, I
VII. Miscellaneous	
24. For several days the students will participate in a game allowing them to "purchase" an unlimited number of items from a department store catalog on credit. Follow–up by discussing buying power, overspending, repossession, garnishee.	A, C, E, H, I
25. The student will take part in the construction of a bulletin board depicting the advantages and disadvantages of credit. Advantages should include usefulness in emergencies, convenience in using a product as you pay for it, providing a record of spending. Disadvantages should include the tendency to minimize comparison shopping, extra costs, overspending.	A, B, C, D, E, H

Table 5–6   *Banking*

Activities	Objectives
I. Class Discussion	
1. List the major functions of banks and discuss how each is used. Students are to determine which service they would most like to use, and	A, B, C

Activities	Objectives
what information an individual needs to use the various services.	
2. Students will discuss the means by which banks earn money. Compare bank services to products sold by other institutions.	A, B, C
3. Students are to discuss competition between savings institutions. As preparation for discussion, students are to clip newspaper advertisements for banks and compare interest rates and premium rates. (Are they going up or down?)	A, B
4. The student will discuss how local area banks facilitate construction and new business.	A, B
5. List some items that the students would like to purchase, but do not have enough money to pay cash. Using several examples, determine how long one would save to accumulate the needed amount of money. Include earnings through interest.	A, B
6. Discuss student opinions about the values in saving. Determine which students have savings accounts, and which students are planning to open accounts.	A, B
7. Students will discuss reasons that money is safer in a bank than at home. Also, discuss interest earned with a savings account.	A, B, C
8. The student will take part in discussing when and why a person would use: a) Traveler's checks, b) certified checks, c) money orders, and d) loans. Discuss the information desired by banks before lending money, and reasons that it is good that banks are careful about who money is loaned to.	A
9. As a group, discuss reasons for having a checking account. Also, discuss joint accounts, and the importance in signing one's name the same as on the signature card. Furthermore, discuss reasons for filling out the check stub before writing the check, and what to do if a mistake is made on a check.	A, C
10. Discuss the meaning and implications of overdrawing one's account.	C
11. The student will discuss what cancelled checks are, and why one should keep them and for how long.	C

Activities	Objectives
12. Students will discuss the variables one needs to consider when deciding whether to put money in a savings or checking account.	A, B, C
13. Discuss the differences between individual, joint, society, and voluntary trust savings accounts.	A, B

II. Role Play

14. Two students are to role play a husband and wife involved in a discussion about whether to borrow money or to save their money to purchase a a) needed item, b) desired item.	A, B
15. Role play husband-wife discussion. Husband wants to keep their savings at home in case they need it. Wife wants to put savings in bank.	A, B, C
16. Students will role play two friends discussing the reasons why one put her money in a savings account, and reasons why the other put her money in a checking account.	A, B, C
17. Role play friends on a shopping trip. One wants to write a check to make a purchase, but has only a pencil to write with. The others explain to him the reasons for not writing checks with pencil.	C

III. Worksheet

18. Students will complete a crossword puzzle that uses key vocabulary words and their meanings, and are associated with services provided by banks.	A, B, C
19. Students will complete signature cards, deposit, and withdrawal slips obtained from local banks.	B, C
20. The student will complete checks and check stubs in response to directions specifying the amount of check, to whom it is made-out, for what purpose, the date, and deposits (if any).	C
21. Students will complete various worksheets on the computation of interest earned through savings.	A, B
22. The student will complete a variety of worksheets on reconciling a bank statement.	C

IV. Class Speakers

23. Invite a bank representative to visit your class to discuss the various services provided by savings institutions.	A, B, C

	Activities	*Objectives*

V. Field Trips
  24. Field trip to local bank. Follow-up by discussing   A
      the various services observed.

VI. Panel Discussion
  25. Divide the class into two groups, those students   A, B
      who agree, and those who disagree with the
      statement that income from savings is not earned
      but is free because nobody has to work for it.

VII. Miscellaneous
  26. The student will construct a bulletin board   A, B, C
      depicting the various services provided by
      banking agencies.
  27. If student income is available, savings accounts   A, B
      may be opened by students and regular
      deposits made under the supervision of the class
      teacher. This may involve weekly class visits
      by the class to a local bank.   B, C
  28. Using flashcards consisting of words commonly
      found on checks, check stubs, deposit slips,
      signature cards, and withdrawl slips, devise
      a classroom game. For example, divide the class
      in half and, alternating from team to team, show
      each student a card. The student must identify
      the word and its meaning to score a point. Go
      through the stack of flash cards two or three
      times, then total points.

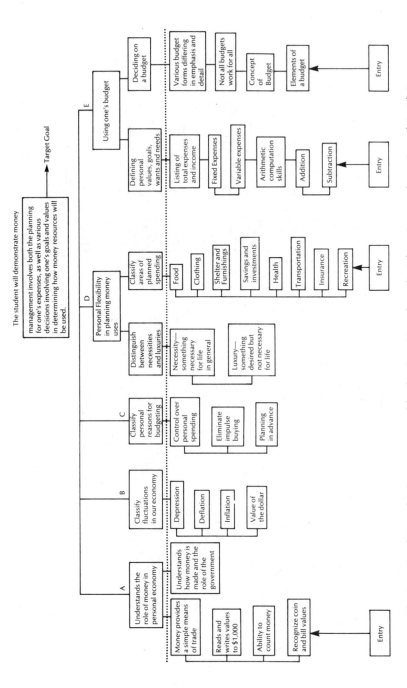

The student will demonstrate money management involves both the planning for one's expenses, as well as various decisions involving one's goals and values in determining how money resources will be used. → Target Goal

A Understands the role of money in personal economy

- Money provides a simple means of trade
- Reads and writes values to $1,000
- Ability to count money
- Recognize coin and bill values

Understands how money is made and the role of the government

Entry

B Classify fluctuations in our economy

- Depression
- Deflation
- Inflation
- Value of the dollar

C Classify personal reasons for budgeting

- Control over personal spending
- Eliminate impulse buying
- Planning in advance

D Personal Flexibility in planning money uses

Distinguish between necessities and luxuries

- Necessity—something necessary for life in general
- Luxury—something desired but not necessary for life

Classify areas of planned spending

- Food
- Clothing
- Shelter and Furnishings
- Savings and investments
- Health
- Transportation
- Insurance
- Recreation

Entry

E Using one's budget

Defining personal values, goals, wants and needs

- Listing of total expenses and income
- Fixed Expenses
- Variable expenses
- Arithmetic computation skills
  - Addition
  - Subtraction

Entry

Deciding on a budget

- Various budget forms differing in emphasis and detail
- Not all budgets work for all
- Concept of Budget
- Elements of a budget

Entry

Figure 5–6   *The learning hierarchy for money and budgeting (Developed with assistance from Darryl Smith.)*

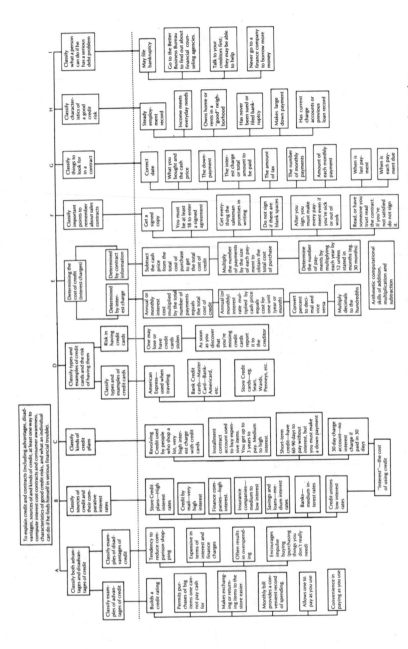

Figure 5-7 The learning hierarchy for credit and contracts (Developed with assistance from Darryl Smith.)

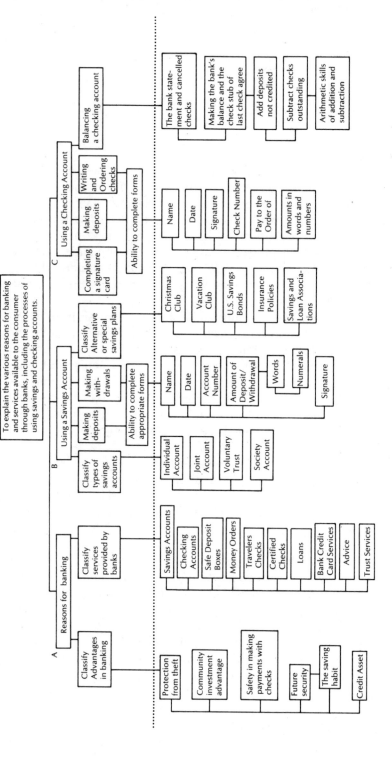

Figure 5-8 *The learning hierarchy for banking (Developed with assistance from Darryl Smith.)*

part 3   Content analysis and criterion testing

If a teacher learns to analyze curriculum content, a great deal of work will have been completed. Yet the task is not yet finished. How can you determine whether an individual learner has or has not mastered the content when instruction is completed? Is it possible that one or more students might have mastered the content before instruction began? To prevent either of these eventualities, we use educational assessment to provide direct feedback—before, during, and after instruction. The vehicles we use are criterion-reference tests prepared by the teacher.*

Recently there has been a substantial shift in emphasis from norm-referenced to criterion-referenced instruments. This parallels the trend to link instruction with frequent assessments of pupil performance. You may recall from reading Chapter 2 that Benjamin Bloom suggests that determination of cognitive entry level is a prime variable in learning success. In addition, P.L. 94-142 mandates that instructional objectives for each child be specified and that measured pupil progress toward these objectives become an integral part of the "Individualized Education Program."

We have seen that norm-referenced testing is useful in sorting and sifting pupils into groups to make instruction manageable. But normed tests are too removed from an individual classroom to be of much utility in identifying an individual's strengths and weaknesses in relation to a particular task—hence, the need for a criterion-referenced test.

Robert Glaser, whose model is used as the foundation for our systems approach to instruction, is credited with coining and popularizing the term *criterion-referenced testing*. Glaser and his colleagues at the University of Pittsburgh developed "Individually Prescribed Instruction" (I.P.I.), a similar program to the one suggested here. Criterion-referenced testing was developed to determine whether an individual has accomplished a particular objective, that is, that a criterion had been mastered.

---

* Refer to chapter 2 for an explanation of "criterion-referenced" and "norm-referenced" tests.

In common use today, criterion-referenced tests are designed to assess specific competencies on an individual basis. The tests are organized into a sequence of tasks from easy to difficult, from simple to complex. When the pupil's level of performance has been determined, the score obtained is viewed from two perspectives: (a) comparison of an individual's performance in one task with that individual's performance on other tasks, and (b) comparison of the individual's score with the criterion for successful performance. In this way, assessment yields valuable data concerning learning successes and weaknesses.

There are five steps in the development of a criterion-referenced test. Notice how they integrate educational goals and assessment and provide a meaningful purpose for the learning hierarchy.

Step 1. Specify the terminal goal for a selected content area.
Step 2. Develop a learning hierarchy in the selected content area.
Step 3. Analyze the hierarchy into content segments.
Step 4. Specify intermediate goals for each segment.
Step 5. Analyze each goal for criterion to be measured.

Application of the Process

This chapter began with Jack Stevens' dilemma—how to analyze a curriculum unit in *Economic understanding for daily living.* We have presented a framework for analyzing this content. To complete the instructional cycle, criterion-referenced assessment measures are needed. The following is a criterion-referenced assessment for "wise shopping," developed from the learning hierarchy presented earlier in this chapter.

Step 1—Specify the terminal goal for a selected content area.
    To explain how the elements of "wise shopping" interrelate to enable one to be a responsible consumer

Step 2—Develop a learning hierarchy in the selected content area.
    The wise shopping hierarchy that follows is a map of the facts, concepts, and explanations to be taught.

Step 3—Analyze the hierarchy into content segments.
    Six segments have been included in the wise shopping hierarchy.
    1. Classify ways to adjust to the effects of inflation.
    2. Classify places and agencies where a person can get consumer protection and advice.
    3. Complete a purchasing transaction.
    4. Demonstrate positive food-shopping habits when purchasing food.

5. Demonstrate positive efficient clothes-shopping habits when planning and purchasing clothing.
6. Demonstrate knowledge of savings when merchandise is on sale.

Each of these segments are criteria that can be referenced to the assessment process. They provide a developmental guide for the presentation of new knowledge as well as the testing of what has been learned.

Step 4—Specify intermediate goals for each segment.

The six main segments of the hierarchy are translated into goals as follows:

1. The student will describe three ways to partially adjust to the effects of inflation, when asked.
2. The student will name six places where a person can get consumer protection and advice, when asked.
3. The student will demonstrate the ability to complete a purchasing transaction when planning and implementing an actual transaction in the community.
4. The student will demonstrate appropriate food-buying skills through planning and purchasing an actual food order.
5. The student will demonstrate appropriate clothes-purchasing skills through planning and implementing an actual transaction.
6. The student will demonstrate knowledge of amount of money saved through wise shopping by specifying the usual price, sale price and amount saved.

Step 5—Analyze each goal for specific criterion to be measured.

This step enables the teacher to individualize instruction. Each objective, with its underlying facts and concepts which comprise explanations, is an incremental step of instruction. The developmental level of the learner can be matched to the complexity of instructional task to insure successful instruction.

Returning again to the learning hierarchy, we will analyze one goal.

1. "The student will describe three ways to partially adjust to the effects of inflation, when asked," is the objective. The concepts related to this objective are the following: (taken from the hierarchy)
   a. Advertising (real and bait)
   b. Door-to-door sales representatives
   c. Guarantees (acceptable and faulty)
   d. Contracts (fair and unfair)
   e. Consumer frauds
   f. Second-hand stores

    g. New vs. used items
    h. Discount stores
    i. Department stores
    j. Specialty stores
    k. Prices in stores
    l. Impulse buying
    m. Shopping list
    n. Inflation
    o. Effects of inflation
    p. Adjustment to inflation

Each of the sixteen concepts can be translated into a series of criterion-referenced test items. For example, a criterion-referenced instrument might include:

1. Find three examples of fair advertisements in the Sunday paper.
2. Find two examples of "bait" advertisements in the Sunday paper.
3. Explain the problems you might have with a door-to-door salesman.
4. List three questions you might ask the sales representative before buying anything.
5. What are "guarantees" for when they come with an item you have purchased?
6. When is a guarantee acceptable?
7. When is a guarantee "faulty" or unacceptable?
8. What are contracts for?
9. How do you know if a contract is fair?
10. What is a consumer?
11. What does "fraud" mean?
12. What is "consumer fraud"?
13. Give an example of a situation which can be called "consumer fraud."
14. What are second-hand stores?
15. Are all second-hand stores the same?
16. Why would you buy things from a second-hand store?
17. Where can you buy new items?
18. What is the difference between new and used items?
19. What are discount stores?
20. What does "discount" mean?
21. Name three discount stores in this area.
22. What are department stores?
23. What are specialty stores?
24. What store has the cheapest merchandise?
25. How do you know which store has the cheapest merchandise?

26. How do you know what the prices are of merchandise in a store?
27. How do you know if a price is low or not?
28. What is "impulse" buying?
29. In what way can "impulse buying" present a problem to you?
30. How can you avoid "impulse buying"?
31. What is the purpose of a shopping list?
32. How do you make a shopping list? What factors do you consider?
33. What is inflation?
34. Give three examples of how inflation affects you.
35. What do I mean when I say "adjustment to inflation"?
36. Why do you need to "adjust to inflation"?
37. List as many ways as you can that help you adjust to the effects of inflation.

The items in the assessment are concrete, specific, and designed to give the student and teacher feedback on student learning. The items included may be read by the student, if the student has the requisite reading skills. They may be read by one student to another, or the answers may be recited into a tape recorder. Or they may be read by the teacher to a small group of students. The students' performance in all cases must be recorded on a data collection sheet.

This process insures that prerequisites are mastered before new concepts are introduced. This monitoring of the instructional process is essential for successful accomplishment of instructional tasks by mentally retarded learners.

Conclusion

At the onset of this chapter, the quandary faced by Jack Stevens was discussed. He was asked to analyze the unit "Money and Budgeting for Independent Living" as part of the larger unit on *Economic Understandings for Daily Living*. His role was leader of the curriculum writing team. His task was somewhat demanding as he was a special education teacher in a secondary school that mainstreams exceptional learners. He realized that his task was to translate a set of broad content goals into a more detailed set of written learning objectives. These would guide teachers in the development of appropriate learning activities and materials for all learners.

Jack also realized that he was uncertain about how this was to be accomplished. His teaching preparation and experience had not taught him to analyze teaching content as systematically and rigorously as would be required to complete his task.

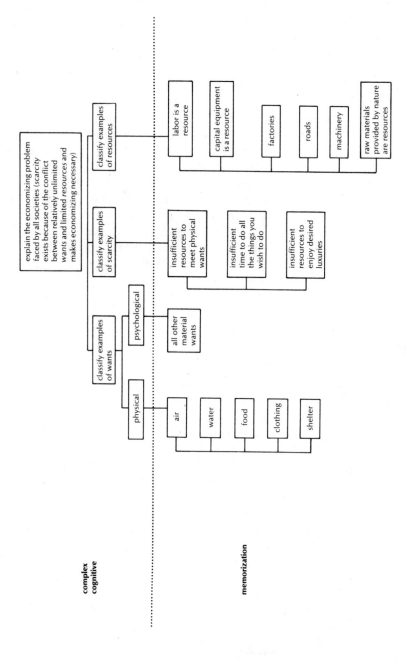

Figure 5–9 A hierarchy of the basic economizing problem facing all societies

207

Jack discovered that the analysis of curriculum can be accomplished through the application of several theoretical models. Subject matter content can be analyzed from the hierarchical frameworks of Gagné and Bloom. Bruner has proposed yet another model for viewing content. Jack also learned that Bloom and his coworkers and Harrow have divided content into three domains: cognitive, affective and psychomotor. The learner as a source of information for curricular analysis holds great promise, Jack now realized, for guiding and individualizing instruction. Criterion-referenced instruments, he also realized, integrate assessment and instruction and provide valuable feedback of learner progress.

Jack wondered why these ideas were so new to him and his special education frame of reference. It soon became apparent, however, that curricular analysis in special education is in its infancy. Yet the learning hierarchy developed by the curriculum writing team represents movement toward a sound approach to curricular development. The hierarchy presented in Figure 5–9 was developed for the school.

REFERENCES

Bennett, A. Reading ability in special classes. *Journal of Educational Research,* 1929, *20,* 236–238.

Blatt, B. The physical, personality, and academic status of children who are mentally retarded attending special classes as compared with children who are mentally retarded attending regular classes. *American Journal of Mental Deficiency,* 1958, *62,* 810–818.

Bloom, B. S. (Ed.). *Taxonomy of educational objectives, handbook I: The cognitive domain.* New York: David McKay, 1956.

Bruner, J. *The process of education.* New York: Vintage, 1960.

Cratty, B. *Perceptual-motor behavior and educational processes.* Springfield, Ill.: Charles C. Thomas, 1969.

Dunn, L. M. (Ed.). *Exceptional children in the schools.* New York: Holt, Rinehart & Winston, 1963.

Ellis, N. R. A behavioral research strategy in mental retardation: Defense and critique. *American Journal of Mental Deficiency,* 1969, *73,* 557–556.

Gagné, R. M. The acquisition of knowledge. *Psychological Review,* 1962, *69,* 355–365.

Gagné, R. M. *The conditions of learning.* New York: Holt, Rinehart & Winston, 1970.

Gagné, R. M. Identifying objectives—task description. In D. Merrill (Ed.), *Instructional design: Reading.* Englewood Cliffs, N.J.: Prentice-Hall, 1971.

Goldstein, H. *Social learning curriculum.* Columbus, Ohio: Charles E. Merrill, 1975.

Goldstein, H., & Siegle, D. M. *A curriculum guide for teachers of the educable mentally handicapped.* Danville, Ill.: Interstate Printers and Publishers, 1958.

Harrow, A. J. *A taxonomy of the psychomotor domain.* New York: David McKay, 1972.

Heinz, P., & Blackman, L. S. Psychoeducational considerations with the mentally retarded child. In I. Bialek & M. Sternlicht (Eds.), *The psychology of mental retardation: Issues and approaches.* New York: Psychological Dimensions, 1977.

Kephart, N. *The slow learner in the classroom.* Columbus, Ohio: Charles E. Merrill, 1960.

Kirk, S. A., & Johnson, G. O. *Educating the mentally retarded child.* Boston: Houghton Mifflin, 1951.

Klein, N., & Safford, P. Effects of representational level of materials on transfer of classification skills in TMR children. *Journal of Special Education,* 1976, *10* (1), 47–52.

Klein, N., & Safford, P. Application of Piaget's theory to the study of the thinking of the mentally retarded: A review of research. *Journal of Special Education,* 1977, *11* (2), 201–216.

Krathwohl, D., Bloom, B., & Masia, B. *Taxonomy of educational objectives, Handbook II: The affective domain.* New York: David McKay, 1964.

Kuhn, T. S. *The structure of scientific revolutions.* Chicago: University of Chicago Press, 1962.

McNeil, J. D. Forces influencing curriculum. *Review of educational research,* 1969, *39,* 293–318.

Phenix, P. *Realms of meaning.* New York: McGraw-Hill, 1964.

Simches, G., & Bohn, R. J. Issues in curriculum research and responsibility. *Mental Retardation,* 1963, *1,* 84–77, 115–117.

Zigler, E. Mental retardation: Current issues and approaches. In M. L. Hoffman & W. F. Hoffman (Eds.), *Review of child development* (Vol. 2). New York: Russel Sage Foundation, 1966. Pp. 167–168.

Zigler, E. Developmental versus difference theories of mental retardation and the problem of motivation. *American Journal of Mental Deficiency,* 1969, *73,* 536–556.

Zigler, E. The retarded child as a whole person. In D. K. Rorith (Ed.), *The experimental psychology of mental retardation.* Chicago: Aldine, 1973. Pp. 267–273.

Writing useful objectives

The school year began 2 weeks ago. It is time to talk to parents. Imagine yourself at a classroom meeting with interested parents, eager to learn about their children's school activities. Put yourself in Miss Jackson's place in the following conversations:

I

Miss Jackson: My goals for the first marking period
(teacher)   center around the development of social
                       studies and reading skills.

Mrs. Demont: (parent)	Miss Jackson, what do you specifically intend to teach my child in social studies?
Miss Jackson:	We will cover topics such as "Getting a Job," "Banking Money," and "Voting."
Mrs. Demont:	That's all well and good, but how will my son Billy be any different at the end of the year than he is today?
Miss Jackson:	I believe that children who are in my class for an entire year get a good education. Thank you all for coming today. Naturally, I'll contact you individually in a month to discuss your child's progress.

II

Miss Jackson:	My goals for the first marking period center around the development of social studies and reading skills.
Mrs. Demont:	Miss Jackson, what do you specifically intend to teach my child in social studies?
Miss Jackson:	The first unit the students will study is titled "Getting a Job." When the unit is completed in 2 weeks, each student will be able to:

1. Locate want ads in the newspaper;
2. Select jobs most suited to his or her needs, experience, training, and ability;
3. Write a letter of inquiry correctly;
4. Conduct a phone and personal interview properly.

Mrs. Demont:	I wonder if we as parents can help you out. This is the first time I've ever known specifically what a teacher expects my Billy to learn. I'd appreciate getting a list of all the material you'll cover each month so I can help out at home.
Miss Jackson:	As a matter of fact, I've prepared just such a list. It describes the major tasks the students are expected to master during the first marking period. There's more

content that will come up as the time progresses, but these are my core objectives to complete by the end of the grading period. Thank you all for coming today. Naturally, I'll contact you individually in a month or so to discuss your child's progress in mastering these objectives. Please feel free to contact me at any time if you have concerns or questions.

In which of the two conversations would you be most comfortable? In which situation would you expect to gain the most parent support and assistance? In which situation would you feel a sense of successful accomplishment?

From our view, the best answer to each question would be the second conversation. The teacher and parent in the second conversation had a meaningful discussion of the expected outcomes of instruction. That is, it was apparent that the teacher had put time and energy into this classroom even before children appeared on the scene. This teacher had made decisions about what knowledge, skills, and attitudes were most worthy for her students to learn.

Furthermore, she translated general goals such as "Getting a Job" into a set of specific accountable tasks and objectives. As a result, the assembled parents felt that the teacher was confident enough to keep them apprised of her goals. And, not incidentally, the parents were encouraged to participate, ask questions, and take part in their children's learning.

Educational Goals and Clearly Stated Objectives

All teachers begin a school year with some idea of their goals. First-year teachers often express these goals as personal prayers to keep "afloat" so they can "survive." Some veteran teachers avoid difficult decisions by trying to cover all the material contained in the various texts they or others have selected. This cover-the-book goal is sometimes unspoken. It may be masked by general goals such as "making better citizens" or "creating socially adjusted youngsters." Most teachers do think through, in general terms, what kind of teacher they want to be or what changes they hope to produce in students.

But more specific goals are needed. Goals must be both specific and focused to help the teacher develop learning activities and evaluation procedures. In Chapter 5, we presented a list of suggested goals in economics for high school graduates. For example, students should be familiar with money management and budgeting facts and concepts. Although these goals are useful in providing a teacher with an initial orientation, they are not specific enough. In order to be useful, a general goal must be translated into clearly stated objectives.

A clearly stated objective is a statement of instructional intent that describes what the learner is expected to know or do at the conclusion of instruction. Four principles are implied in this definition. A clearly stated objective must:

1. *Contain only one learning outcome.* There must be only one learning outcome stated in each instructional objective the student is expected to complete. For example, "the student will be able to make change from one dollar after a $.45 purchase with 100% accuracy" requires one outcome.

2. *Be expressed in terms of what the* **student learns,** *not what the teacher does.* The objectives are written for student behavior, not vice versa. For example, the objective above clearly states that the *student* will make change for one dollar after a $.45 purchase.

213

3. *Describe observable behavior.* It is important that the words used in the objective let the teacher observe whether or not the behavior has been attained. For example, "be able to make change" can be readily observed; "understand how to make change" cannot.
4. *Orient both teacher and student to the way the objective is to be evaluated.* The objective should state what the student will do, so that the teacher can plan instruction and the student will know what to expect.

There is, clearly, an intimate relationship between content goal analysis (as discussed in the previous chapter) and clearly stated objectives. A thoughtful analysis that produces a structured hierarchy of learning functions is the "map" from which individual objectives are developed. Such a hierarchy helps the teacher incorporate two of the four characteristics of clearly stated objectives. Since the hierarchy is constructed from separate elements, the probability that the instructor will focus on only *one* learning outcome for each objective is increased. Second, the psychological analysis that is an integral part of the hierarchy ensures that objectives will be written in terms of student rather than teacher behavior.

Writing Clearly Stated Objectives

In Chapter 5 we looked at two approaches to learning processes. One, the objective-taxonomic approach of Bloom and his colleagues, involved three learning domains—the *psychomotor, cognitive,* and *affective* domains. These domains provide useful categories for writing clearly stated educational objectives. The psychomotor domain includes objectives that involve physical skills, i.e., motor development, auditory and visual perception, and combinations of those. In a curriculum for the mentally retarded, psychomotor objectives may focus on handwriting training, manipulative activities for small motor development, eye-hand coordination, physical development, and manual arts training. For example, "the student will write his name and address using manuscript letters" is one such objective.

The affective domain includes emotional content such as interests, attitudes, and values. Affective objectives in a curriculum for mentally retarded children might include expression of needs and feelings, working cooperatively in groups, and helping students cope with the demands and pressures of everyday adult life—for example, "the student will demonstrate group cooperation by cooperating with the manager of the volleyball team."

The cognitive domain includes information that must be memorized and various kinds of thought processes. A balanced curriculum would include both memory objectives and those that help students classify information and solve complex problems.

Again, a clearly stated objective must "describe what the student is expected to know or do at the conclusion of instruction." Examine the following objectives. Are they primarily psychomotor, affective, or cognitive? Are they clearly stated?

1. Students can discriminate between wet and dry objects using sense of touch.
2. Student can successfully hold a utensil in hand, using either the fist or fingers.
3. Each child must complete a 40-yard run.
4. You will be able to successfully position as many rivets as possible in the shortest time.
5. Students will be able to orally recite the initial consonant letter and sound of 20 words pronounced by the teacher.

These objectives are primarily psychomotor and are clearly stated. They conform to the four guiding principles of clearly stated objectives—include only one learning outcome, expressed in terms of what the student learns as opposed to what the teacher does, describe observable student behavior, and orient both teacher and student toward the way the objective is to be evaluated. Most teachers have little difficulty writing clearly stated objectives in the psychomotor domain because the learning process described is directly observable. As a result, the relative success of student performance can be easily assessed.

Cognitive and affective objectives are not so easily written. Compare the two lists of verbs below. What are the differences between the verbs in List I and those in List II?

I	II
Analyze	Run
Memorize	Throw
Show interest	Reproduce sounds
Increase self-concept	Sing
Value	Swim
Think	Manipulate
Evaluate	Button

The verbs in List II denote psychomotor processes that are directly observable. Consequently, objectives constructed from them will usually be clearly stated. On the other hand, the verbs in List I denote cognitive and affective learning processes that cannot be observed. The learning processes described by the objectives (analyzing, memorizing, appreciating) are psychological behaviors that we think occur within the brain. To evaluate student performance in the cognitive and affective domains, we must find some observable *indicator* that the student has actually accomplished the objective; that he has analyzed a paragraph or appreciated a musical selection. Thus we must modify the third guiding principle for writing clearly stated objectives.

> Clearly stated objectives describe observable behavior (psychomotor) or include an *observable product or activity* (cognitive or affective).

Thus, to make the verbs in List I conform to the guidelines, we would add to each one:

> Analyze *in a one-page essay*
> Memorize *the list on the blackboard*
> Show interest *by attending optional performances*
> Increase self-concept as *indicated by answers to a questionnaire*
> Value *as demonstrated in a simulated supermarket shopping list*
> Think *by solving open-ended questions in a small group*
> Evaluate by *writing a letter to the editor expressing your opinion*

To further reduce the ambiguity commonly found in cognitive-domain objectives, a teacher is wise to use, wherever possible, only verbs that form the cognitive categories in either the Bloom (1956) or Gagné (1960) taxonomies.*

Bloom	*Gagné*
—Recall	—Memorize
—Comprehend (understand)	—Classify
—Apply	—Explain relationships
—Analyze	—Solve (complex problem)
—Synthesize	
—Evaluate	

Because the taxonomy verbs communicate a well-defined learning process, using them helps the teacher systematically present instructional intent. "Recall" or "memorize" communicates that the student

---

* Research appears to support the teacher who informs students of the learning objectives at the onset of instruction. Preknowledge of what is expected is helpful to students as they begin their study. If you choose to translate the objectives for your students, you will need to employ more familiar verbs. For example, "classify" becomes "pick out," "analyze" becomes "break down," "synthesize" becomes "put together," and so on.

is to retain specific information taught during the lesson or unit. "Apply" and "classify" involve the ability to recognize examples of a general category being taught in an unfamiliar context. "Evaluate" requires the student to apply a reasonable set of standards in judging the relative value of something. These taxonomy verbs are listed in order from simple to more complex. Moving in this order is essential for retarded students.

Following is a series of goals and objectives. Read them and decide which ones conform to the principles of clearly stated objectives.

1. From a list of people who have been important in American history, students can recall those who were active in establishing the new nation.
2. The teacher will cover the elements of a nutritionally sound diet.
3. We will all learn how to "Get a Job."
4. Given a situation where the student must solve the problem of making change for up to and including $5.00 after various customers purchases, he will do so correctly.
5. You will be able to develop an awareness of what it is like to be involved in the election process.
6. Students will show their understanding of the personal interview by verbally evaluating given simulated interviews.
7. We will cover the four steps of proper phone interview procedure.
8. The student will explain how school used to be.
9. You will find success in what you have learned to do.
10. You will be able to apply your knowledge of the correct use of capitalization and punctuation by writing a letter to a friend.

Give yourself 100% if you identified numbers 1, 4, 6, and 10 as clearly stated objectives. Notice that in each of the correct examples an observable student or activity is included in the objective.

1. Recall *from a list.*
4. Make change *given $5.00 and various customer purchases.*
6. Understand personal interviews *by verbally evaluating given simulated interviews.*
10. Apply your knowledge *by writing a letter to a friend.*

Each of the incorrect examples can be fixed to eliminate the errors that kept it from being a clearly stated objective.

2. *The teacher will cover the elements of a nutritionally sound diet* (teacher objective, not student objective; verb "to cover" unclear; no observable product or activity).

Possible modification: Each student will apply concepts taught in this unit by planning a one-day nutritionally sound diet on a form provided by our nutritionist.

3. *We will all learn how to "Get a Job"* (verb "learn" unclear; no observable product or activity).

   Possible modification: Each of you will be given a problem to solve. You will play the role of an unemployed person with particular characteristics. I want you to explain out loud how you intend to "get a job."

5. *You will be aware of what it is like to be involved in the election process* (no observable product or activity).

   Possible modification: When the unit is completed, students will respond to the following sentence: "Learning about the election process has made me aware of. . . ." You may write or talk into a tape recorder as much as you wish. This assignment will not be graded. Do not sign your name.

7. *We will cover the four steps of proper phone interview procedure* (verb "to cover" is unclear; no observable activity or product).

   Possible modification: Given a written account of a phone interview, students will classify examples of the four steps of a proper phone interview.

8. *The student will explain how school used to be* (no observable activity or product).

   Possible modification: The student will explain how school used to be by interviewing two adults and reporting the information on an audio tape.

9. *You will find success in what you have learned to do* (objective unclear; no observable activity or product).

   Possible modification: You will be able to see your progress in tumbling by watching your performance at the beginning and end of the unit on the video playback screen.

The next group of objectives are all clearly stated. If the objective is in the *cognitive* domain, the Gagné or Bloom category verb is italicized and the observable activity or product is italicized. If the objective is in the *affective* domain, only the observable activity or product is italicized.

1. Each student will *synthesize* the elements of a colonial planters' home in Williamsburg *by constructing a model of one.*

2. *When given a series of advertising presentations,* students will *classify* those which are factual and those which are misleading.
3. Students will indicate their interest in the "Nutrition" unit by *listing the nutritionally sound diet* they have followed for 1 month.
4. You will demonstrate your ability to *apply* the concepts "root words," "prefixes," and "suffixes" by *successfully passing a posttest* that will require you to identify root words and add prefixes and suffixes to them.
5. Students will *classify* the 10 given emergencies in the following categories—"fire," "police," "poison control," or "operator or assistance" *in a homework assignment.*
6. You will be able to *recall, when given written examples,* the sound of an initial consonant.
7. When asked to *recall* self-identifying information *in an oral discussion,* the student will correctly state his name, address, phone number, birthdate, age, and sex.
8. Students will be able to *explain* how each person in a business or industry is important *by creating a skit* that shows what happens to other workers when one worker fails to do his job.
9. Students will *solve* the following problem: Given the task of going to the supermarket and getting the best buy on cereal, milk, and canned sliced pineapple, they will *write a report* of their findings. The report will compare the cost of various product brands.
10. You will demonstrate your recall or the steps involved in insertion of paper in the typewriter *by actually doing so for me.*

Adding Criteria for Successful Performance

Until now we have considered only the question of the *clarity* of instructional objectives, that is, whether an objective clearly communicates what the instructor intends to teach and, more importantly, what the student is expected to do when instruction is finished. There is an additional concern in writing clearly stated objectives. How can an instructor provide information concerning the *quality* of the performance expected from the student? Consider one of the objectives presented earlier.

> You will be able to recall, when given written examples, the sound of an initial consonant.

It would be impractical to expect all the students to complete this objective successfully with 100% accuracy. All classrooms have students at varying levels of competencies. Each learner has particular learning strengths and weaknesses. Some may be proficient in math but weak in grammar and spelling. One student may be weak in all academic areas but quick and agile in activities requiring manual dexterity. Given the variety of student abilities and previous experience, a teacher must qualify instructional objectives by attaching a realistic criterion against which to evaluate the students' performances.

Because of the varied learning rates and styles among retarded learners, a criterion-referenced approach is more useful than the normative approach teachers frequently use. A normative-based objective would be stated as follows.

> When given written examples, *70% of the students* will be able to recall the sound of an initial consonant.

This "7 out of 10" model is particularly problematic with retarded students. What happens to the three who can't recall the initial consonant? Do we forget about them or what? As an alternative model for specifying criteria for performance, the objective could read as follows.

> When given written examples, students will be able to recall the sound of an initial consonant with 70% accuracy.

In this case, all students are expected to perform at the minimum level established by the criterion in the objective. This model provides a standard for specific performance of all students on particular tasks.

Another consideration in specifying standards for performance can be called *minimum acceptable number*. This model focuses on the quantity of responses and assumes each is 100% accurate.

> When asked to recall the vowels, the student will list five of the six vowels verbally.

Some material requires more than specifying standards for performance. One additional consideration related to performance is time. For example, in the following objective, the criterion is not only task completion, but doing so in a stated amount of time.

> The student will sort 30 nuts and bolts of three different sizes in *3 minutes.*
>
> or
>
> The student will demonstrate recall of the steps involved in assembling a bicycle brake by correctly doing so in *90 seconds.*

or

The student will run ½ mile in *6 minutes.*

or

The student will swim 20 yards in *2 minutes.*

The students' individual levels may also be incorporated into objectives. For example,

The student will swim 20 yards and break stride *only one time.*

or

The student will complete the 18-piece puzzle looking away from the task no more than *two times.*

or

The student will copy the list of spelling words from the board with *no more than one error.*

or

The student will print the name on the check but *sign his name in cursive.*

or

The student will complete the math assignment in *15 minutes with no assistance from the teacher.*

or

The student will complete the math assignment *and ask for help when needed.*

These additional phrases included in objectives give the teacher specific criteria by which to measure performance. For instance, in the last example, the student may complete the math assignment, but with many errors. The teacher has decided that an important goal for that student is to know when she needs help and to ask for it. This learning need has been incorporated into the objective. This practice lets the teacher specify particular behaviors for individual students.

With retarded students, the more information included in objectives, the better the teacher can monitor and foster educational growth. These objectives are designed to guide instruction. The more specific the information in the objectives, the better the individualization can be.

In all these examples, the purpose of the criterion is to establish an acceptable level of performance against which to assess students' performance. Hopefully, the criterion is challenging but is not so imposing as to be overwhelming. It is important to let the retarded learner be successful as well as challenged.

A second type of performance criteria is used for complex problem-solving tasks such as writing creative papers, constructing models, or sampling community opinion on a controversial issue. In these cases, the teacher may need to add a quality criterion that can be used to assess the final product. In this way, students can plan their tasks better. The following two objectives contain quality criteria that the students can use in organizing their work.

> Students are to create a skit to illustrate a potential safety hazard in the home. When working on the skit they must
>   a. Keep skits to no more than 5 minutes in length.
>   b. Plan for at least 3 speaking parts.
>   c. Be consistent with the safety suggestions discussed in class.
>
> Each student is to construct a model of a favorite store. In the construction of the store, the following rules are to be observed:
>   a. Only the front view of the store is to be completed (see movie set diagram on bulletin board).
>   b. Raw materials are available from industrial arts teacher.
>   c. Paint, utensils, design, and assistance will be provided by the art teacher.
>   d. Finished product should be consistent with photographs of "stores we buy from" in the class photo album.

Writing Worthy Objectives

Even though an objective may be clearly stated, it may not have any educational value. Examine the following objectives. Do they conform to the guidelines for clearly stated objectives? Would they be a valid example of your educational goals?

1. Students will be able to recall the definitions of *check, bank, deposit,* and *withdrawal* and write them exactly as taught.
2. Each student will correctly spell 90% of the names of the U.S. Presidents from oral dictation.
3. Students will be able to write a letter of inquiry for a job with no margin or spelling errors and no erasures. Letters that are incorrectly prepared must be done over again.
4. Each student will memorize his social security number and bank account number.
5. Students will recognize the names of signers of the Declaration of Independence with 90% accuracy.

It would be difficult to argue that the listed objectives were not clearly stated. Yet a particular objective may be clear, but it may also be trivial or close minded. For example, the objective "Each student will correctly spell 90% of the names of the U.S. Presidents from oral dictation" communicates intent but is of marginal educational worth, for either retarded or nonhandicapped students.

Although in these examples it was relatively easy to determine whether the objectives were worthy or not, the concept of a "worthy objective" requires explanation. A worthy objective has three characteristics.

1. It is written for a particular group of students.
2. It is generated from a logical and psychological analysis of a content goal.
3. The content goal which subsumes the objective is useful for the target group of students in understanding and solving important life problems.

Each of these three characteristics deserves further explanation. First, the objective must be written for a particular group of students because our concept of "worthiness" in part relates to the classroom where the objective is to be learned. What are the important learning characteristics of the students? What have they previously learned? How is the objective woven into their interests? Are the students motivated to learn, or are they difficult to reach? How old are they? How mature are they? What general aptitudes and specific abilities do they have that will affect the objective? In addition to student characteristics, the instructional environment includes other factors that may affect the selection of objectives. The size of the classroom, the physical arrangement of desk and open areas, time considerations, and resources available within the school and in the surrounding community are factors that may be considered.

Second, worthy objectives are generated from logical and psychological analyses of a content goal. As we discussed in Chapter 5, content analysis is a vital stage in instructional development. Thoughtful analyses yield a series of objectives that help produce maximum learning for students. Jerome Bruner (1960), a leading educational psychologist, compared a careful subject analysis to the image of a fully bloomed tree. The trunk and major branches are comparable to the central explanations, the remaining branches the concepts, and the leaves compare to the related facts. Bruner (1960) suggests that instructional focus on an explanation and its concepts and related facts is better than concentration on isolated elements of information.

Third, the larger content goal from which the objective is derived must be of use to the students in understanding and solving problems in the world outside the classroom. Content goals that involve the explanation of useful concepts such as "money," "sexuality," and "citizenship" assist students to cope with life's problems. The goals should help the students learn to solve problems on their own. Too many teachers seem to use a "right answer" approach. In classes for everyone from the mentally retarded to the gifted, subjects for study are chosen because "right" answers are easily discriminated from "wrong" answers. Some teachers opt for factual teaching because ambiguity is reduced and the students find learning facts easy and satisfying.

The problem here is that the world outside the controlled classroom is quite complex. Problems where no "right" answers are available surface; decisions must be made only after the advantages and disadvantages of various options have been assessed. Students who are nurtured on a steady diet of memorized learning and right answers have trouble when they try to transfer the problem-solving methods they learned in the classroom to the confusing real world. And mentally retarded students often have extra difficulty transferring ideas across situations, so they need many opportunities to practice new skills and use new concepts and ideas. They need to learn to look for alternative answers rather than a single one. Teachers should expand investigation rather than restrict it. For example, at the conclusion of a unit on "Banking" the teacher asks the class, "What do you think might happen in the U.S. if all the banks would close their doors tomorrow and never open again?" Another teacher begins a class with, "If you had only a single one of the five senses, which one would you choose, and why?" In a unit on biology, a creative teacher has the students list the possible effects on our lives if we had no thumbs. Teachers who value this kind of *divergent thinking* permit their students to create their own concepts and explanations for common phenomena. Only after the students complete their investigation would the teacher begin to present the commonly accepted answer. Then the class can compare and contrast it with their answers. In this way, the process of investigation becomes as prized as the ultimate answer or answers.

The value of education is both in the process and product of the experience. Thus, the avenues that a student uses to find an answer may be as important as the answer itself. Creative teachers have already discovered that enhancing the process of education can serve to both motivate the learner as well as heighten his learning. Reflect upon your own teaching: Are you using your own creativity to strengthen the process of your students' education? A good objective will not only be clearly stated; it will help the student learn to learn.

Conclusion

The translation of general educational goals into clearly stated objectives is a vital step in effective instruction. Clearly stated objectives permit communication among teachers, parents, and students. They let the teacher design activities and evaluation procedures that correspond to the instructional objectives. They permit the teacher to evaluate the performance of students and the effectiveness of the instruction.

But the use of clearly stated objectives, as vital as it is, is subordinate to the process of developing worthy objectives. Instructional objectives are worthy when they pass three tests. First, they must be written for a particular group of students. Second, they must be generated from a careful analysis of a content goal. Last, they must lead to learning that assists young people to understand and solve problems in the world outside the classroom.

When instructional objectives are both clearly stated and worthy, the most difficult hurdle in instructional development is overcome.

REFERENCES

Bloom, B. S. (Ed.). *Taxonomy of educational objectives, Handbook I: The cognitive domain.* New York: David McKay, 1956.

Bruner, J. *The process of education.* New York: Vintage Press, 1960.

Gagné, R. *The conditions of learning.* New York: Holt, Rinehart & Winston, 1960.

Selecting and implementing learning activities

This dialogue was heard in the teacher's lounge of an elementary school.

Mr. Collins:	I'm really angry at the children in my class. They were so restless and irritable today.
Ms. Harris:	I know what you mean. What happened?
Mr. Collins:	I'm not really sure. When they came in this morning I told them to get out their pencils, pick up a worksheet from my desk, and get right to work. They moaned and groaned and grumbled about it.

Ms. Harris:	How do they usually behave?
Mr. Collins:	They're usually much more cooperative. They do the same thing every day and should know what to expect by now.
Ms. Harris:	Maybe that's the problem?
Mr. Collins:	What is?
Ms. Harris:	The fact that they do the same thing every day. Maybe the kids are bored with the same activity.
Mr. Collins:	How else are they going to learn the material?
Ms. Harris:	Maybe you could offer them a variety of activities. There are a couple dozen kinds of activities to choose from.
Mr. Collins:	What other kinds of activities did you have in mind?
Ms. Harris:	Well, it really depends upon what you're teaching and how children learn best. Not all kids learn in the same way. Some kids need specific directions; others

Selecting and Implementing Learning Activities

	need only suggestions, and they follow up on their own.
Mr. Collins:	Give me some specific examples of activities.
Ms. Harris:	O.K. Suppose you want your children to learn spelling words. They could match them on a worksheet, fill in the missing letters on the board, test each other, construct a treasure hunt where they find letters hidden in the room to make their words, find the words in "hidden word" games, put all the letters of the alphabet on children in the room with some extra letters available, and have a child spell a word by selecting children who are wearing the correct letter, and on and on. There is no end to spelling activities.
Mr. Collins:	You amaze me! I've never really thought about doing things that way. Give me some ideas like those for social studies.
Ms. Harris:	Okay! Let's say you want to teach your students about voting. You could give a lecture, assign a reading segment, use audiovisual materials, do role-playing situations, do classroom simulations, have directed discussion groups, write letters to the editor of newspapers, conduct a classroom campaign and nominate candidates for classroom "mayor," conduct candidate interviews, take field trips to city hall and the board of elections, or have outside speakers make presentations.
Mr. Collins:	I can't believe you just listed all those activities. How do you decide what to use, when to use each, and whether the children know about voting when you're finished?

This dialogue focuses on a critical issue in the instructional process—the selection of appropriate activities. Clearly, there is a rich variety of learning activities available to the teacher. The more inventive and creative the teacher, the more exciting the learning activities can be.

In this book so far, we have discussed the "who" (learner), "where" (assessment), and "what" (functional-life curriculum) of instruction. We will now look at the "how" of instruction—learning activities.

In this chapter, we will look at how to select and implement learning activities and suggest a set of guiding principles to assist the teacher. Finally, we will focus on individualizing learning as it relates to classroom learning activities.

Models of Teaching

There are no "right" or "wrong" activities; there are no "perfect" methods. Hundreds of studies have been conducted combining a particular method with a grade level or ability level in the hope of improving instruction across the board. Unfortunately the data are surprisingly ambiguous, confounding, and inconclusive.

Joyce and Weil (1972) have identified a series of categories or models of teaching based on what teachers do in classrooms (their learning activities). These models range from strategies to develop abstract mental powers such as problem solving and other cognitive skills to the use of classical operant conditioning techniques.

This is an interesting way to view teacher behavior. Instead of a focus on the learning activity itself, they generalize from a group of activities to create an idealized set of teaching models. Our approach is learner centered, which means that both the method of teaching and the content are derived from the needs and interests of the learner. It combines several of the models described by Joyce and Weil: inductive teaching, inquiry training, science inquiry, concept attainment, developmental, social inquiry, and operant conditioning. We believe that each of these approaches is relevant to the Functional Life Curriculum.

Framework for Activity Selection

The underlying framework of this book is a theory of development that assigns the child an active role in learning. The child is not a passive receptacle but a continually developing organism. This view is basically cognitive-developmental. The interactions between the child's developing mental structures and the environment foster changes in behavior that we call "learning."

This developmental-interactionist viewpoint has been espoused by such writers as Bruner (1961), Dewey (1938), and Kohlberg (1968). All of these writers highlight the critical role of the environment in fostering children's intellectual development. Another important factor is the relationship of feeling to thinking. Cognitive and affective development in the child are closely intertwined. These developing processes must also be seen within a social context, such as the classroom. Children's interactions with peers, teachers, other adults, and siblings are central to their development as effective social people. Thus, classroom activities should foster the on-going *total* development of the child. But where does the teacher begin?

The Process of Learning

Bruner (1961) identifies three almost simultaneous processes that occur during the act of learning: acquisition, transformation, and evaluation. *Acquisition* involves taking in new information that could run counter to, may integrate with, or replaces what the individual already knows. *Transformation* is the process of manipulating knowledge to fit new tasks. The individual must apply new information in other areas and other situations. *Evaluation* is the process of determining whether the way in which information was manipulated is adequate. Evaluation, although most frequently done by the teacher, may also be done by the child.

The *acquisition* stage actually consists of two substages: acquisition and retention. In other words, a child may take in new information, but he must also retain it in order to have fully "learned" it. Both processes are necessary if the child is to move beyond acquisition. In other words, the child must internalize new information (a combination of acquisition and retention) as the first step toward transformation—the ability to use, modify, or adjust information.

Purpose of Learning Activities as a Selection Principle

Given that learning activities must facilitate three interrelated processes—acquisition, transformation, and evaluation—a wise instructional designer begins by classifying activities according to these three purposes. Some activities—lecture, A-V presentation, reading—are most useful for acquisition. For transformation we would look for activities that require the students to manipulate ideas and materials. Puzzles, worksheets, or discussion exercises are excellent transformation activities. Finally, evaluation activities such as various tests or projects complete the instructional cycle.

In addition to the three specified purposes of activities, classroom experiences have an additional more generalized purpose—to interest a child in the world of ideas. Bruner (1961), in commenting on this general purpose, suggests that high quality activities may increase

> the inherent interests of materials taught, giving the student a sense of discovery, translating what we have to say into the thought forms appropriate to the developing child, and so on. What this amounts to is developing in the child an interest in what he is learning, and with it an appropriate set of attitudes and values about intellectual activity generally. . . . If teaching is done well and if what we teach is worth learning, there are forces at work in our contemporary society that will provide the external prod that will get children more involved in the process of learning than they have been in the past. (p. 73)

Clearly, the phrase "if teaching is done well" is the critical factor. It is to that issue that this chapter is addressed.

Other Principles for Activity Selection

There are many, many kinds of activities available to the teacher. They range from highly structured programs such as the Systems 80 teaching machines to open-ended inquiry discussions. Assuming that the purpose of the activity has been decided and an appropriate group of activities has been gathered together, what additional principles can the teacher use to select the most appropriate activity for a particular learning objective and a particular group of students?

The selection of activities can best be determined by adherence to "the principle of the match." This principle has five subparts, each a factor in determining a match. The subparts include a *match* between an activity and: (a) the instructional objective; (b) the needs and interests of particular learners; (c) the individuality of the teacher; (d) the demands and requirements of the real world; (e) the physical surroundings of the classroom.

The "match" to the instructional objective. The instructional objective is a major consideration in choosing an activity. Recall the characteristics of a systems approach to instruction—purpose, integration, and feedback. In a systems approach, the relationship between the learning objective and the activity must be communicated to the students. It is not sufficient to announce that the two are related; students must understand the relationship.

The hierarchy used for analysis of content goals in Chapter 5 is a useful framework for matching objectives and activities. To understand how this is done, look at Figure 7–1. The hierarchy suggests learning activities. For instance, the problem of "following direc-

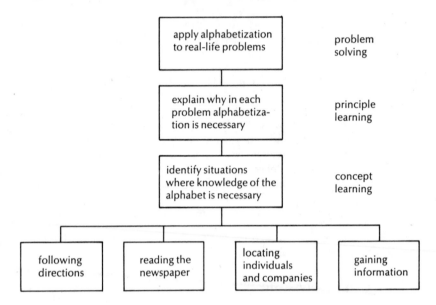

Figure 7–1

tions" can be explored through map work or written directions on a board game. A child may be asked to find an apartment for rent in the want ads to establish the importance of "reading the newspaper"; the phone book may be used for "locating individuals and companies." Searching through encyclopedias and a dictionary for the meaning of words can be the activity used to demonstrate "gaining information."

Using learning activities that are derived from the various levels of the hierarchy also guarantees that they will match the prescribed "levels of learning" suggested in the instructional objectives. In the alphabetization example, the instructor can see that one activity must be at the *problem-solving level,* probably a number of activities will need to be designed at the *concept level,* and *memorized information* will need to be provided in some fashion for following directions, reading the newspaper, locating individuals and companies, and gaining information. Once a meaningful hierarchy has been created, it is relatively quick and easy to list learning activities that closely match the instructional objectives.

The objective and the activities that relate to it must also be in the same domain of learning. Affective objectives should be carried out through activities that give the student an opportunity to acquire or transform interests, attitudes, or values. For example, if the objective is in the area of social development (i.e., "the child will intro-duce himself to a visitor in the classroom"), then the activity for teaching the objective should begin with introductions to classmates and other familiar persons. It is much more difficult to learn to interact effectively with people using pencil-and-paper worksheets that ask, "what do you say when you meet someone?" Pencil-and-paper activities do not meet the qualification for match to objective when human interactions are the focus. The same analysis can be made for psychomotor objectives. They need activities that let stu-dents perform the physical skills.

Finally, an objective and activity must match in regard to materials required. Where possible, activities should involve the same mate-rials as those listed in the objective—particularly at the acquisition and retention level. For example, if the stated objective is "When given ten coins of varying denominations, the child will be able to correctly identify each one's value," coins are the material to use. By the same token, if an objective focuses on differing characteristics of people, we would expect activities might focus on the children's height, weight, glasses, and hearing aids.

The match with the needs and interests of particular learners. Piaget and Bruner both suggest that the process of intellectual development follows a continuum from sensorimotor learning through formal operations. During the early stages, children's mental work consists primarily of establishing relationships between action and experi-ence. They are primarily interested in manipulation as the basis for learning. As they progress to more advanced levels of intellectual functioning, children are able to deduce operations and compre-hend more abstract levels of reasoning. Classroom activities must be directed toward each child's present level, with opportunities to experiment with new information to extend or challenge what the child already knows.

There is a "right time" for learning—that moment when children eagerly and intently involve themselves in an activity that enables them to acquire, transform, and evaluate new knowledge. This pre-cious moment is an unforgettable memory for teachers who man-age to capture it. There are several factors involved in the "meshing" of learner needs to activities. The child's age is a factor. If a child is 8 or 9 years old and has not learned to classify objects, he needs activities that will help him learn to do so. The selection of age-appropriate materials, however, is an important consideration. Where for young children a teacher might use toy forks and spoons,

Gayle Boss Monday, May 16, 1978
Honest person that
should tell truth sometime
and you get more
friends get a job and
they don't stealing
they don't lie alot
they don't cheat and
are dependable fairly
nice And friendly and
are not shy you should
stealing any stuff
like candy or money
or gum

John Hobbs
5th Ave 5th
5/16/78

Honesty
Honesty is being truthful so
stealing, lieing, cheating Being
honest to yourself.
Let of it yes I always tell the
truth. Like giving people money
and returning money back.
Because if you get a job.
you should tell to boss
if your a friend is doing
something wrong.

Sharon Smith 3°   5-16-78
Honesty
honst to yourself truthful
My friend is honest because I gave her money
to buy me some gum

Because I asked her to buy me some gum and I asked
her to buy stuff for me before that's why I trust her

                    Gary Reynolds soc.st.
Honest you depend on a other person
and a person is truthful on a job
they don't lie cheator steal & you
they are dependable person.
    the person is dependable
to another, they help you

STUART
Honesty HOBBS
1 Honest to yourself
2 Honest to your mom And Dad
3 Honest to your friendes
4 Honest to your sister
5 Tell the Truth all the time when
   ever you are and don't lie never

6 don't stealing gum, candy, pop,
7 Honest and don't turn your dark
   (and say you tell the truth)
8 fact the fakes that you stealed it

Mike Doolye
Honest one who tells the truth
one who don't steal, one who don't
cheat. one who don't lie.
I was honest to tell want
I broke at home

Maria Young   May 16, 1978

Honest person tell the truth
abot everything like if you
see something and you was
there you should Honest and tell
the truth like if some boy
take a ladies pack book
and you saw him that
person may ask you
for lie but you should
not lie Because at the
court house you can
get money for Being Honest
and you can I have more friend pay

for older children more age-appropriate materials such as food, clothing, sports equipment, and small hardware would be used.

Activities that "match" the needs of the learner are expected to enhance curiosity and interest in learning. According to Bruner (1961)

> Somewhere between apathy and wild excitement, there is an optimum level of aroused attention that is ideal for classroom activity. What is that level? Frenzied activity fostered by a competitive project may leave no pause for reflection, for evaluation, for generalization, while excessive orderliness, with each student waiting his turn, produces boredom and apathy. There is a day-to-day problem here of great significance. Short-term arousal is not the same as long-term establishment of interest in the broader sense. Films, audio-visual aids, and other such devices may have the short-run effect of catching attention. In the long run they may produce a passive person waiting for some sort of curtain to go up to arouse him. . . . Perhaps it is in the technique of arousing attention in school that first steps can be taken to establish the active autonomy of attention that is the antithesis of the spectator's passivity. (72–73)

In determining the "match" between the learner and the activity, it is perhaps helpful to remember that the ultimate aim of education is to help students think independently for themselves. That is what we mean by the ability to function effectively in our complex society. Thus, another factor to be considered in the match is the degree of independence the activity affords the learner. Some retarded students are not able to cope with much independence. Others, if given the opportunity, could function quite independently in a given activity.

In short, activities are most effective if they are tailor-made for particular students. Teachers should sit down with students and talk *with* them, rather than *to* them, to find out what excites them. Teachers can test themselves about how well they know their students by listing their preferences, interests, hobbies, and character traits that could be used in selecting interesting activities. If a teacher doesn't know the students well enough to identify their needs and interests, he or she might schedule interviews to get to know them better.

The match with a teacher's individuality. This topic may come as a surprise. Many writers eloquently describe the individuality of students, but few discuss the individuality of teachers. Often we speak of "the teacher" as though one uniform set of characteristics, interests, and competencies would describe *all* teachers. Of course, that is ridiculous.

Teachers have varying levels of interest in and knowledge about certain subject areas. The teacher's own interests and competence obviously influence, either consciously or unconsciously, his or her selection of activities. A teacher who is interested in science may find science activities exciting. Teachers who enjoy art and other creative activities may find that they heighten their own enthusiasm for teaching.

Some teachers will avoid activities with which they feel uncomfortable. Some teachers refuse to use activities in the area of sex education ("that stuff doesn't belong in school"; "I can't deal with that material with my kids, I'm uncomfortable and embarrassed"). Activities may be avoided by the teacher for other reasons: "I don't know how to present the digestive system in an interesting way"; "I feel uncomfortable talking about handicapping conditions"; "I don't understand basic math myself, so how can I teach it or even help children understand the principles involved?" "I find that I am more successful at small group activities than I am when I work with the entire class."

Thoughts and feelings like these are often expressed by teachers. They should influence the selection of activities. We believe that teachers can share their knowledge and expertise with each other— not as "subject" specialists, but as "activity" specialists. They can talk with other teachers and find out what they do well. They can either teach each other or help out in other teachers' classes. Teachers can learn and teach just as children both teach and learn.

There are other factors involved in the match of the teacher to activities. Selecting a particular reading program, for example, requires some knowledge on the part of the teacher. Some teachers prefer structured reading programs such as DISTAR (Engelmann & Brunner, 1969) and feel confident and satisfied when using them. Others are quite uncomfortable with any tightly structured program and prefer a more open approach, like that suggested by Sylvia Ashton Warner in *Teacher* (1963) or the experience–chart story approach. Again, the teacher should use an approach that he or she is comfortable with.

We believe that teaching can be fun—we are teachers. We feel most comfortable when we use activities that are successful and foster our students' growth. We as teachers sometimes feel uncomfortable, however, when we move into new or untried areas of teaching and learning. That's true for children also. There is always a certain degree of discomfort associated with learning. Learning sometimes requires hard work—an expenditure of total effort. As you learn to do new things, try new activities, learn more about

Jennifer is learning to make basic home repairs.

yourself and about your students and how they learn, however, your choices for activities will become enlarged. As teachers broaden their own range of knowledge, take risks in trying new activities, and increase their receptivity to learning, they can derive greater pleasure from their teaching.

The match with the real world. The Functional Life Curriculum is built upon society, the learner, and subject matter, filtered through the philosophy of normalization. This philosophy says that retarded students should learn, live, work, love, and participate in society just like everyone else. School must help prepare them to do that.

Activities in the Functional Life Curriculum should be applicable to problems and experiences of the "real world" outside the school. For example, in the area of social skill development, there are many opportunities to take children out of the class into social situations. Places such as stores, the library, the supermarket, the zoo, the theater, and concerts (to name only a few) give children an opportunity to practice their newly developing skills.

Visualize the entire community as a source of learning activities. That is the "real world." The more the children are out there, the better able they will understand and adjust to it.

The community is filled with resources that can be used to enhance learning for retarded children. Career educators have integrated this idea into their curricula. Their programs frequently consist of taking children out to observe, first hand, the actual jobs people do in various careers. These direct experiences let children understand career alternatives better. Bringing speakers into the classroom to describe and demonstrate their expertise is another valuable activity.

Many retarded students who have always had difficulty in school are not interested in school demands, particularly when they see them as *irrelevant*. Relating learning activities to the world of work and helping students understand why something is necessary can enhance their motivation. For instance, explain that math is used in making a budget, a plan for spending *your* money.

One "test" to see the "match" between an activity and the real world is, "Can I justify it in terms of normalization? Will this activity help the student become more independent and a responsible, productive citizen?" If the answer is "probably not," perhaps the teacher should consider an alternative.

The match with the physical surroundings of the classroom. The physical dimensions and physical arrangement of the classroom also influence the selection of activities. The choice of active games is restricted by both the size of the room and the noise imposed on nearby classrooms. The size of the room is fixed, obviously, and activity selections must be made accordingly.

The arrangement of the classroom is another matter, however. In classrooms where desks are fixed in neat rows, the selection of activities is limited by that arrangement. The more flexible the classroom environment, the larger the range of activities available. The learning centered classroom described in Chapter 2 is an example of a flexible classroom environment. It allows several activities to be conducted simultaneously. The "noise" level that accompanies certain activities is also a factor in selection.

Selecting activities that will help the student achieve specified instructional objectives is a systematic process. Employing activities that are appropriate to the specific purpose of the task—to acquire, transform, or evaluate—and then applying the "principle of the match" enables the instructor to select a suitable activity for each instructional situation. The match between the nature of the in-

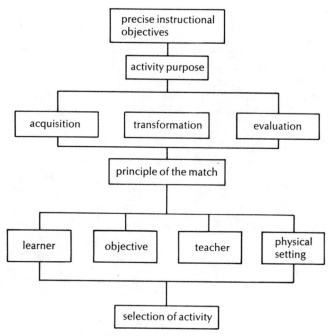

Figure 7–2   *Process of selection of an appropriate activity*

structional objective, the learner, the teacher, the real world, and the classroom is important to consider in the selection. The total selection process is represented in Figure 7–2.

The Implementation of Learning Activities

The next task is to put the activities into action. Before that can be done, however, there are several considerations for the teacher. Will he use media? Will the students be in a large or a small group? How much structure is required? These are some of the factors which the teacher must consider before implementing classroom activities.

Implementation is the actual meeting of instructor and student, either face-to-face or through learning materials. The nature of this "meeting" between student and teacher is the focus of this section of the chapter. There are four principles to keep in mind during this stage:

1. Active learning,
2. Variety,
3. Practice and overlearning,
4. Feedback and reinforcement.

Steve prefers to stand while completing his work.

The "Active Learning" Principle

Children are not merely empty vessels waiting to be filled with knowledge. Rather, they are developing people who learn by manipulating materials within their environment. Children can best understand the properties of materials through direct interactions with them. They must learn the properties of things and how to distinguish among them. For instance, feeling the roundness of a ball and the squareness of a box can help the child learn the concept of shapes. By the same token, smelling an onion, a rose, and a chocolate bar helps the child learn "smells," and it has the added advantage of using a sense that is often neglected. Active learning does not mean that the students must move about the classroom, though physical activity is often desirable. The principle of active learning does mean that potentially passive activities such as reading and listening should be structured to require immediate responses. For example, an oral presentation should be brief or broken into episodes with student responses to questions or discussions following each episode. Reading should be paired with a written response sheet, a programmed learning worksheet, or perhaps a dramatization of the story. As increasing attention is focused on basic skill learning, the instructor must not forget to provide active learning systems for students. Figure 7–3 shows a written response lesson that is one approach to creating active responses to reading. The same model may be used with small discussion groups.

The active principle may be applied to all content areas of instruction. Young children need materials to act upon; older children need materials in addition to interesting ideas to act upon. For example, the use of Cuisinaire rods with young children helps them find relationships for themselves. The materials developed by Montessori (1965) are fine examples of things children can manipulate in learning. Lessons in social behavior, problem solving, and expressive language may involve dramatic presentations, role-play situations, and classroom simulations. Science concepts, by the same token, can be taught through classroom experiments, breeding live fish and animals, growing plants of many kinds, and using a microscope to look at small living cells.

Each of us learns by doing. This is especially true for young children or retarded students who have difficulty generalizing information or learning abstract material. The more opportunities students have to act upon ideas and materials, the better able they will be to acquire, transform, and evaluate information.

The Variety Principle

If we can be sure of a single learning principle, it is the importance of instructional variety in teaching. For our purposes, we shall analyze variety in terms of (a) multidimensional aspects of learning activities, (b) dominance patterns, (c) grouping and interaction patterns, and (d) structure of learning activities. Activities must be varied to hold student interest, provide practice, and meet the students' needs.

Variety and multidimensional activities

Sensory learning. We take information in through our five senses. A young child walks into the house and says, "Oh good, we're having spaghetti for dinner." His sense of smell gave him a clue that he related to a previously known experience; he then reached a conclusion.

Figure 7–3

Written Response Lesson
(Secondary Level)

Two kinds of written response lessons can easily be designed.
One is heavily structured, requiring students to make frequent responses.
The other approach places more responsibility on the student to draw out
and synthesize information. Students can choose either approach.

Objective: After hearing and reading the following story, the student will
describe in writing a society with limited freedom.

"Tortoise Model"	"Hare Model"
Reading	*Reading*

"Tortoise Model"

Reading

Paragraph 1 (describes political
control over the population)

What is the main idea of this
paragraph?

_____

_____

_____

Paragraph 2 (describes economic
control over the population)

What is the main idea of this
paragraph?

_____

_____

_____

Paragraph 3 (describes social
control—censorship, laws cover-
ing marriage, child rearing, etc.)

What is the main idea of this
paragraph?

_____

_____

_____

From your reading of this story,
describe a society with "limited
freedom."

_____

_____

_____

_____

_____

"Hare Model"

Reading

From your reading of this story,
describe a society with "limited
freedom."

_____

_____

_____

_____

_____

Each sense, as a source of information, contributes to a child's understanding and interpretation of the environment. Although the senses operate independently, they assist learning through a process of integration. For example, a mother has prepared a new recipe for dinner. Seven-year-old Steven sits down, looks at the casserole, and says "What's that?" His visual sense has not provided enough information for him to decide whether he wants to eat it or not. His mother says "That's a ground beef casserole." Now Steven says "What's in it?" (seeking additional information). He sniffs the aromas as he asks the question. The mother responds, "Ground beef, macaroni, tomato sauce—all the things you like." Steven receives this auditory response, processes it (perhaps congering up pleasant taste sensations associated with those familiar foods), and responds "O.K., I'll taste it." That is the final test—the information gathered from the first taste is the determining factor in the decision "to eat it or not." In this example, Steven has used information from four of his five senses before deciding whether to try the new meal. The final sense of touch will be used during the process of eating. The information from each sense, although separate, is integrated, related to past experiences, and brought to bear on the situation at hand.

Children's earliest learnings are dominated by the senses. The infant hears her mother's voice, sees her mother's face, and soon associates sights and sounds with mother. Sensory domination characterizes learning for young children in school as well. They can be observed touching, listening, tasting, viewing, and smelling objects with great intensity. Since all senses are relevant to learning, activities should include materials related to each of them. Most instructional experiences are auditory and visual. For young children particularly, this practice fails to stimulate the development of the other senses as sources of learning.

The following dialogue is a case in point.

I

Teacher:	Here are three pictures of foods we like. Tell me which is your favorite? Lamar, which do you like?
Lamar:	The chocolate pudding.
Teacher:	Good, now Helen, which do you like?
Helen:	I don't know what that is in the middle picture.
Teacher:	That's chili.

Helen:	What's that?
Teacher:	Who can tell Helen what chili is?
Juanita:	I can. That's meat and beans and tomatoes and chilis and it's real good.
Teacher:	Good explanation, Juanita.

II

Teacher:	I am going to blindfold each of you and ask you to taste three foods. When you do, see if you can tell what each is and whether you like it or not. Lamar, here's a spoon; you try first.
Lamar:	This is chocolate pudding. I like it. This is ice cream, maybe vanilla. This is hot, I don't know what it is. It tastes awful.
Teacher:	That's chili. You don't like it?
Lamar:	It's bumpy and hot and I like the pudding better.

In the first example the teacher is using auditory and visual stimuli for instruction on food and tastes. In the second example, taste itself is the basis upon which decisions are made. Which do you think is the more productive approach to developing sensory awareness?

Activities that relate to the stimulation of the senses can also be aimed toward the integration of sensory information. Sandpaper letters, for example, give children an opportunity to feel, hear, and see the letter simultaneously. Thus, several sources of information are stimulated; children can relate all three as they strive to learn the task. Reading activities can be structured to include more than auditory and visual stimuli as well. Let's use the word "car" as an example. The child is shown the printed word *car* with a picture of it. The teacher says "What is the word?" The child says "car." "Find the object" (from a group of objects that is on the table) "that is the same as the word." The child picks up a car. He can now feel it, say it, and point to the word that he reads as "car."

Multisensory activities are those that provide information from many senses. Children must first become aware of sensory stimuli and helped to interpret their meaning as the first steps toward integrating the information. Activities such as feeling materials of varied textures as they say words such as "soft" or "rough"; shaking cylinders of varied sounds as they match the contents to rice, beans, and peas; and smelling extracts of varied odors as they match them to assorted fruits stimulate individual senses and are additional sources of receiving information.

Creative, expressive activities. Creative, expressive activities are an important source of variety in classroom instruction for several reasons: (a) they are vehicles for self-expression, (b) they are enjoyable, (c) students cannot fail in them, (d) they are not stressful, (e) they provide an opportunity for children who have difficulty in academic areas to excel, (f) they encourage social interaction, (g) their products can be shared and admired, and (h) they can reinforce developing skills.

For some children, freely expressing ideas and feelings is difficult. Some children may not have the language they need to express themselves out loud. Others, though quite verbal, are unable to verbalize their feelings in an appropriate, productive manner. Teachers can use art, music, and movement activities to help all these children express themselves.

For example, a child who is angry, quick to fight, and quick to tear up his paper in frustration may be unable to express his feelings in words. He may, however, find satisfaction in doing an "angry" dance or creating an "angry" picture to be shared with the class. These activities encourage children to express their feelings in socially acceptable avenues. Helping a child understand that angry feelings are natural and that they can be expressed in alternative, acceptable ways is an important part of helping a child develop affectively.

Creative, expressive activities have no right or wrong answers, so children can be free of the fear of failure. Even children who have difficulty in basic skill areas can excel in creative, expressive activities. As a result, children usually enjoy these experiences.

Because of the enjoyment that comes from these activities, teachers may encourage children to work together, choose projects, perform for others, or work individually on selected tasks. In addition, basic skills can be reinforced through art, music, and movement. For example, repeating verses in songs, drawing a field trip experience, or pantomiming a story are all skill-oriented and fun.

Let's return to the Functional Life Curriculum for an example. Suppose you were working with the concepts of necessities and luxuries. You might ask a group of elementary children to draw all the "luxuries" they would most like to own some day. They may then choose to model some of them in clay. Older children might build a luxury home, boat, or automobile of their choice.

Physical and perceptual-motor activities.   The earliest actions of young children are motor activities. Learning to control and manipulate their bodies helps children gain confidence and self-direction. Physical activity in the form of games is fun; it makes children feel good. Even as children mature and move on to more sophisticated intellectual activity, physical activity continues to be of importance in a well-rounded, satisfying life.

Development of basic perceptual-motor skills is essential to success in other academic areas. These skills include auditory skills, tactile skills, kinesthetic and visual perception (including eye-hand coordination), directionality concepts, and the position of the body in space. There are many classroom activities that incorporate these skills. For example, from the Functional Life Curriculum, one area of study includes the application of technology to everyday living. Auditory discrimination skills can be developed by comparing and contrasting sounds from the machines of the industrial age. Jumping activities can be related to "jet" jumping, "helicopter" jumping, "train" jumping, and so on.

Physical activities can be fun, heighten motivation, and enhance learning. For young children learning the concept of "up" and "down," moving up and down so that they actually feel and experience the concept enhances learning. The same can be said for "in" and "out," "under" and "over." Using an empty, large box, a child can be instructed to "get in the box," "sit under the box," and so on. These learning experiences help the child internalize concepts while adding variety in the classroom.

Physical activities can also help children relax. There are many relaxation exercises that can increase children's ability to control and relax their bodies. Other exercises increase flexibility and movement, muscle control and development, and general motor ability.

Physical activities in the classroom can provide an important interlude during the class day. They are a change of pace. Also for children who have difficulty in academic areas, these activities allow them to demonstrate their physical proficiency and prowess to their peers and teacher. Another advantage is that routine physical activities can help children to get into the habit of exercise—a life-long activity.

Combined activities.   Certain activities involve only one modality or fall into only one of the three domains—a math worksheet, for example. These have their place in the curriculum, particularly for purposes of evaluation. But many learning activities aimed at specified objectives can involve several dimensions. They are called *combined activities.* Several sensory modalities, actions, and domains may be combined within a single classroom experience. For example, a classroom game that involves moving to music while stepping on numbered cards on the floor as they are identified by the teacher includes music, movement, and numbers. Musical chairs is another example of a combined activity. String painting (wriggling a string on a newly painted picture) to music that has both fast and slow tempos is still another example.

Combined activities give the teacher a chance to incorporate less palatable tasks into high interest areas. For example, a child who needs practice counting may enjoy making "hash marks" as she counts the number of times her classmates jump to music. Creative teachers often find it an exciting challenge to develop combined activities that mesh both fun and practice with basic skills.

Other activities will stress social interaction, cognitive development, and verbal expression. Games such as "Twenty Questions," role play situations, and discussion groups all integrate several dimensions.

Young children can act out reading stories or favorite library book stories or invent their own stories in creative dramatics. Older children may wish to write, produce, and direct plays related to the content of the Functional Life Curriculum. These efforts may include creating sets, costumes, and publicity. These endeavors provide practice in organizing, writing, directing, planning, performing, and accepting responsibility for tasks. Perhaps most important of all, these activities are fun and encourage the children to interact with their classmates.

Language-oriented activities. The ability to communicate ideas, thoughts, and feelings through words is highly valued in our society. Certainly verbal communication is the primary mode of social interaction and classroom exchange. Expressive language skills are an area of weakness for many retarded children. Several authors (e.g., Klein & Safford, 1977) have found that mentally retarded children can demonstrate "internalized" or receptive language but are unable to express their thoughts adequately. Thus classroom activities should focus on language to the maximum extent possible.

Language activities can further the development of certain psycholinguistic abilities. This orientation can be carried out in language arts, math, science, social studies, and physical education lessons in activities that require auditory memory, auditory decoding, and visual and auditory sequencing. For example, auditory decoding can be developed through activities that require the student to repeat several statements, sing songs with many repeated verses, or play the telephone game.

The teacher can increase the child's verbal facility by providing "new" language in classroom situations. Children can be encouraged to use materials in new and varying ways. These experiences give teachers an opportunity to express the language for the child. For example, in an activity that focuses on objects that float and objects that do not, the child can experiment with several objects and observe their actions. The teacher can then introduce the words "sink" and "float" to label the actions the child has already observed.

The child's receptive language provides clues to what he thinks about and the way in which he reasons. The teacher should use this information to select learning activities that will interest the child.

Variety and the issue of dominance. A second way to vary classroom activities is to vary the dominant role. That is, some learning activities are dominated by the instructor, who regulates the pace of the activity and the sequence of events. The teacher-delivered lecture on the digestive system is an example; a directed discussion lesson when the teacher questions and students respond is another. Student-dominated activities place the student in a central role. A student may lecture, or several students may participate in a group discussion that they organize and control.

A third group of activities may be considered media-dominated, since the pace and sequence of learning are controlled by a film, slide-tape presentation, or game board. Media-dominated activities, which are also called *mediated* lessons, are different from the traditional teacher with A-V supplements. Mediated activities involve a self-contained instructional sequence such as a slide-tape presentation, programmed learning program, film, filmstrip with worksheet, or computer-assisted instruction (Heinich, 1970). Advocates of mediated activities forecast that with their increasing use the teacher will be free

> to do what the machine never can do—motivate, counsel, and lead students to those high order functions which are the primary goals of education—to question, imagine, invent, appreciate and act. The teacher need no longer be the purveyor of information or even the developer of basic skills and understanding. (Heinich, 1970, p. 155)

Variety and grouping and interaction patterns. Grouping and interaction patterns among students and between the teacher and students is still another type of variety. Some instructional goals lend themselves to large-group instruction, such as a lecture. A lecture is efficient, though its effectiveness depends upon the content and style of presentation. A large-group presentation is usually more effective when followed by small-group discussions that allow students to explore ideas and concepts more fully.

Grouping patterns may also include small groups organized for discussions, projects, or class meetings. Depending upon the size of these groups, they may provide the students with the opportunity to interact. The smaller the group, the more interaction is possible.

Peer tutoring is another grouping pattern. In this model, a fellow student tutors one or two peers who need assistance in a specified area. Peer tutoring can be very effective for helping handicapped students in the regular classroom.

Student needs are an important consideration in the selection of grouping patterns. For example, a quiet, reserved child may respond more openly in a group of two or three students who are working on a specific task or project. Certain students work better together than others. Obviously, the teacher's knowledge of the students is the best tool in putting together a group.

Variety and the structure of activities. The degree of structure required for activities can also provide variety. Structure is the number of intermediate, predetermined, subtasks contained within a task. Each subtask normally consists of a set of instructional stimuli followed by appropriate student responses. These responses may be oral or written or involve some other type of physical movement. If

we put structure on a continuum, a highly structured activity such as programmed learning would form one end of the continuum, and at the other end would be one with low structure, like discovery learning.

Moving along the continuum, the degree of structure varies depending upon the task and the needs of the learner. The Systems 80 teaching machine provides a high degree of structure. The student sits in front of the machine, listens to the auditory direction, and responds by pushing a button. There can be only one correct response. The student attends to many S-R sequences before the task is completed. There is little freedom for the student with this machine. In contrast, a discovery learning activity affords the student much freedom; there is very little imposed structure. The intermediate steps in a discovery learning task are not predetermined either by the teacher or instructional developer; structure evolves from the nature of the task. The student is free to create her own limits as she identifies principles and ideas to explore.

There are several considerations to consider in determining the degree of structure necessary for a given task. Learner characteristics are one set of considerations. Those learners who act anxious, insecure, and dependent upon adult feedback require relatively highly structured tasks that have built-in feedback. For example, DISTAR (Engelmann & Brunner, 1969) is a highly structured reading system that provides consistent feedback to the learner at each successive step. The experience chart story approach to reading has much less structure as the steps are not predetermined by the teacher, although the teacher does give feedback as the steps unfold.

Helping a student function effectively with less and less structure may be an instructional goal for some learners. In order for students to be fully independent, they must learn to operate in situations that have no predetermined steps. Activities can be modified to be more or less structured on the basis of learner need, as the learner develops increased tolerance for less structure.

The characteristics of the task also determine the degree of structure inherent in a task. Compare the following classroom dialogues.

I

Teacher:	Bill, only a natural-born American can be a president. A natural-born American is one born in the U.S. or whose parents were American citizens. Can a person born outside the U.S. to citizens of another country become a U.S. president?
Bill:	No!
Teacher:	Good! Now what if my parents were American but lived in Germany when I was born. Can I become president?
Bill:	I don't know.
Teacher:	The rule states that my parents have to be American citizens. Does it mention where they live?
Bill:	No.
Teacher:	Then make a guess. Can I become president?

Bill:	Yes.
Teacher:	Good! As long as my parents are American citizens I can become president of the U.S.

II

We learned that a president of the U.S. has to be at least 35 years of age. Now I want you to examine these four individuals; two can be president and two cannot. Tell me why. Your answer will identify another requirement to become a U.S. president.

1. Ling How was born in Canton, China. With his parents he moved to the U.S. when he was 2 years old. (NO)

2. Mary Stewart was born in Canada. Her parents, who were U.S. citizens, had been on a trip when she was born. (YES)

3. Mela Sankis was born in the U.S. while his parents, who were Greek, were vacationing in the U.S. (NO)

4. Peter Petash was born in the U.S. His parents were immigrants from Poland. They never became U.S. citizens. (YES)

Teacher:	Why were Mary and Peter able to become citizens?
Bill:	Mary's parents were citizens. Peter was born here.
Teacher:	Right. What you have just learned was the requirement that the president must be a natural-born citizen, which means born in the U.S. or born to American citizens.

How do the two instructional dialogues differ? Dialogue I shows a step-by-step process directed by the teacher (high degree of structure); performance feedback to the student follows each step. Dialogue II is a more open process (low degree of structure); students investigate data and arrive at a conclusion. The teacher gives feedback in response to ideas presented.

Another significant difference between the two lessons relates to their logical structure. Dialogue I is a deductive process of logic. Deductive lessons proceed as follows.

1. Instructor defines a concept or explains the relationships imbedded within a principle.
2. Instructor provides relevant examples and nonexamples.

Deductive approaches are the most common in classrooms at all grade and ability levels and in all subject areas. A deductive approach is appropriate when time is limited and the material is to be learned at the recall level. If the material is to be learned at the concept level, a deductive approach may still be appropriate if the concept is clearly defined and involves physically describable characteristics. A useful way to classify concepts is to divide them into two categories. *Either-or* concepts have a clearly defined rule that can be used to discriminate examples from nonexamples. All concrete concepts, like "man," "woman," "table," or "fork," are either-or concepts. Abstract concepts may also be either-or concepts. For example, the concept "citizen" is abstract, in that citizens look no different from noncitizens. Yet we can, by definition, discriminate one from the other. Consequently, citizen is an either-or concept. "Middle class," "verb," and "symbol" are also either-or concepts and may be taught deductively.

The second category of concepts, those that have *more-or-less* rules, involves inductive learning. More-or-less concepts are abstract, and the rules that define them cannot be used to clearly discriminate every example from every nonexample. "Freedom," "justice," and "beauty" are examples of more-or-less concepts because reasonable persons often disagree when faced with a particular decision about them. More-or-less concepts involve comparison and judgment, which make learning to apply them difficult. Consequently, it is best to teach them inductively. Inductive approaches to learning activities proceed as follows.

1. Student is presented with examples of a principle or concept to be learned.
2. Student infers the existence and the qualities of the principle or concept.

Inductive approaches are more time-consuming than deductive approaches, but they provide the best option for learning abstract, more-or-less concepts. They also provide practice for thinking through problems and seeking solutions. Tasks related to inductive reasoning objectives are, by their very nature, relatively less structured. On the other hand, tasks organized deductively, those tasks with clear rules that lead to right or wrong answers, have a higher degree of structure. Many tasks can be structured in more than one way, depending upon the preferences and needs of the learners.

The Principle of Practice

Everyone needs to practice in order to develop their skills and talents and remain proficient. Professors read, analyze, and discuss ideas to develop them. Great musicians practice for many hours each day. At the age of 80, Pablo Casals spent 6 hours each day playing Bach's cello sonatas!

Practice can be defined as the "act of performing repeatedly in order to learn." Some teachers of mildly retarded children bemoan the fact that Johnny knew a word yesterday, but has forgotten it today. The fact is that Johnny had insufficient practice with the new word; he really hadn't "learned" it in the first place. Some mentally retarded children seem to have memory-processing difficulties that impair their short-term memory. They may need to practice new skills and knowledge several times during a day, for several weeks or even years, in order to truly "learn."

The teacher may need to devise several activities that focus on the same objective to provide the necessary practice for the child. For example, suppose the objective for Lashawn is that "he will name 10 parts of the body." These body parts can be identified on the child himself, on others, as he is doing physical activities, during art, during music ("put your finger in the air"), and as he is putting on his clothing to go home. Because repetition of the same activity can result in boredom for retarded as well as nonretarded students, the practice activities should be varied.

Not only must activities provide practice, but the teacher needs to know exactly what areas the child needs practice in. As they learn to accept responsibility for part of their own learning, children can identify their own needs for practice.

Some writers say mentally retarded children need practice in order to "overlearn" (Kirk, 1972). We prefer the term "internalize," which essentially means that a child has learned a skill when he can repeatedly perform it correctly. College students who cram for a final often have not internalized the material. Learning takes time; activities that provide time for practice enhance learning for children.

Principle of Feedback and Reinforcement

Each of us wants to succeed. As we strive toward our own goals, we seek feedback on our progress; positive feedback guides our further efforts. Children also need feedback and positive reinforcement for their school performance. Because many retarded children have experienced failure throughout their lives, they are often more dependent upon adult feedback than other children. Thus, feedback and positive teacher responses have great impact on these students.

Activities should be selected and presented so that the mechanism for feedback is apparent to both the teacher and student. If the child is engaged in a task, the teacher should be sure she is aware of the feedback process. Feedback can be structured in several ways: (a) verbal feedback from teacher observation, (b) nonverbal, tactile feedback (a pat or a squeeze), (c) written teacher feedback, (d) verbal peer feedback, (e) written peer feedback, (f) verbal group feedback, (g) a combination of verbal, nonverbal, and written feedback from either teacher or peers, and (h) feedback directly through learning materials, i.e., programmed learning.

Some tasks lend themselves to written feedback. When providing such feedback, the teacher should be careful in identifying errors. A question mark beside an incorrect response (Are you sure about this one?) conveys the same message as a big red slash. Feedback may

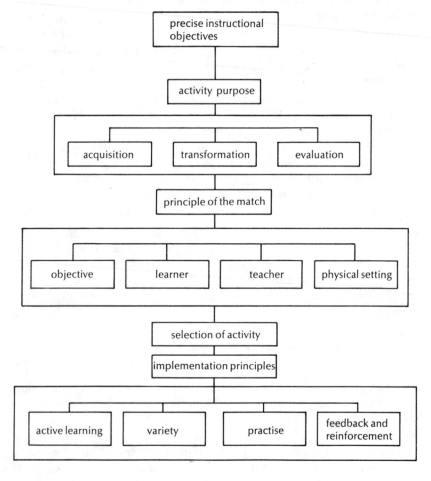

Figure 7–4   *Selection and implementation of learning activities*

identify accuracy or errors; the teacher can facilitate the child's using the feedback to correct errors or to apply it to new tasks.

Positive reinforcement is closely allied to feedback. Positive reinforcement is an effective way to identify desired behavior for the child and maintain it. Positive reinforcement is most effective when it is immediate and specific. "Good boy" conveys less information than the statement, "You completed the assignment in science very well today. I'm proud of how hard you worked on your project."

Positive reinforcement takes many forms. Verbal praise from the teacher or peers, written praise using words, stars, or checks, a smile, a pat, a note to parents, a private comment to a child are alternatives. Class meetings or group discussions can also be used to provide positive reinforcement from the group.

Figure 7–4 summarizes the selection and implementation principles that have been discussed in this chapter. In the next section of the chapter we will look at two examples from the Functional Life Curriculum—Candle Production and Life Cycles.

Two Sample Activities from the Functional Life Curriculum

Candle Production

This activity involves a class of elementary school children. They live in a city that offers many cultural, sports, and community activities. The students have identified three field trips they wish to take: an afternoon baseball game, a matinee at the Playhouse, and an overnight hike. They have also discovered that these excursions cost money, more money than they have.

The class has explored sources of income and decided they must become producers and manufacture a product that will bring a profit to pay for the field trips. They have decided to produce candles. The class has established a step-by-step process to follow:

1. Need for candles (market analysis)
2. Factors of production
   a. Labor
   b. Rent, light, heat
   c. Capital
   d. Advertising
   e. Profit
3. Cost of production

4. Production process
   a. Raw materials
   b. Personnel needs and deployment
   c. Space
   d. Time
5. Production steps
   a. Manufacturing
   b. Packaging
   c. Pricing
6. Distribution and sales
   a. Advertising
   b. Marketing
   c. Financial transactions
   d. Bookkeeping

Market analysis. After much discussion, four students have been selected to do a market analysis. They develop a questionnaire that they present to each class in the building. The questions are related to (a) Would you buy candles? (b) How much would you be willing to pay? (c) How many would you probably buy? (d) What colors are your favorites? The children go to each class, explain the purpose of the survey/questionnaire, and wait for students to complete them. Upon completion, they tabulate their results.

Factors of production. Another group of students studies the factors of production related to their candle project. They have analyzed each factor and established a dollar price for each candle.

Cost of production. Another group is responsible for determining the cost of production. They have investigated sources of wax and the cost of equipment needed for production. They determined that a capital investment of $50.00 is required.

Process of production. Another group has identified the required steps in the production process and secured the necessary materials (thanks to the capital investment). They have secured sufficient raw materials to produce only enough candles to provide additional capital for reinvestment.

Production. The entire class is involved in production. One group is responsible for raw materials, another for equipment, a third group for the actual manufacture, and a fourth group for packaging.

Distribution and marketing.   Having completed production of their goods, the class is now divided into distribution and marketing groups. Some students are responsible for advertising and taking orders. Some are packing orders. Others are distributing leaflets to homes in the neighborhood in an attempt to foster additional business. Two students are responsible for keeping the financial records —costs, sales, and available capital. The class must decide when to take out their profits and go on their field trips, whether to expand production or close the factory.

This activity can be used with elementary school or junior high level students. Each segment can be analyzed for prerequisite skills. Candle Production meets the criteria for active learning and variety. The principle of the match can be used as students assume task responsibilities.

Life Cycles

This activity also involves an elementary school class, where the teacher wants to bring the idea of the cycle of living things into the classroom. After several discussions, the students have identified three classes of living things for study: animals, plants, and humans. The students have been divided into three groups, each of which will focus on a particular class. As a total group you have identified critical factors in a life support system:

1. Germination or conception,
2. Nutrition (food, light, and water),
3. Care.

Each small group will now identify how the class with which they are concerned relates to life cycles.

Plant group.   The plant group has identified the needs of plants in the life cycle. Each member of the group will visit the Garden Center to learn about plant species, needs, and care required. Each will then identify two different species to grow himself. The teacher will help the students find plant cuttings. The students will identify plant needs and materials required to meet those needs and submit a plan for securing the required materials.

The group will also grow beans, root potatoes, and carrots to compare the plant growth systems. The teacher will help them secure materials.

The group has decided to build a terrarium and has designed a schematic for it. They have identified a heat source (a light bulb), natural light sources, and moisture needs. They will need plywood, thick plastic, hinges, small nails, and masking tape to make it.

As the terrarium dimensions are being determined, the group has rearranged the classroom to house it. Each member of the group has begun caring for individual plants. The terrarium is ready to be built. Two students are keeping records of plant needs and growth —amount of light required and frequency of watering as related to growth.

There are some students who wish to experiment with plant varieties; they are talking with people at the Garden Center to learn how to generate plant hybrids.

Animal group. This group has gone to the Natural Science Museum. As a result of their visit and conversations with the museum staff, they have decided to raise white mice. Although other animals were considered, the group wanted white mice because they found them most interesting.

The group has now identified the factors necessary for a life support system: food, room temperature, a glass cage, cedar bedding, toys, and water. The teacher will help them get the necessary equipment. Each group member will be responsible for maintenance of a particular piece of equipment.

The students have determined that they need to know how to provide on-going care for their mice. The librarian was very cooperative and gave them several books. The group also visited three pet stores and talked to their owners about caring for white mice. They are now ready to establish a plan for care.

During their pet-store visits, the students compared the prices of white mice. They found a store whose prices they could afford and decided to purchase the mice. The equipment was brought into the classroom, and they were ready to study their mice.

The group decided to study weight, length, and varying characteristics related to the use of toys, wheels, and hiding places. A record-chart format was decided upon, and each student is responsible for recording his or her own mice's development and behavior. Comparisons among the mice will be made daily.

The group decided to get only female mice until they choose to increase their mouse population. One member of the group wondered what effect a black mouse would have on future generations. They will consider this topic for possible future study.

Human group. After viewing a film that describes the process of human conception and then fetal development in the womb, the group chooses to focus on infant care from birth to age 12 months. They visit a pediatrician who permits them to attend examinations, talk to parents in the waiting room, and help the nurses with simple chores. The teacher then suggests that each student in the group prepare a chart illustrating both the growth process during the first year and the baby's nutritional requirements from milk and formula through solid food. Some students select particular charts that feature physiological maturation, others select emotional growth, still others prefer to concentrate on language acquisition. In addition, different students in the group choose report topics that reflect their special interests. Among the subjects selected by the children are breast vs. bottle feeding, infant danger signals, sleeping patterns, and the father's role in infant care. The pediatrician has agreed to act as a resource person for each child and to appear in the classroom and assist the students as they present their individual topics. The hospital and library have interesting films the group will use.

Individualizing Learning Activity

Another perspective from which to view "variety" is to look at the individual student rather than the classroom unit. With this perspective, the question becomes one of providing enough alternatives that a match is created between the learning activity and each individual's interests, abilities, achievement level, and preferred learning style. To do this, the teacher must individualize learning activities.

Assume that we assign a student to visit a classroom where individualization is normal practice. Upon her return, the visitor would report that the individualized classroom appeared to function without teacher control or management. The teacher was rarely found in the usual teaching stations—in the front of the room or behind a desk. Instead, she could be found in the midst of the students, assisting individual students or small groups. Students would begin or finish activities without the teacher being there. Upon closer scrutiny, the visitor was startled by the fact that the students were using a variety of learning materials and media; some students were doing arithmetic work while others were completing social studies assignments. One child was doing a science experiment. Moreover, within the largest group of students, those working on arithmetic problems, it was obvious that some children had progressed much farther in their study than others. Although the majority of the group were practicing long division, some were completing multiplication tables and others were beginning a programmed learning sequence

Peer tutoring provides extra opportunities for practice.

that explained the concept of fractional numbers. The visitor summarized her report by exclaiming, "Not only are many kinds of variety implemented in an individualized classroom, but they are implemented all at once!"

Individualization: The Problem of Definition

Individualization of instruction—Independent study—Individual study—Personalized education—Individually guided education—Child centered instruction—such a confusing list of ideas; they appear to express similar ideas with slightly different words. How can they be differentiated one from another? After all, if a dedicated teacher wants to individualize, he or she will need to describe what classroom changes are necessary. He will also need to compare and contrast his approach with others that are being utilized in other classrooms within the school or district or described in the literature.

One kind of individualized learning is *independent study*. Independent study is a curriculum concept that permits an individual student, possibly in consultation with an instructor, to select his own curriculum goals.

One of us taught for a number of years in a secondary school where independent study was a common practice. Two kinds of independent study were featured. The first was called *depth*. Student *depth* projects were developed when an individual student chose to study some previously learned course content in unusual detail or scope. In that event, the instructor might release the student from the usual curriculum to conduct a special investigation. When the student completed the self-study, he would return into the flow of the prescribed curriculum. One sample suitable depth project emerged from study of a unit on the newspaper as a communication medium. A student compared the approaches to news gathering and reporting taken by a large city newspaper and a newspaper published in a rural village.

A second kind of independent study was labelled *quest*. Quest activities were an accepted option for students in all subject areas and grade levels, in all ranges of ability and achievement. The concept was described by David W. Adams (1972) in the context of its use with a Learning Activity Package (LAP). A LAP is an individualized curriculum unit that provides opportunities for all types of learning options.

> Quest, like depth, can be interpreted as a form of independent study. At my own school it meant that a student could break away from the curriculum altogether for the purpose of studying a subject of particular interest to him and yet still justifiable within the broadest context of the area in which he was studying (science, social studies, etc.). The extent to which this option is made available by the instructor depends largely upon the teacher's philosophy as to what is a "justifiable" topic for study. My own team's philosophy on this point was a liberal one. In our world history course it was not at all unusual for a student to approach one of us after his completion of a LAP, let us say on the Ancient World, and to request permission to study Buddhism or even the problems of the inner city for a quarter. Since either request would seem to be within the boundaries of appropriateness for social studies, it would be most assuredly granted. It might be decided also that the student would meet with an instructor on a weekly basis to guide his study and that the student need not attend class during the period under consideration (although teachers differed on this latter issue considerably). The point to be made is that quest, if properly handled, can be a most effective means for individualizing instruction in terms of the different needs, abilities, and interests of students. (p. 4)

A second example of quest can be observed in physical education programs. For most people, physical education is a large group activity. In the independent study school, students were encouraged to select an individually tailored course of study from any area of physical activity. These options ranged from physical fitness to basketball. Interestingly, even before the recent move toward equality of the sexes, physical education in this school was coeducational except where injury could be expected. Students could use any of the numerous types of equipment and all of the facilities. The basic requirement was that each student develop an individual learning system—objectives, activities, and an evaluation plan including assessment criteria. Our classroom visitor would have been quite amazed at the difference between her experiences and those of the students in this P.E. quest program.

A second term that requires definition is *individualized instruction*. We prefer a concise, descriptive approach to the definition of *individualized instruction*. Individualized instruction is the process that permits an individual student, possibly in consultation with an instructor, to select how he will pursue a given learning goal.

The various ways that curriculum goals and instructional methods are selected can be displayed on a 2 by 2 matrix. Four options are possible. Option A (the most individualized) assigns both the responsibility for goal selection and methodology to the student. There are two mixed combinations. In Option B, the student selects goals, and the teacher selects instructional methods. In Option C the teacher selects goals, and the student selects instructional methods. Option D is the traditional pattern where the teacher retains control over both the curriculum and instructional processes.

Curriculum goals

	student selected (independent study)	teacher selected
Student selected (individualized instruction)	A	C
instructional methods teacher selected	B	D

Types of Individualized Instruction

What are the possible ways that instructional methods can be individualized in a classroom? We shall discuss four options available to special education instructors: (a) varying the pace; that is, permitting the students to decide how fast or slowly they learn, (b) providing content options, (c) developing alternative approaches on the basis of difficulty level, and (d) creating learning style options.

Pace options.   Many definitions of individualized instruction refer only to the variation of pace (Blake & McPherson, 1973). This is because there are many sophisticated self-pacing systems available to instructors. These student-controlled pacing systems, if maintained with integrity and efficiency, require a rigorous system of assessment and record-keeping. Self-pacing systems are normally found in schools with flexible grade-level placement policies. Schools with a philosophy of ungraded classes and a commitment to individualization almost invariably use self-pacing options.

As special educators confront the instructional changes mandated by new federal law, it is impossible to escape the conclusion that self-paced programming is a necessity. Other types of individualized instruction will also be desirable features of new programs, but self-pacing is inherent in the IEP concept. (See the discussion of the IEP in Chapter 2.)

Instructors and school officials who are experienced in the design and implementation of self-pacing instruction and who advocate its use claim it has a number of advantages for both the child and the teacher in contrast to traditional instruction.

For the Child:
1. It enables him to proceed at his own pace through the study of each subject.
2. There is a one-to-one relationship between him and the subject he is studying.
3. It permits him to get an immediate response to his answers; immediate satisfaction is gained.
4. It enables him to understand better the structure of the subject he is studying.
5. It enables him to study in greater depth those aspects of the subject which diagnostic tests indicate he needs, and to move with greater speed on those materials with which he is more familiar.
6. Instruction is nongraded; each child can proceed in a subject as far as his ability will permit.

For the Teacher:
1. It frees the teacher from teaching many of the routine basic skills of a subject.
2. It enables him to meet more accurately the instructional needs of each child.
3. It furnishes him with diagnostic devices.
4. It allows him to spend more time with students who need the most help.
5. It enables him to bring a structured, carefully thought out program to his pupils.
6. It brings about a higher degree of job satisfaction.

7. It helps the teacher to serve not only as a lecturer but also as a guide to the pupil in his efforts to increase his knowledge of a given subject. (Blake & McPherson, 1973, pp. 13–14)

Content options. Adams (1972) describes a less common concept of individualized instruction—content individualization. With this option, students study different content under the same basic study topic. The material shown below is taken from a curriculum unit titled *justice* written by a secondary English team. It is part of a language arts unit. The teachers analyzed the concept "justice" into a series of themes, stated in the form of questions. Under each theme several assignments were conceived.

LITERATURE OPTION #1
Theme: What is justice? How does it affect each of us?
Selected Movie: *People First* (introduces several handicapped children)
Group chart story about what justice is to each of us. Student-generated play on justice.

LITERATURE OPTION #2
Theme: What is due process of law? What happens when due process of law is not granted or not carried out? How does it affect you in schools?
Role Play Activity: Student has been dismissed from school with no warning or reason given.
Due Process Booklet: Students will identify school-related situations that involve due process and create a booklet to distribute to other classes.
Small Group Discussion: P.L. 94-142, Section 504 regulations.

LITERATURE OPTION #3
Theme: What is prejudice? How does it affect you?
Personal Experience Sharing: Each student will share a situation in which they or someone they know has been a victim of prejudice.
Selected Movie: *Jackie Robinson Story*.
Selection from: *Autobiography of Miss Jane Pittman*.
Student stories of prejudice that affects their lives.

This format enables students to create movies, stories, or plays as well as use material provided by the teacher.

Level of difficulty options. Some subject areas, especially those subjects where reading skill is needed for subject mastery, are particularly suited to individualizing by establishing alternative tracks according to difficulty. In schools where mildly retarded youngsters are placed in least restrictive environments, there is no reason why these children require a separate curriculum or placement in segregated classes. A more appropriate strategy is to modify instructional materials to match each child's cognitive entry characteristics. As Bloom (1976) maintains, almost all children can fulfill objectives if the instruction is consistent with their level of ability and achievement. In language arts or social studies, alternative reading selections will be necessary. For example, while studying the concept of "totalitarianism" in political science, some children could read statements of philosophy written by political leaders; others could read what ordinary people observed and heard and experienced while living in a totalitarian state; still other children might read a selection from Orwell's *Animal Farm* (1946). In each case, the learning goal is identical; the options provide an opportunity, through varying levels of reading difficulty, to meet the needs of individual children.

Learning style options.   As we focus directly on "how" each person prefers to learn, another set of individualizing options surfaces. These are described as "learning styles." The first subset involves the medium of instruction. The two most common media in use in classroom instruction are face-to-face-interaction and learning through printed materials such as books and worksheets. These commonly used media provide a useful example of how learning style options increase learning output. Some students prefer interactive instruction. They enjoy listening and responding to the teacher and other students. Others prefer interacting with printed materials—reading, worksheets, programmed learning. When filmstrips and film loops are added as additional options, another learning style is recognized. Adding sound to visual presentations in the form of slide-tape presentations or films provides still another option. It seems self-evident that when children are encouraged to select from alternative presentations—interactive, print, oral, visual, tactile— their attitude may be influenced positively. Consequently, their motivation, attention, and perseverance may increase. The result is predictable: a greater acquisition of additional subject matter.

The same analysis can be made with a second subset of learning style options, those that involve grouping and interaction patterns. Some students prefer to remain inconspicuous and learn as a member of a large group. Others opt for more interaction and activity as a member of a small group. Still others prefer learning from materials in individual study or in a tutorial session with a peer or teacher.

The final subset of learning style options fit the general rubric of *structure*. Some students prefer learning in small increments, with frequent feedback and reward or correction. This kind of students often pop up in front of the teacher with questions or work to show the teacher. Other students prefer less close supervision and more freedom to develop ideas and investigate alternatives. Those students are uncomfortable with programmed learning methods that break learning tasks down into small, incremental units. They prefer divergent or problem-solving activities that let them structure the task themselves.

Creating a Climate for Individualizing Learning

Selecting and implementing learning activities that make individualized learning possible are the technical aspects of teaching. The realization of the goals of this instructional view will be fulfilled only when the classroom climate fosters a spirit for learning. What are the elements which comprise this spirit? Certainly an atmosphere where learning is expected and appreciated by an involved teacher is necessary. In a classroom where rigid discipline, tension, anger, apathy, and boredom abound, individualized learning—learning in general—will be severely limited. On the other hand, in a classroom where the teacher consistently shows respect for each individual child, where rules are clearly defined and consistently applied and protect the rights of children, where openness is valued, individualized learning is enhanced. We believe that involving children in establishing rules helps them understand the need for rules. In addition, the children can help decide what consequences will occur when the rules are broken.

The relationship that develops between a teacher and the students is a powerful tool—it can contribute to or detract from learning, however. All children want to learn, to succeed, to please others, especially adults whom they respect and value. The teacher's ability to develop an initial sense of trust from the students will put him on the path to success. Once children trust the teacher, they are more able to take risks, to try; in short, they are more able to learn, and thus a "spirit for learning" evolves.

This essential element in the instructional process can be translated into specific guidelines. We hope they will assist you in individualizing instruction within a climate that fosters a "spirit for learning."

1. *Individualized instruction is a strategy that requires creativity, planning, communication, and evaluation on the part of the teacher and other supportive staff in the school.* This is probably the most difficult but necessary part of achieving a successful individualized program of instruction. These instructional experi-

ences are not available in the teacher's guide from the basal reading series, nor can they be purchased from a commercial materials catalogue. Individualized instruction programs are the result of the teacher's and other colleagues hard work. The quality of the program is a direct result of the thought and effort that goes into the program. Learner interests, strengths, weaknesses, and previous history are the data from which such programs are derived. There is no short-cut to quality education. However, putting time and effort into individualizing instruction can yield benefits to both the child and the teacher.

2. *Individualized learning tasks must be prescribed for children.* In order for the processes of acquisition, transformation, and evaluation to occur and result in optimum learning, each task must be appropriate for the child's developmental level. Through observation and formal and informal assessment the teacher can devise tasks that encourage a match between the activities and the child's developing structures.

3. *Individualized instruction requires continual modification of objectives.* As children progress through activities and master new material, additional objectives must be developed to keep the child an actively involved learner. "More of the same" leads to boredom.

4. *The teacher is the facilitator of learning, rather than the giver of all knowledge.* The physical and human environment can provide rich resources for the learner. Thus the teacher's role is one of guiding the learner through experiences and tasks, helping the child question and clarify when necessary. In addition, the teacher is responsible for facilitating social as well as academic learning. Pairing a quiet student to serve as tutor with a more out-going student can encourage a social interaction that might not occur on its own.

5. *The teacher is a powerful model in both academic and social learning.* The use of modeling as a teaching strategy has been effectively employed in many levels of classroom instruction. The teacher models the kind of behavior she expects from children in the classroom. The teacher models interest, concern, and problem-solving skills that are necessary for classroom success. The manner in which the teacher respects individual differences, responds to individual student needs, tolerates frustration, and accepts her own errors provides the model to be emulated by children. The importance of the teacher as model places enormous responsibilities on her. She can't say to the children, "Do as I say, not as I do," and expect them to follow that advice. Whether

we like it or not, children will copy our behavior. The quality of the model depends upon each teacher.

6. *Individualized instruction means planning, implementing, evaluating, and if necessary, going back to the drawing board.* We have advocated a systems approach to instruction. Implicit in this perspective is the need to assess the child's progress; instructional decisions must be made on the basis of the data. For example, if a mildly retarded child has been using a basal reading series for one year and has made little progress, perhaps another "method" is required. What about trying "Words in Color," "DISTAR," "programmed reading"? Individualization requires matching characteristics of the learner to particular characteristics of a method most suited to him. The assumption that the child can and will learn when offered materials that foster learning is the guiding principle underlying the notion of individualized instruction.

7. *Individualized instruction is facilitated by seating and desk arrangements.* We need not dwell on the inappropriateness of bolted-down desks and row seating to the implementation of individualized instruction. Musgrave (1975) has provided an illustrated analysis of seating arrangements. His numerous seating options are summarized here. We have added additional possibilities.

1. Whole group formation (children seated in a large circle);
2. Round table discussion (children seated in rows around a table);
3. Small group discussion (children seated in groups of four or six);
4. Individual work formation (children's desks placed together to form a large rectangle);
5. Interest stations (instructional centers placed in the classroom for short periods of time);
6. Interest centers (materials available for long periods of time for children to use at their leisure);
7. Whole class debate (two groups of two parallel rows, facing each other);
8. Simultaneous combination (round table discussion, small group discussion, interest stations, and interest centers);
9. Individual selection (child chooses a quiet place in the classroom).

Conclusion

This chapter has presented several principles for selecting and implementing learning activities. In addition to the purposes of learning activities—acquisition, transformation, and evaluation—the "principle of the match" is the guide an instructor should use to select activities. The implementation of activities is governed by the principles of active learning, variety, practice, feedback, and reinforcement.

The concept of individualized learning can involve either independent study or individualized instruction. Individualized instruction can be accomplished by varying the pace of instruction and providing content options, level of difficulty alternatives, and alternatives based on student learning styles. Finally, a set of principles for establishing a "spirit of learning" to support an individualized learning system were presented.

We have mentioned within this chapter that certain activities are inherently enjoyable and fun. We believe that learning, while difficult at times, is fun when it parallels the child's natural curiosity and interests. Have you ever watched a group of children playing baseball? Have you noticed the intensity with which they are involved? There seems to be no limit to their organizational skills in games. They try their best to perform at the level expected by their peers. There is no question that in games group achievement is valued, but the emphasis is still on the individual. Players are valued for different reasons—some for their speed, others for their throwing arm, still others because they hit for power or a high average. Very rarely does one youngster perform all these activities equally well. The basic requirement is to give to your all and encourage your teammates.

To an observer, the pleasure children have while participating in a game of their choice is obvious in their faces, comments, enthusiasm, and the length of time they are involved in the game. Game players appear to value the actual playing (the process) as much as the final score (the product). Of course, they prefer to win, but losing is tolerated until next time.

We believe that classroom activities can be like these games. They can foster and stimulate children's interests and involvement; carefully selected activities can be as much fun for children as those they choose themselves. That is the real challenge that confronts the teacher in selecting and implementing activities that elicit positive, enthusiastic responses from the children while helping them to be independent, productive citizens.

REFERENCES

Adams, D. *Providing curricular options: A teacher's view of the learning activity package.* Iowa City: Westinghouse Learning Corporation, 1972, 4 (4).

Blake, H., & McPherson, A. Individualized instruction—Where are we?" In J. E. Duane (Ed.), *Individualized instruction: Programs and materials.* Englewood Cliffs, N.J.: Educational Technology Publications, 1973.

Bloom, B. S. *Human characteristics and school learning.* New York: McGraw-Hill, 1976.

Bruner, J. *The process of education.* Cambridge: Harvard University Press, 1961.

Dewey, J. Education as growth (1938). Cited in C. Silberman (Ed.), *The open classroom reader.* New York: Random House, 1973.

Engelmann, S., & Bruner, E. C. *DISTAR: An instructional system for reading instruction.* Chicago: Science Research Associates, 1969.

Heinich, R. *Technology and the management of instruction.* Washington: AECT, 1970.

Joyce, J., & Weil, M. *Models of teaching.* Englewood Cliffs, N.J.: Prentice-Hall, 1972.

Kirk, S. *Educating exceptional children* (2nd ed.). Boston: Houghton Mifflin, 1972.

Klein, N., & Safford, P. Application of Piaget's theory to the study of the thinking of the mentally retarded: A review of research. *Journal of Special Education,* 1977, *2,* 101–115.

Kohlberg, L. Early education: A cognitive-developmental view. *Child Development,* 1968, *39,* 1013–1062.

Montessori, M. *The Montessori method.* Cambridge, Mass.: Robert Bentley, 1965.

Orwell, G. *Animal farm.* New York: Harcourt, Brace, 1946.

Musgrave, G. R. *Individualized instruction: Teaching strategies focusing on the learner.* Boston: Allyn & Bacon, 1975.

Warner, S. A. *Teacher.* New York: Simon & Schuster, 1963.

Classroom evaluation

Imagine yourself as a first year-teacher about to meet parents across the table for the first time to discuss their child's progress in your class. Consider the thoughts that might rush through your mind, increasing your nervousness and anxiety. Do I look all right? Will I project confidence and control? Can I be articulate while under pressure? Will I get across my desire to be a good teacher? To be helpful to my students? Can I establish a good working relationship with each parent? As the thoughts come and go, one set of questions gives you the greatest concern. Have I evaluated the child fairly and appropriately? Can I provide evidence to support my conclusions? Am I sure that it was the child's performance being assessed, or was it the quality of my instruction? What should I tell the parents? Will they be angry with me or with their child?

Teachers are generally uneasy about evaluating students. Consequently, it is predictable that a teacher's concerns about evaluation and grading predominate when it's time to report to parents. What is surprising is the extent to which misunderstanding of the nature and functions of evaluation has exaggerated the problem. When anyone involved—teacher, student, or parent—has a different concept of evaluation from the others, the result is often bad feelings, loss of confidence, and ultimately student learning failure. To prevent this, an instructor should establish an evaluation process that can be defended. This process requires the teacher to understand the concept of evaluation and apply a set of established principles to reduce judgment errors. This precise evaluation process must then be communicated to both students and their parents so that all parties concerned are fully informed about the criteria the teacher is using.

Concept of Evaluation

What precisely is evaluation? How does evaluation differ from the process of assessment we discussed in Chapter 2? You may recall that we defined assessment as the "determination of the aptitudes, skills, and competencies an individual possesses." A wise instructor looks for information on students' ability and performance during all stages of a task-related instructional sequence. Still, assessment information is indispensible at two critical periods in an instructional sequence: (a) prior to instruction, to assess a learner's entry level and (b) after instruction, to assess how much the student has learned and the quality of instruction. Again, we assess to gain data for two purposes. First, the data will be used to identify and place learners who are expected to benefit from special education. Second, the data are useful as the basis for programming decisions. These decisions result from judgments as to whether a particular student has mastered a particular task and whether instruction was successful.

Educational evaluation is a *judgment concerning a learner's potential or achievement in preparation for educational decision-making*. Figure 8–1 shows how evaluation relates to special education.

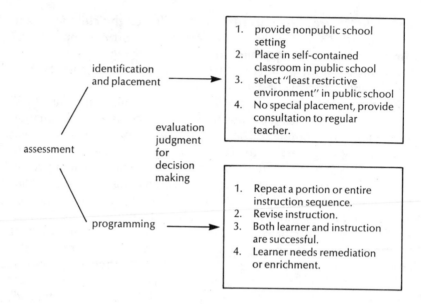

Figure 8–1 *The process of educational evaluation as it relates to special education*

As shown in Figure 8–1, a placement evaluation has several possible results. For instance, a particular mildly retarded student might be learning math concepts as expected and thus be placed in a regular classroom, or a student in a regular classroom might benefit from remedial assistance from a resource room or itinerant teacher. In the programming arena, a number of options are possible also. Assessment information might reveal that a particular student is having difficulty in performing a particular motor skill. The decision might be to repeat the instructional sequence with additional feedback and instructor encouragement. Or the decision might be to teach the skill beginning at a lower level of difficulty.

Evaluations occur so frequently in our daily lives that we are often unaware of their frequency. Words such as *like–dislike, good–bad, fair–unfair,* and *beautiful–ugly* are examples of common evaluative comparisons. In most evaluations, there is an inherent emotional response to whatever is being evaluated. This emotional response forms a part of the data used to form the judgment. On many occasions, the emotional reaction is the most significant factor in the response. In most situations, that is quite appropriate. You see a painting and decide to buy it. Assuming price is irrelevant, the emotional reaction is the basis for decision making. You do not need to defend a personal decision like that.

In educational evaluation, emotional responses must be recognized and controlled. There is no way they can be avoided. Most teachers prefer attentive, neat, attractive, polite, middle-class children. They prefer quiet, reflective, docile youngsters rather than loud, impulsive, aggressive ones. If teachers let their emotional responses form the basis for educational evaluation, they could be rightfully accused of arbitrariness and discrimination. Obviously, when a teacher reports to parents concerning their child's school performance, overly subjective judgments are inappropriate.

Parents of school children have the right to expect teachers to make skilled evaluations that they can defend with experience and reasoning. Parents should not expect teachers to be correct in *every* evaluation, but every judgment must reflect an analysis of student performance. The teacher should be able to explain the decision in concise, clear language. Furthermore, the decision must be justified with appropriate reasoning and supportive evidence.

The Role of Objectives in Evaluation

Within a systems approach to instruction, evaluation is the final stage in an instructional design. A systems approach requires *purpose, integration, feedback,* and provision for *redesign.* The evaluation stage permits the designer to determine whether a learner has achieved one or more of the prescribed instructional objectives. It is this pivotal assessment that supports the judgment and decision-making phases of evaluation. Before we discuss evaluation as a design stage, we should examine the relationship between instructional objectives and evaluation. You may recall the meeting with parents that introduced Chapter 6 on writing useful objectives. In the second, preferred version, Jackson shared with parents her "Getting a Job" unit. She told parents, "When the unit is completed in 2 weeks, each student will be able to

1. Locate want ads in the newspaper;
2. Select jobs most suited to his or her needs, experience, training, and ability;
3. Write a letter of inquiry correctly;
4. Conduct a phone and personal interview properly."

If teachers use this approach in writing clear objectives, creating evaluation procedures becomes less burdensome. The evaluation procedures are more closely related to both the predetermined objectives and the learning activities. Consider the four objectives in the "Getting a Job" unit. Since the objectives are so clear, it is easy to generate evaluation procedures. For example, suppose the objective for a student is that the student will write a letter of inquiry correctly. During the teaching process, all of the elements of such a letter must be clearly specified, then taught. These would include an accurate and appropriate heading, the correct salutation, clearly stated questions directed toward the information sought, an address for sending a response, and the appropriate closing. Such specificity allows evaluation to be directed to appropriate sections of a multi-faceted task.

Without clear objectives, evaluation cannot be used to identify any weaknesses of the instruction. Thus the instructor can never be sure whether the student failed because he did not study or because the lesson was poorly designed. For the evaluation to work as a monitor, the instructional objectives must accurately describe what the student is expected to know or do when instruction is completed. Cloudy or confusing objectives produce inaccurate, often useless evaluation decisions.

A Climate for Evaluation

The climate in which an evaluation is conducted can enhance or detract from its full value. For example, if evaluation procedures are misused, the students may see them as punishment. If the teacher responds to a student's misbehavior with the retort "Keep it up! We'll see how much you don't know when you take the spelling test tomorrow," then the spelling test becomes a punishment for improper behavior. It is important that the teacher be aware of the ways evaluation can be used as a threat or punishment for some students. Certainly, the threat of punishment diminishes the objectivity in well-conceived evaluation.

Proper use of evaluation, on the other hand, results in valuable information for both teacher and student. For the teacher, it provides feedback on the benefits of instruction for individual learners. If a student has not mastered a skill or concept, valid evaluation techniques will tell the teacher. By the same token, the student also benefits from systematic evaluation. Valid evaluation instruments show the students those areas where they have mastered skills and those areas in which they still need practice. From this perspective, "tests" are not punishment, but rather a source of helpful information. The established class climate influences the message the student receives.

Evaluation and Measurement

Although evaluation is defined as a judgment, most people include the idea of *measurement* in their concept of evaluation. Before any judgment is made, the teacher must determine how he or she is going to measure whatever is to be evaluated. Measurement can be defined as a *systematic procedure used to obtain information that will be used to describe and/or predict behavior.* Measurement procedures are often equated with tests, but it is more useful to consider a test an instrument used to assess achievement (performance in response to objectives) or aptitude (general ability).

Again, tests can either be standardized by a commercial testing company or teacher-made. Whether commercial or teacher-made, most tests are formal, in the sense that a special environment or set of conditions are present during the testing period. Informal tests such as checklists and rating scales are less common. In addition, other checklists, rating scales, and anecdotal records are useful as unobtrusive observation tools. Finally, there are self-reporting instruments that let youngsters assess their own behavior. Questionnaires are also useful as reporting instruments. For a further discussion of different types of assessment instruments, refer to Chapter 2. Children vary; thus evaluation procedures should include a variety of methods to accommodate these differences.

In educational controversies centering on evaluation (for instance, the debate over the meaning of IQ scores), the issue is often whether the measurement instrument or procedure that undergirds the evaluation is defensible. Defensible measurement procedures follow established principles. These principles can be grouped within two general categories. The first of these is validity. A measurement procedure has validity *if it actually measures what it promises to measure.* To understand the concept of validity, interpret the following imaginary dialogue.

Headwaiter:	Bill, we have a problem, you and me!
Bill:	What kind of problem?
Headwaiter:	You're fired for incompetence.
Bill:	What! Why am I fired? I'm very reliable, here 10 minutes early, haven't missed a day of work. I break fewer dishes and spoil less food than anyone on the floor.
Headwaiter:	All that's true, but you also can't be trusted to get an order correct. Just 5

minutes ago a customer angrily claimed
he requested the diet lunch and you
served him macaroni and cheese with an
extra rich malt. If you can't provide the
right recipe for a customer, I don't care
how reliable you are.

Teachers have to select the "right measurement recipe" to assess
their objectives. A teacher can neither describe a student's past performance nor predict future performance if the measurement procedures do not test the subject matter or the learning process
prescribed in the instructional objectives. The term *content validity*
describes the need to assess the appropriate content. Common sense
dictates the knowledge taught should be the knowledge tested. Yet
many teachers include a couple of questions on content not included in the unit to reward those who learn on their own. It can
be difficult to convince them of the principle of testing only what
you taught.

Construct validity refers to the need to assess the learning process
described in the instructional objectives. As you recall from Chapter
5, learning can be subdivided into a number of categories. The par-

ticular categories depend on the conception of learning the teacher selects to use. To illustrate the principle of construct validity, consider this dialogue.

Teacher: I can't understand why you are complaining about the spelling test. I told you to learn those words.

Student: But in class we used the new words in sentences. We developed paragraphs using as many of the words as possible. I assumed we would be asked to do that with different sentences on the test. How come you required us to define each word exactly the way you wrote the definition on the board? You didn't tell us that was important? I just don't think it's fair! I really knew those words!

It appears that this teacher has a construct validity problem. The learning activities in class were at the application level; the test required strictly memory. That teacher might be quite embarrassed if he were required to defend that test to someone knowledgeable in measurement techniques.

One useful way to reduce content and construct validity errors is to use a table of specifications in constructing a test. A table of specifications (see Table 8–1) relates content and the learning processes described in the instructional objectives to insure that the correct proportion of content and learning levels is included in the test. In the table, the numbers refer to the portion of the test to be allocated to a particular combination of content and process. For example, the teacher decided to organize the test so that 10% of the total test would relate to the objective "students will be able to recall the various services performed by banks." Another cell of the table indicates that 5% of the test ought to be reflected by one or more items at the complex cognitive level related to the "advantages of banking." Specifically, one item was selected—"Explain to a friend why banks are a better place to store your money than is a mattress. Give at least three reasons."

You might ask how the percentages are selected. There is no hard-and-fast answer except that the percentages should reflect the time the student is expected to spend in learning the particular objectives. This time would reflect both in-class and out-of-class

Content	Memorization (recall of specifics, computation skill)	Complex cognitive (classifying, explaining, problem solving)	Total
Banking services	10	20	30
Advantages of banking	10	5	15
Opening and maintaining a savings account	15	5	20
Kinds of savings accounts and plans	5	5	10
Writing a personal check	10		10
Balancing a checking account	15		15
Total %	65%	35%	100%

Table 8–1   *Table of specifications—Using banking services wisely*

activity. The teacher too should spend the most time teaching those objectives that are most highly valued.

The second measurement concept that must be considered in evaluation is *reliability*. Where validity concerns "truthfulness," reliability protects "accuracy." Accuracy is closely related to consistency. A consistent procedure will generate similar results each time it is used. As a result, teachers can place their faith in the accuracy of the procedure. Remember that the goal in educational evaluation is to make judgments about student ability, performance, or the quality of instruction in order to make decisions. Keeping in mind the concept of reliability, teachers might wish to establish a set of rules for themselves. First, since they are going to measure student learning in response to instruction, a pretest is always desirable. The pretest will indicate what students know or are able to do before instruction begins. They will learn if any students have mastered the objectives; if so, it would be inappropriate to teach those students what they already know. And some students may not have learned the prerequisite concepts or skills that would permit them to begin instruction with any hope for success. Remedial work may be needed. In either case, the pretest will reduce reliability errors by more accurately assessing the real growth that directly comes from the instruction.

A second principle involved with reliability cautions teachers to carefully examine the instructional objective to be assessed. In the case of a complex objective, more than one evaluation procedure may be required. If only one procedure is used, the results may not be consistent with the results obtained by a different procedure. Let us examine a particular case. Assume an instructor had the following problem-solving objective.

> Students will be able to select an appropriate banking service that fits their needs and actually follow through to take advantage of it.

One procedure to assess the objective might require the student to "establish a savings or checking account." But analyzing the objective shows that one dimension is not assessed by that procedure, that being the selection of a banking service that fits the student's need. A second procedure could be created to meet that need. The teacher might invent a series of situations, each of which suggests a different banking service. When required to respond, each student would then select an appropriate service and justify the selection. Thus two assessment procedures would provide greater reliability than either one alone.

Multiple assessments have a second advantage. Two or more different assessments provide extra insight into student performance. A written test provides information on student knowledge, ability to work under the pressures of time, and ability to understand and manipulate verbal or mathematical language. A written test tends to reward students who have breadth of knowledge, not necessarily in any great depth. On the other hand, a student-created product spreads out the time pressure and permits the student to respond to the objective in ways that can compensate for language difficulties. The student-created product rewards such traits as creativity, organization, patience, and diligence. It rewards a student who seeks depth of knowledge in a way that a written test often does not. Viewing the two assessments, written testing and student products, in tandem, it is apparent that they complement each other by sampling different traits and abilities. As a result, the assessment will be more reliable.

Just as instruction must be individualized, evaluation procedures should be chosen to fit each learner. Some students prefer precise written evaluations. Others like the opportunity to respond out loud.

Still others perform more effectively on projects or other application measures.

There are also other useful approaches to multiple assessments. Instead of using different types of assessment procedures, the same type can be used repeatedly. For example, in the banking service unit, role playing teller and customer roles might be both the entry level pretest and the posttest exercise. The student's growth in knowledge of banking procedures and services could then be assessed. In addition, since learning activities would provide practice in the same tasks, we have created a set of multiple assessments for our banking service unit.

Still a third way to view multiple assessments involves the concept of informal and formal testing. Many school objectives are reality-based. That is, the teacher expects the student to transfer his learning from the controlled environment of the formal testing situation to behavior that is unregulated.

One of the authors has been an evaluator for a nationally disseminated social studies curriculum project whose purpose is to reduce the incidence of adolescent disruptive behavior. How could that goal be evaluated? Within the controlled class environment, cognitive tests are used to determine if the students who have studied the curriculum can apply the concepts in the program to solve simulated problems. The teacher is also expected to monitor in-class student grades and behavior. Yet in both cases, students are more or less aware that they are expected to perform in a prescribed manner. The most informal measure of the project's success in reducing disruptive behavior would be to monitor out-of-class behavior. To accomplish this, all the discipline referrals in the school are examined to compare pretreatment and posttreatment effects. Grades in all subject areas are also compared. Finally, a class not

most controlled				most natural
objective and essay exams	student performance or products exhibited in controlled environment	unobtrusive observation in controlled environment (checklists, self-reports, rating scales)	out-of-school assignments and activities (homework, projects, student logs and diaries)	unobtrusive measures in an uncontrolled environment (observation in the community, lunch room reports, discipline referrals, parent conferences)

exposed to the curriculum treatment is compared to one that has experienced it.

From this example, a controlled environment–natural environment continuum for evaluation can be constructed. In many situations behaviors observed in formal or controlled testing situations will also be present when the learner is on his own.

Alternative Evaluation Constructs

In the traditional pattern, the teacher assumes full responsibility to conduct all evaluations. Alternative systems relieve the teacher of full responsibility. One of these alternatives is best described as *peer evaluation*. In peer evaluation, one student or a group of students make evaluation judgments concerning the ability or performance of classmates. Consequently, students develop their own evaluative skills and a sense of responsibility, and have experience in giving and receiving critical feedback. For example, two students may take turns spelling words for each other, interactively or by using a tape recorder. This procedure would be agreed upon by both students involved, in consultation with the teacher; the students would be responsible for conducting and recording the evaluation data.

Bill provides Jim with peer evaluation and support.

Peer evaluation is also useful for small group projects. In this instance, students have specific responsibilities for given tasks in a small group; group members develop an evaluation instrument and evaluate the performance of their peers on the specified criteria. It is important that the teacher help the students develop fair criteria for process as well as for content considerations.

Peer evaluation may take the form of class meetings. Here students give each other feedback on specific behavior objectives that have been identified previously by the students and teacher. This format is especially valuable for social skills. At least initially, the teacher must set up ground rules to prevent some students from getting picked on. For example, one rule might be to share positive things first. Then one student may share a negative comment, but the group has to suggest ways to help the child improve before the next negative comment may be shared.

Peer evaluation is also an effective mechanism to evaluate the teacher. A group of students might be instructed to select criteria for evaluating a given lesson, for conducting a project, or for any other task the students and teacher agree upon. The teacher must willingly open up for student feedback and criticism, but the procedure can yield vital information. Teachers evaluate students all the time, and students evaluate teachers (at least behind their backs). We think teacher evaluation is best brought "out of the closet." If teachers allow students to evaluate them, they model the kind of behavior they expect students to exhibit when they are evaluated. Clearly this is a possibly threatening, nontraditional view of evaluation. However, there are enormous potential benefits to those teachers who are willing to take the risk and teach their students to be critical evaluators of others as well as themselves.

That leads to another option for evaluation—*self-evaluation*. Again, traditional procedures rarely include an opportunity for students to evaluate themselves. Certainly self-evaluation is a critical skill in much of adult life. We must evaluate our performance on the job, in personal relationships, as citizens, and as consumers. Students *can* learn critical and valid self-evaluation. Having students rate their performance and compare their ratings with those of their peers and teachers is one possibility. Students can rate their performances in a skill area (using an objective scale developed along with the teacher) and compare that rating with their performance on an objective test. This format helps the students to know their own skills and evaluate their performance realistically. While students should not underestimate their strengths and abilities, they also should not overestimate their performance levels.

As Gwen evaluates her own work, she discovers it is all correct.

There is one final source of evaluation information that can be a valuable resource to both teacher and student—the *parent*. Objective evaluation can be an aid in the process of communication between parents and teachers. Parents are also a source of information. For example, the parent can tell the teacher how the child does her homework. Does she need constant attention and help, or does she do it independently? Is the math homework more of a problem than projects the child is assigned? What other observations has the parent made that would help the teacher teach that child? Remember, the more data the teacher collects, the better able he or she is to meet the varying needs of the children in the classroom.

One final perspective on evaluation should be discussed. Teachers may wish to evaluate the *process* of education as well as its content. Process is the various ways that teachers, other adults, and students interact within the school. Some instructors consciously develop instructional objectives that assess on-going process in order to improve the instructional climate. In that event, evaluation of those objectives should not be neglected. Even when no particular objective is written, process evaluation can provide information that can improve the learning environment for all content objectives.

A last word concerning process evaluation relates to the role of the observer who may be asked to participate in data gathering.

Teachers may find it helpful to ask other school personnel to assist in evaluating the process in their classroom. If so, it is essential that the teacher and the observer set up time for communication. The information the observer gains only has value if the teacher fully understands it and uses it to modify the classroom procedures. The teacher must trust the observer, decide without pressure to have the observer collect information, and accept the feedback openly and without being defensive. The observer should be someone for whom the teacher has respect and whose input he or she values. Otherwise the whole procedure is a waste of time for all concerned.

Unfortunately, teachers are not usually rewarded for asking for help. In fact, in many school systems, the teacher who does so is viewed as inadequate and incompetent. The culture of the school discourages teachers from self-scrutiny and self-evaluation. This prevailing practice inhibits or even prevents instructional improvement. To counter this negative attitude, a teacher must have both courage and a strong commitment to being a highly effective educator.

Process Evaluation Information

Process evaluation is much more difficult to conduct than content evaluation. It is not easy to design valid and reliable instruments or procedures that assess the process of learning. As we have suggested, process evaluation is best done through direct observation. An observation form will help clarify specific areas to be observed. Such considerations as the quality and duration of student interactions, the dependence of students on adults, the independence of students in completing tasks, the responses of students to adults, and the responses of adults to individual students are all relevant dimensions of process evaluation.

Student involvement with each other and the task may be determined by time-sampling. An observer can select a student and take measurements of that student's time on task, time on productive interactions, and time off-task. For example, some children may devote 2 minutes to a task, 5 minutes looking out the window, 3 minutes interrupting other students, and 10 minutes seeking help from other students or the teacher.

One of the most reliable methods for observing the instructional process is through the use of graphs. For example, a chart can be used to evaluate social behaviors. Cooper (1974) suggests that the teacher use squared graph paper and plot the frequency or duration

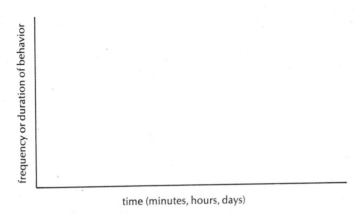

time (minutes, hours, days)

of a particular behavior along a vertical axis and the observation time on the horizontal axis.

The teacher then gathers baseline data that establish a level or amount of behavior during a given observation period. This procedure is used to determine accurately if a behavior is occurring to such an extent that intervention is necessary. Baseline data are usually recorded for a minimum of five sessions. For example, a teacher is concerned about a student who leaves his seat during directed math

Reading to a friend allows John to show off his progress.

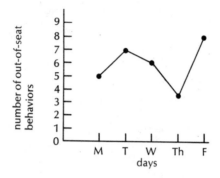

Figure 8–2   *A graphic representation of baseline information*

instruction. The teacher records the number of out-of-seat behaviors during math instruction for five consecutive days. The teacher verbally corrects the student when out-of-seat behavior occurs. The numbers of inappropriate out-of-seat behaviors are 5, 7, 6, 3, 9. Figure 8–2 graphs this information.

It is obvious that intervention is needed. The teacher has several options of intervention. In this case, the teacher decides to reinforce the student verbally for appropriate in-seat behaviors and to ignore out-of-seat behaviors. The intervention will extend for 5 more days. The results of the intervention indicate that out-of-seat behaviors decreased as a result of the intervention. The numbers of out-of-seat behaviors are 5, 3, 2, 0, 1. Figure 8–3 shows these data.

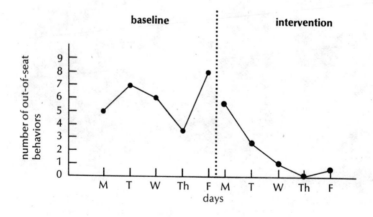

Figure 8–3   *A comparison of observations*

This is an excellent form of evaluation for the teacher because it clearly shows that the intervention strategy did change the student's behavior. This visual evaluation is clear to both student and teacher. In addition, the line graph format can easily be taught to students so that they can record their own behaviors—academic or social—and therefore become more competent self-evaluators. They can record and evaluate the times they come to school on time (or are tardy), the number of spelling words mastered, the number of math facts learned, or the number of assignments completed.

The line graph can be used to teach academic and social behaviors simultaneously. For example, a student may be tardy for class because of a difficulty with telling time. In order for the student to improve this behavior, a teacher might help the student graph his arrival time at school. The vertical axis indicates the time of day, and the horizontal axis relates the days of the week. Upon arrival in the classroom, the student reads the clock, finds this time on the graph, and marks the corresponding time. The student then checks the vertical line to see if he is on time or tardy. Figure 8–4 represents this procedure.

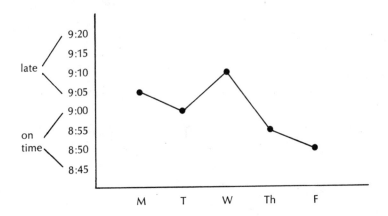

Figure 8–4   *Representation of on-time behaviors*

This graph displays to the student the times that he arrived in the classroom and shows that he was on time for 3 of the 5 days. Individual charts could be designed for several students with a particular color or shape assigned to each student. In this way, the teacher could easily discriminate who was on time, late, or absent.

A multiple-line graph can also be used to chart only academic progress. For example, Bob, Ray, and Jim are all 12 years old. They feel that their math skills are terrible and they only see the problems that the teacher marks as "wrong." The teacher is seeking a way to help them focus on their progress. He decides to design a multiple-line graph and assigns each student a separate symbol. Bob is a O (circle), Ray is a △ (triangle), and Jim is a □ (square). The teacher designs the chart so that each student can record the number of problems he computed correctly over a 2-week period. It is not important that the boys are working on different skills; the teacher is only interested in graphically communicating to each one that he is making progress on his own tasks. The boys are instructed to count the number of correct problems on their papers and to record this information on the chart. The results of this procedure are presented in Figure 8–5.

All three boys can see that they are making progress on a daily basis, even though the gains may be small. This also opens up new avenues for instruction and evaluation. The students could count the number of correct responses for a week and add them together

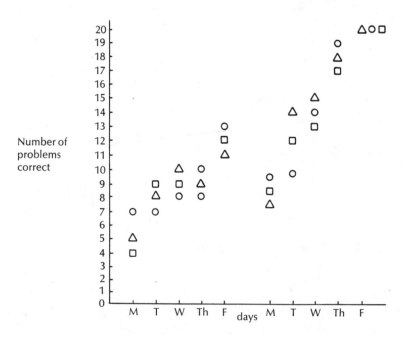

Figure 8–5   *Number of problems correctly computed by three students: Bob (O), Ray (△), Jim (□)*

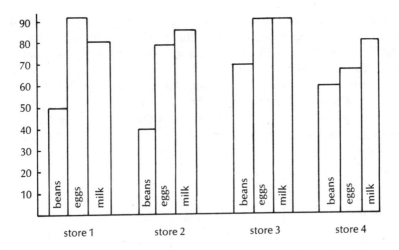

Figure 8–6   *A bar graph*

to get a total number. The concept of "average" score could be introduced, and the boys' division skills could be evaluated.

Another type of graph that can easily be used for evaluation is the bar graph. For example, in an instructional context students record the prices of foods after comparative shopping and then chart the rise (or fall) in prices over a monthly period. Figure 8–6 is a bar graph of comparative prices.

The bar graph provides a very clear picture of several pieces of information for comparative purposes. It is educationally relevant, especially in regard to functional life skills. It is easily designed, implemented, and understood by students.

The bar graph is also useful in evaluating a variety of behaviors—academic, social, and physical. The behaviors must be clearly stated, the criteria established, and the time specified. The teacher may decide which behaviors to graph, or the decision can be one arrived at by both teacher and student.

For example, suppose the teacher and student decide to graph time on-task, number of correct math problems, and time spent exercising. All three behaviors would be identified, criteria established, and recording procedures specified. The monitoring decision would then be made: Who will record the performance? This can be done by the student, a peer, adult observers or the teacher. In this case, the teacher and student have decided the student will do the recording. The teacher has provided the student with a clock and the graph in Figure 8–7 has been designed.

This same evaluation procedure can be implemented for the entire class for one or several specific performance variables. Each student's progress can be recorded in a different color so that the chart can be easily read.

The bar graph is particularly useful for monitoring individual progress toward objectives stated in the students' IEP's. As each student progresses, he can see his progress toward each goal. He can carry the chart to his various teachers, and take it home for his parents to see.

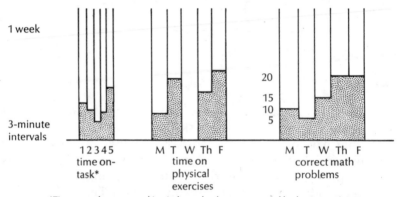

1 week

3-minute intervals

20
15
10
5

1 2 3 4 5	M T W Th F	M T W Th F
time on-	time on	correct math
task*	physical	problems
	exercises	

*Time on-task means working independently on money and budgeting project without disturbing another student.

Figure 8–7   *Multiple behavior graph*

Line and bar graphs are but two examples of systematic recording methods for evaluation of student progress. Teachers can create their own variations that fit the behavior, the content to be evaluated, the age of the child and his individual needs. A comprehensive and sophisticated description of usable procedures can be found in *Measurement and Analysis of Behavior Techniques* (Cooper, 1974).

Making the Evaluation Decision

Assuming a valid and reliable measurement procedure has been created or selected, how does the information get translated into a decision? Before instruction began, the teacher had to design a series of information-gathering assessments for *formative evaluation*. In formative evaluation, the teacher seeks information to use to adjust the instructional system while corrections are still possible. The pretest is a formative evaluation procedure. Other examples include quizzes and student and parent conferences. Input from process assessment is often very useful for formative evaluation. As a result of input from formative evaluation, an instructional treatment for a given learner can be altered in one of several ways: (a) an objective can be revised, (b) an activity can be repeated, (c) a substitute activity can be implemented, (d) more or less time can be allocated to instruction, or (e) the postinstructional assessment can be altered. In any case, formative evaluation permits the instructor to make changes in the instructional process while the changes can still affect final student performance.

In contrast to formative evaluation, formal tests and student products are often used for summative purposes. In *summative evaluation*, teachers seek information to determine the extent to which a learner has been successful in mastering one or more instructional objectives. When this is determined, the decision-making phase is used to decide what must be done. As was described earlier, these options include a decision to require the learner to repeat some portion of the instruction or to change the treatment by substituting, adding, or deleting learning activities. Hopefully, the decision would be to congratulate both the learner and the instructor for a job well done.

Evaluating Children with Special Needs in the Regular Classroom

One of the most controversial and perplexing problems for educators is how to evaluate the work of children with special needs who are students in regular classrooms. After social and adjustment problems have been addressed, the teacher still must make a judgment about and often assign a grade to individual students' academic performance.

The issue of evaluating retarded learners placed in regular classrooms is especially pressing when the student reaches junior and senior high school levels, since many elementary schools do not specify letter grades for performance. For example, Mr. Sanford teaches math in a junior high school. He has some knowledge of retarded students and has three special education students enrolled in his eighth grade business math course. After careful assessment, he finds that all three retarded students perform at the third grade level in arithmetic. Mr. Sanford plans individual work for these three students. The students feel valued in this class, are interested in the content, and attend class regularly. Their high level of motivation has helped them reach the mastery level on all the criterion-referenced measures Mr. Sanford designed and administered. However, it is report card time for his school system, and he is required to assign grades to all students.

Should Mr. Sanford assign grades to the retarded learners relative to their peers? If he does, none of the three will receive a grade higher than "D" because they are certainly not exhibiting the same eighth grade math skills as their class peers. On the other hand, a grade of "D" would not accurately reflect their level of performance relative to the teacher's expectations for them. In addition, that grade would only discourage these students from continuing their work. In fact, a grade of "D" might well lead to the students stopping work or not attending class. Given that traditional comparative evaluation procedures would be both inaccurate and unfair to some of the students in the class (Mr. Sanford realizes that not only his retarded students are affected), another method of evaluation must be sought. The use of class quizzes, graded on a bell-shaped curve, is clearly not appropriate for this group of students.

As an alternative, Mr. Sanford has decided to assign grades to the retarded students in relation to each student's progress, using the criterion-referenced tests that he designed as the basis for grading decisions. In this way the students know exactly what the grading criteria are. This procedure helps to maintain the student's motivation, a critical factor in learning. The teacher has chosen an instructional process that individualizes both instruction and evaluation. A consequence of this decision, Mr. Sanford realizes, is the potential reaction of his other students and parents to this nontraditional approach.

We believe that the establishment of performance criteria and student evaluation based on specified criteria is the most precise and most equitable method of evaluation. This evaluation procedure redirects attention from comparative to individualized evaluation. This departure from the established, long-entrenched normative methods currently in use in most public schools presents problems for students, parents, and college entrance requirements. But change in any arena is difficult to effect. Those who will be affected by the change must be fully informed and involved from the beginning. This implies, then, that students and their parents must participate in the evolution of new procedures for student evaluation. In addition, their advice, concerns, and views must be sought in order to develop a procedure that has the support and endorsement of the parents as well as the students themselves.

Enrolling retarded students in less restrictive environments such as regular classrooms, regular physical education classes, and similar mainstreamed educational settings will require that all educators take a fresh look at their evaluation practices. The issue of normative versus criterion-referenced evaluation is one area that clamors for attention. Another area which must be addressed is the actual reporting system used by both regular and special education personnel. What reporting options are available to educators?

Reporting Systems: The Report Card

It is not carved in any stone educational textbook that all children must receive the time-honored report card. Of course many parents and students want to maintain the traditional report card as a method of communicating student progress. If these report cards suffice for the majority of the school population, then they should not be abandoned for retarded learners. We are not rejecting the idea of the report card. We are, however, rejecting the traditional format for grading. To develop a fair, accurate recording system that truly reflects the performance of retarded learners in regular school classrooms, it will be necessary to design a new type of evaluation report. The teacher should design report cards that designate the skills accomplished that relate to the objectives stated in the IEP. It would be unreasonable for each student's card to contain all of his long- and short-term objectives. Thus, objectives listed on the card must be carefully chosen and reflect the focus of classroom activity for each grading period. The criteria for objectives are the basis for grading in the major areas. If the stated objectives are derived from the Functional Life Curriculum areas, then each student's objectives could be applied to these areas. An example of this report card can be seen in Figure 8–8.

This process of evaluation may at first appear to run counter to the more traditional methods. This method could be used as a supplement to traditional methods for all students. It promises that the needs of the retarded learners, the needs of their regular classroom peers, and the needs of their teachers could be met in an appropriate and judicious way. Evaluation of individual students would be reported in a flexible, yet accurate manner. Teachers would be more motivated to individualize instruction and evaluation. In this

Classroom Evaluation

Name _____

Home Room Teacher _____

Teachers Responsible for Evaluation   Subject Area

1. _____   _____

2. _____   _____

3. _____   _____

4. _____   _____

Curriculum area	IEP Referral	Grade
I	Objective #3 #4	
II	Objective #6 #8	
III	Objective #1 #3	
IV	Objective #10 #13	

Other areas

Grading Criteria
A = Mastery—Excellent Performance
B = Performance Near Mastery—Very Good Performance
C = More Progress Needed—Acceptable Performance
D = Lack of Progress in Reaching Objective—Unacceptable Perform-
*   ance*
F = Objective Frustrating Individual—Frustration

Figure 8–8   *A model secondary school report form for individualized performance assessment*

way, students—especially retarded learners—could more fully realize their learning potential.

Reporting System: Anecdotal Records

Another available reporting system is anecdotal records. These short narrative accounts of individual performance provide more detailed information regarding student performance than could be communicated by a single number or letter grade. These anecdotes should be related to each objective stated in the IEP and contain information regarding both quantity and quality of performance.

Reporting System: Student's Work Records

Another reporting system that provides detailed information on student performance is the student work record. This system includes both evaluation of student performance and the actual work of the student. This system may be used along with anecdotal records, the more traditional report card, or in place of these systems. Each of the student documents included should relate to a specific objective to demonstrate the student's performance. Bar graphs and line graphs of social and academic performance can also be included as documentation.

Reporting systems should be devised so that the maximum amount of information is communicated to both student and parent. They are not the vehicle for punishing students, nor should they be posed as a threat. Their purpose is to communicate performance. The teacher should select the system or combination of systems that maximizes the amount of information the teacher wishes to convey to parents and students.

As you develop your reporting system, imagine that you are the parent reading the information. Put yourself on the receiving end for a moment. Consider what you would want to read about your child, as the parent, and what kinds of information would be most helpful in conveying the facts about your child. Teachers should not withhold negative evaluations and only report the "good news." But they should include negative information in a manner that conveys concern for the student. Furthermore, when it is necessary to convey negative information, the teacher should include a request to meet with the parent and some specific suggestions for activities that the parent might do at home with the child to work on the problem. No parent enjoys receiving negative information about his or her child. All parents want their children to succeed. Thus, parents often are able to accept the negative reports more fully when they are helped to understand what role they can play in contributing to the child's more positive performance.

Conclusion

Evaluation involves judgments about student learning success and the quality of instruction. Process evaluation, the assessment of the interaction in the classroom, can often provide additional information concerning the quality of instruction.

Measurement is the central ingredient of evaluation. Formal tests and various informal measurement techniques must be both valid and reliable. In a systems approach to instruction, validity is defined as testing what the objectives prescribe. This means that a test must reflect the behavior and the learning levels that are stated in the objective. Reliability implies consistency of results when measurement procedures are repeated with the same or similar learners. To insure maximum reliability, instructional designers are encouraged to use pretests, multiple assessments, measurement in both a controlled and a natural environment, and posttests.

Teachers should also be aware that alternative evaluation systems —peer, student, and parent evaluation—which transfer partial responsibility for evaluation to others are often useful in accurately judging student behavior.

Regardless of whether the teacher alone makes the evaluation decision or whether he is assisted by others, the decision must be made. It should be made both in the formative period of instruction and at the conclusion of instruction, as a summative judgment.

As instruction of children with special needs becomes more and more a role assumed by the regular teacher, the issue of the wisdom of a traditional grading policy must be examined. New grading policies and reporting procedures are needed.

REFERENCES

Cooper, J. *Measurement and analysis of behavioral techniques.* Columbus, Ohio: Charles E. Merrill, 1974.

Analyzing curriculum materials

Jim Kerr's Dilemma

Jim Kerr has been a special education teacher for 15 years. He has worked with mildly retarded youngsters of all ages, although most of his experience is with children aged 9 to 12. During the past 15 years, special education has grown into a high priority concern in the minds of parents, boards of education, administrators, and teachers. Although the changes in the education of handicapped learners mandated by federal and state legislation have excited Kerr, the complexity and rapidity of change are perplexing.

Kerr is active in the local chapter of The Council for Exceptional Children. He has not, however, attended a state convention for many years. The state C.E.C. convention is being held in his home town this year. The convention program includes several interesting workshops and announces a display of curriculum materials appropriate for mildly retarded students. Jim is seeking new ideas to recharge and revitalize his own curriculum, so he decides to attend the convention.

Jim's first activity at the convention is a visit to the displays of books, audio-visual projects, learning programs, and other materials. This section displays all the latest products available to teach reading, mathematics, social skills, science, and every other kind of subject matter. Each stall seems to attract the potential user with claims that this product or that one produces extraordinary achievement results or is useful in a program of individualized instruction. Slogans such as "high interest," "low readability," "attractively packaged," "suitable for mainstreaming" overwhelm him. Each exhibitor has evaluation data that purports to demonstrate that his materials are best for retarded learners. "In whose hands are they 'best'?" Jim wonders. Jim collects brochures, catalogs, and advice from publisher representatives, in addition to all the other assorted free materials that are available to convention participants.

When Jim gets back home he begins to sort through the materials he has collected with the express purpose of selecting some appropriate materials for the children in his class. Furthermore, since many of his students are being placed in regular classrooms, many of his colleagues will be asking him about selecting appropriate materials. Jim begins to realize the importance of this selection process.

Rather than finding this task easy, Jim finds the selection process difficult and confusing. He begins by sorting the materials into groups—textbooks, sophisticated learning programs, paper-backed books for enrichment or optional reading, spirit masters, programmed materials, audio-visual products, games, and a very large category for miscellaneous items. Many of the items in the various categories are expensive; he can purchase only those materials that will be most beneficial to his students. His frustration grows as he realizes that he has not developed a systematic process for discriminating worthy materials from those that are not. Jim is uncertain about what criteria he should apply in the evaluation process.

What kinds of materials should he select? Would a complete reading or math program be best? Best for whom? Some of the programs he examined are certainly sophisticated and richly endowed with required and optional materials; they are also quite costly.

Should he invest in an assortment of games, puzzles, paper-backed books, and worksheets? Since he has limited funds, should he spend them on one item or several smaller ones? Jim must decide whether to purchase printed material exclusively, a mixture of print and nonprint materials, or primarily nonprint materials. Which materials are most appropriate for his newly developed Functional Life Curriculum? Which products are most likely to help the youngsters survive and be successful in the world outside the classroom? Are all the materials appropriate for all the learners? How does one choose discrete subject-matter products for an integrated subject-matter curriculum? Spending money was never so difficult.

Jim's confusion mounts as he continues to scan the materials. He is ready, at this point, to throw all this new stuff out, spruce up his basal readers, worksheets, and math and spelling workbooks, and let the regular classroom teachers fend for themselves. Realistically, though, he knows that he is responsible for his students' learning. He also is eager to help other teachers select and analyze curriculum materials systematically.

Jim's problem is a very common one for special and regular educators as well as curriculum planners. Recently there has been an explosion of new, expensively packaged educational materials available. Many of the products developed and marketed by the

publishing companies are worthy and useful in instructing mentally retarded learners. However, there are other products that appear to be merely watered-down content, uninteresting or commercially prepared worksheets that simply provide busy work to keep children occupied. Some products consist of printed material whose readability level is erratic, generally inappropriate, or not really suited to his students' assessed needs.

You may recall the Jack Stevens' case presented in Chapter 4. Just as Stevens was uncertain and anxious about the analysis and design of curriculum units, Jim Kerr feels the same confusion when he grapples with the evaluation of existing materials. In both situations, the teachers need an organized systematic framework for analysis.

The ways students use materials provide one source of information for evaluation.

This chapter has three purposes. First, it reviews the curriculum and analysis process already presented. Thus, the key principles involved in goal selection, assessment, writing objectives, selecting learning activities, and evaluation will be applied to existing curriculum materials, both teacher-made and commercial. Second, specific materials are discussed. We will focus on one teacher-made material, a Learning Activity Package (LAP), which is an entire instructional unit.

Third, since curriculum materials come in various sizes, shapes, and types, we shall present a classification system with appropriate evaluation criteria to help a teacher select materials.

But two cautions are necessary. First, no single material or group of materials will improve the learning performance of all children. No single curriculum program, no matter how elegant and sophisticated, will be the best approach for all children. Second, we must again trust the individual teacher as a rational decision maker. The teacher cannot be shunted into a secondary role during the instructional process. No set of materials can and should replace the teacher. Although the emphasis on the teacher may vary in some instructional patterns, the role of the teacher is nevertheless crucial.

Traditional Models of Curriculum Development

Most school districts use a subject area or grade-level committee for curriculum development and planning. Teachers and other personnel are charged with developing or adopting a curriculum program for a group of age-related children. The committee represents a small sample of the teachers who are expected to use the program; in many cases the program is to be used throughout an entire school system. Furthermore, a decision to use a curriculum normally translates into thousands of dollars spent on instructional materials and in-service education.

Although the traditional curriculum committee is often praised because of its cost effectiveness and efficiency, there are other issues that should also be considered. One issue is that of investment—not financial, but the personal investment that comes from being involved in curriculum development. Only the members of the committee who make the purchasing decisions will have the excitement and commitment needed to make a program successful. Selecting goals, analyzing these goals, translating the goals into objectives, designing learning activities, and selecting curriculum materials are all parts of an interrelated process. When the traditional committee does the work, the teachers who are not on the committee, who were not directly involved in the process, are expected to carry out someone else's creation.

That is not a realistic expectation. Personal investment and enthusiasm is diminished by a committee approach. It is much more fun to be on the ground floor.

For example, imagine that you were involved in an argument with a colleague on the committee. You were pushing for a scientific inquiry unit involving several procedures. Your colleague said it wouldn't work; it was beyond your students' abilities. Following that friendly debate, you went ahead with the activity to field test it and discovered that your students not only grasped the basic concept and principles, but they asked surprisingly sophisticated questions. This experience is not only a victory for your students, but for you as well.

Again the teacher, as the person primarily responsible for the education of retarded children, must be directly involved in the development of instructional goals, objectives, and activities for his or her class. Through this direct involvement, teachers can learn what to teach and teach what they learn. And finally, the teachers are the evaluators of the products they have created. It is commonly accepted today that if an educational innovation is to be used by teachers, they must be able to understand and identify with the innovation. It no longer was developed "out there"; it is now the creative property of the user. Applying this principle to curriculum development, you can see that the greater the role teachers play in the creative process, the greater the identification with the program.

Working with colleagues as a part of the teaching responsibility may also increase the teacher's motivation and enthusiasm. Productive, task-oriented groups can provide an opportunity for fun, learning, and developing an esprit de corps unavailable to many teachers. Scheduling time for creativity shared among colleagues is one highly desirable alternative to the usual teachers' meetings with which teachers are all too familiar.

Team Approach

An alternative approach to individual decision making is a team approach. Teaching teams are useful in curriculum and instruction problem solving, in teaching, in developing curricula. One author has been involved with a project to institute team planning in a number of elementary schools in a large urban school district. In this project, teachers who have worked along with the principal to make curriculum decisions and implement the system in the classroom had positive changes in their attitudes toward the children and their own job satisfaction. In addition, there was almost unanimous support for the concept of team planning.

As professionals, teachers have few chances to work cooperatively; they often have little opportunity to interact at all. It is startling to realize how little adult interaction occurs in an elementary or secondary school. The teachers within individual schools rarely share or discuss curriculum or instructional ideas with their colleagues; in fact, they have little adult stimulation during the school day. Seymour

Sarason and his colleagues, in their discussion of the loneliness of teachers, observe that:

> Although a teacher is in the room throughout the entire day with 20 or more children, teaching is basically a lonely profession. A teacher presents material to children and she may correct their work. On occasion, she may share a child's ambitions, his fantasies, or his worries but it is rare that a teacher has the opportunity to discuss her problems or successes in teaching with anyone else. (Sarason, Levine, Goldenberg, Cherlin, & Bennett, 1966, p. 74)

Curriculum development team.   The curriculum development team may be made up of teachers, parents, and (where appropriate) retarded students themselves. The task of material selection follows that of selecting goals and objectives. Many possible materials should be carefully reviewed and tested. Those that are useful should be shared with the group. In that way, the curriculum budget can be extended. Pooling resources can enhance instruction for an entire department or school.

If, however, an individual teacher finds that a school system is unwilling or unable to organize a group curriculum effort, this problem should not change the teacher's desire to become a curriculum planner. It is better to have one teacher planning alone for a classroom of children than to abdicate the responsibility completely. A cooperative effort is always preferred, but this goal may not be realistic. A systematic analysis of curriculum materials by an indi-

Small-group learning activities can help children generalize concepts.

vidual teacher that matches teacher–learner needs and interests can still provide an excellent individualized instruction program.

Instructional Systems and Elements

This final chapter focuses on the selection and evaluation of instructional systems. An instructional system is a body of content that includes an integrated set of learning objectives and specified procedures for evaluation. It may be a single lesson that takes up one classroom hour; it may be a unit that takes several hours or even weeks to complete; it may be as large as a course of study or a program of studies. Consequently, within a total instructional system, there may be several subsystems. In any case, an educational product is an instructional system if it includes learner objectives and matching evaluation procedures.

In contrast, *instructional elements* are the vehicles or devices through which information is presented to the learner. Instructional elements do not have a clearly identified structure. They do not include an integrated set of learner objectives and specified procedures for evaluation. Instructional elements may be books, films, worksheets, puzzles, and so on. They can be evaluated by themselves, the way you would evaluate any book you read or film you see. Still, instructional elements are best evaluated within the context of the learning activity in which they are placed. In that way, they are ingredients in an instructional system. This chapter focuses on systems as opposed to elements.

Evaluating Instructional Systems

The curriculum development process that we recommend is summarized in Table 9–1. The table is divided into three columns. The first column consists of separate categories for each of the stages of the curriculum process: (a) goal selection, (b) educational assessment, (c) learner objectives, (d) learning activities, and (e) evaluation procedures. An educator who intends to use the chart to evaluate an existing instructional system would use the second column for descriptive characteristics of the system. The third column is used to assess system characteristics against the criteria for judgment identified as critical or successful instruction of EMR learners. Although the chart is primarily a tool for evaluation and selection, it may also be used to guide the development of instructional systems.

The first stage of the process is goal selection. The key questions involved in goal selection are: Is the subject matter an integrated

Table 9–1   *Evaluating instructional systems*

Curriculum process	Descriptive characteristics	Criteria for judgment
A. Goal selection	Describe the goals of the system.	Do the curriculum goals explicitly or implicitly represent a philosophic commitment to one or more "sources of information"?
		If so, is this commitment to a synthesis of subject matter and student needs and interests and the needs of contemporary society?
		In general, are the broad goals worthy of study by EMR learners?
		Are the goals consistent with the normalization principle?
		1. Do they help EMR learners become productive members of society?
		2. Are the goals consistent with a "mainstreaming approach" in a "least restrictive environment"?
B. Educational assessment	Describe any diagnostic tests or other assessment procedures or information.	Does the system demonstrate an understanding of the EMR child as a learner? (learner analysis)
		1. Developmental tasks.
		2. Enhancement of attention.
		3. Meaningfulness.
		4. Active learning.
		5. Rewards and encouragement for success.
		Do the goals indicate an understanding of content analysis (task analysis)?
		1. Are principles and concepts stated or easily discovered?
		2. Is there a logical relationship inherent in the tasks?
		a. Concrete to abstract.
		b. General to specific or specific to general.
		c. Complex to simple or simple to complex.

Curriculum process	Descriptive characteristics	Criteria for judgment
		3. Do the goals seem consistent with some organized hierarchical view of learning (Bloom, Gagné, or other)?
C. Learner objectives	Generate a list of the objectives (if the system extends beyond a single unit, select objectives for a typical unit).	Are the objectives clearly stated? 1. Observable behavior or activity. 2. Method of measurement. 3. Criteria for successful accomplishment. Are the objectives logically related to the broad learning goals?
D. Learning activities	Describe a set of learning activities (if the system extends beyond a single unit, select activities from a typical unit).	Are the activities consistent with the "principle of the match"? 1. Logically related to objectives. 2. Able to be implemented in typical classroom settings (or with environmental requirements clearly stated). 3. Consistent with EMR learners' needs and interests. 4. Provide "active learning." 5. Can be implemented without special teacher in-service training. 6. Provide real world experience. Are the activities consistent with the principle of "instructional variety"? 1. Multidimensional. 2. Large group, small group, individualized. 3. Teacher dominated, student dominated and mediated. 4. Structured and unstructured. Do the activities provide for "individualized instruction"? 1. Provide opportunities for learners to work at their own pace.

Curriculum process	Descriptive characteristics	Criteria for judgment
		2. Provide content options within conceptual goals.
		3. Provide learning style options for a set of learning goals.
E. Evaluation procedures	Are evaluation procedures/ instruments provided and/or described?	Are the evaluation procedures related to the learner objectives and activities?
		1. Consistent with behaviors.
		2. Consistent with levels of learning.
		Do they sample the full range of instructional content?
		Are the testing directions clear? Is the scoring reliable?
		Are the measurement instruments normative or criterion-referenced?
		Are their formative evaluation procedures?
		1. Pretests.
		2. Repeated measures for diagnostic purposes.

approach to content? Are the goals worthy of study by EMR learners? Is the instructional system consistent with the concept of "normalization"? Does the instructional system lend itself to mainstreamed education? These questions relate to our philosophy of education. The broad goals in any instructional system for retarded learners should meet the criteria implied by these questions.

In the second stage of the process, educational assessment, the diagnostic tests or other assessment procedures must be identified. These tests are then subjected to a set of questions that determine the comprehensiveness of the learner analysis. The criteria for judgment include: Do the materials demonstrate an understanding of the EMR child as a learner?

1. Structured in terms of developmental tasks?
2. Enhancing learner attention?
3. Concern for meaningfulness?
   a. Pairing known with unknown?

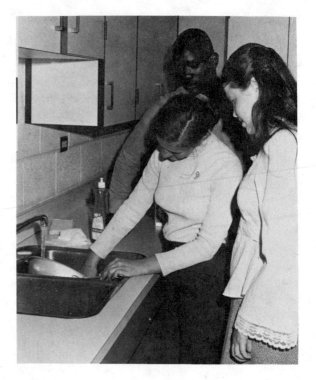

If students are to be successful in the real world, they must master basic home-making skills.

    b. Using verbal and pictorial mediators?
    c. Concrete to abstract?
4. Active learning?
5. Encouraging and rewarding success?

These criteria must be met if the assessment is to meet the needs of retarded learners.

    Besides fitting the individual learner, the system must be appropriate for the curriculum content. This can only be accomplished through a content or task analysis that results in

1. Clearly stated or easily discovered principles,
2. A logical relationship of content within a task (concrete to abstract, general to specific or specific to general, simple to complex),
3. A hierarchical view of learning that begins with facts and builds to concepts and finally to principles (explanations).

    After evaluating a system's goals and assessment procedures, the teacher is ready to examine the learner objectives. If the product is a small system, there will be few objectives. On the other hand, if the system is a large system that will be used for a long time (weeks, months, or year), there will be more objectives. A basal reading series is an example of this type of large system. The DISTAR Reading Program (Englemann & Brunner, 1969) would be another example. The science, math, and reading programs developed by SRA (Science Research Associates, 1971) are yet another example of a larger instructional system whose use consumes large time blocks.

In evaluating instructional objectives for instructional systems, the criteria suggested in Chapter 6 must be applied. To be *clearly stated*, the system objectives must contain descriptions of

1. Observable behavior or activity,
2. Methods of measurement,
3. Criteria for successful accomplishment.

Each objective in the instructional system must be related to the system's broad goals. Mentally retarded pupils have a great deal to learn during the time they are in school. The sad fact is that there is never enough time to teach all of the skills and knowledge that teachers would like these students to learn. The more efficiently teachers plan instructional time and the more meaningful the instructional systems, the more benefits children will derive from their educational experiences.

Manipulative materials provide opportunities for learning and fun.

The next stage in the curriculum process is the evaluation of learning activities. Learning activities must be consistent with the principle of the match. This principle involves matching activities and

1. System objectives;
2. Classroom facilities, time, and equipment requirements;
3. The needs and interests of particular learners;
4. Critical learning principles such as "active learning";
5. Teacher competence;
6. The realities of the world in the larger community.

By the same token, instructional systems must follow the principle of instructional variety. To optimize learning, there should be variety in the following areas:

1. Multidimensional;
2. Large group, small group, or individualized options;
3. Dominance patterns—teacher, student, or media;
4. Structured and unstructured options.

Finally, an instructional system contains a set of evaluation procedures. These procedures determine whether the system has been successful with particular learners. The following criteria identify essential characteristics of properly constructed evaluation procedures.

1. Are the procedures consistent with the learner objectives required by the system?
2. Are the procedures consistent with the levels of learning contained within the objectives?
3. Are the "testing" directions clear?
4. Is the scoring reliable?
5. Are the measurement instruments normative or criterion-referenced?
6. Are there formative evaluation procedures?

The model for evaluating an instructional system—whether a lesson, a unit in economic education, or a class meeting designed to let students communicate effectively—is a systematic process. At each step in the process of evaluating and selecting an instructional system, there are criteria that can be applied to determine the appropriateness of a particular system. This approach is an alternative to the hit-and-miss model that is found in too many classrooms across the country.

Evaluating a teacher-made instructional system. We have chosen a particular content area—sex education—to illustrate the curriculum evaluation process. Within that large instructional system, one particular junior high school EMR teacher has developed a 3-week Learning Activity Package to teach the causes and effects of venereal disease and its proper treatment. Remember that a LAP is a teacher-made curriculum unit, designed through a systems approach, that has a number of student learning options. Since the LAP on venereal disease has both objectives and matching evaluation procedures, we shall use it to illustrate the evaluation of instructional systems. The analysis can be seen in Table 9–2.

Table 9–2   *A Learning Activity Package: Understanding venereal disease*

Curriculum process	Descriptive information	Criteria for judgment
A. Goal selection	LAP is derived from a broad educational goal *Understanding oneself and others* within the Functional Life Curriculum.	Sex education should be contained in curriculum.
	This particular topic—venereal disease—is a 3-day experience as part of a three week unit on "Sex Education for Junior High Students."	Rise in V.D. and teenage pregnancy make sex education a necessity for Functional Life Curriculum, especially for retarded learners.
	Broad goals To have students learn that: 1. People progress through developmental stages. 2. Boys and girls develop physical differences during adolescence. 3. Sex drive occurs at this time and society has rules about it. 4. Sexual intercourse may result in pregnancy if some method of birth control is not used. 5. Venereal disease is communicable and requires prompt medical care.	Normalization: Retarded learners have the same sex needs as peers and need education to remain productive members of society. With least restrictive environments, sex information is necessary for social skills as well as survival skills.
B. Educational assessment	Information must be gathered via criterion-referenced	Learner analysis 1. *Prerequisite struc-*

	measures (visual and audio cassettes). Examples:
	  What is venereal disease?
	  What are two types of venereal disease?
		ture: Understanding of terms: *disease, infection, sore, sexual organs, sexual intercourse, pus, discharge, rash, brain disorder, blindness.*

	What could an open sore on a penis mean?
	How do you contact a venereal disease?
	What happens if you have sexual relations with a person who has V.D.?
	What are two signs of gonorrhea?
	What happens if you do not have medical treatment for syphillis?
	Can V.D. be cured?
	List three places to go for treatment of V.D.
	Does a doctor have to tell your parents that you have V.D.?
	How can you prevent V.D. and still have sexual relations?
		2. *Attention:* high interest for adolescents.
		3. *Meaningfulness.*
		  a. *Paired learning:* Knowledge of bodily functions and diseases that can occur.
		  b. *Concrete to abstract:* Physical activity to physical discomfort to disease to social problem.
		  c. *Interesting tasks:* Pictures, films, models.
		4. *Reinforcement concepts:* Reassess #1 in different context or stress semantic differences in terms.
		5. *Active learning:* Role-play, small group discussions (note myths and inaccuracies).
		6. *Rewards & encouragement for success:* Audio cassettes, inquiry.

	(See synthesis of learner and content analysis in Figure 9–1)	*Content analysis.* 1. *Concepts:* V.D. is a disease that can

Curriculum process	Descriptive information	Criteria for judgment
		ruin your life and cause problems for others.
		2. *Logical relationship:*
		a. Sex with infected person can infect you; you can infect others.
		b. V.D. germs infect genital areas. Germs can cause medical problems.
		c. Medical attention is required for all V.D. problems.
		Facts: Stages and symptoms of V.D.
		Concepts: Disease, V.D., communicable.
		Principle: Since V.D. is both communicable and dangerous to health, prompt medical attention is required.
C. Learning objectives	1. During a role-playing activity, the doctor will explain to the patient why venereal disease is dangerous and requires medical treatment.	Clearly stated and logically related to broad learning goals.
	2. When asked, the student will orally state that the two most common types of V.D. are syphillis and gonorrhea with 100% accuracy.	
	3. After listening to an audio-cassette describing a case of gonorrhea or syphillis, the student will	

Curriculum process	Descriptive information	Criteria for judgment
	identify the disease as gonorrhea with 100% accuracy.	
	4. After reading a article on V.D., the student will orally describe to a small group the process by which V.D. is passed on.	
	5. After viewing a filmstrip on V.D. treatment, the student will write a list of three places an infected person can go to receive medical help with 100% accuracy.	
	5. Following a classroom lecture, student will make an audio-tape listing the untreated results of syphillis and gonorrhea with 100% accuracy.	
D. Learning activities	1. Medical doctor from free clinic will meet with class and show film on gonorrhea and syphillis, and have class question-and-answer session.	Meets all requirements of principle of match. 1. Objectives. 2. Student needs and interests. 3. Teacher developed. 4. Real world.
	2. In a role-play situation, one student will be a doctor and one patient with V.D. The patient will list his or her symptoms, and the doctor will confirm or deny.	Instructional variety 1. Multidimensional. 2. Small group, large group, and individual grouping patterns.
	3. An audio-tape in the learning center will list the symptoms of V.D. Students can listen, check with prepared visual materials, and write a record the correct answers.	3. Varying dominance patterns.

Curriculum process	Descriptive information	Criteria for judgment
	4. Field trip to free clinic to provide information or how to get there and explain services provided.	
	5. Class discussion on prevention of V.D. if one engages in sexual activities.	
	6. Written case studies and audio-tapes describing actual experiences with V.D.	
	7. Teacher-led presentation on concept of "communicable" as it relates to V.D. and other diseases.	
E. Evaluation procedures	Criteria levels listed in instructional objectives. Answers written to direct questions: lists, procedures, etc. Answers taped on audio-cassettes. Teacher evaluation/observation of information exhibited in small group discussions.	Criterion-referencing allows for learning that is consistent with behaviors and the levels of learning. Learning is sampled via written answers and oral communication in small and large groups. Field visits and role play allow for individualization of instruction. Pre- and posttests are required for all learning centered activities and also allow for practice of repeated measures.

Evaluating commercially produced instructional systems. Because of the abundance of commercially developed instructional materials available, it is essential that a teacher view them in an organized systematic process. As Jim Kerr, our special education teacher,

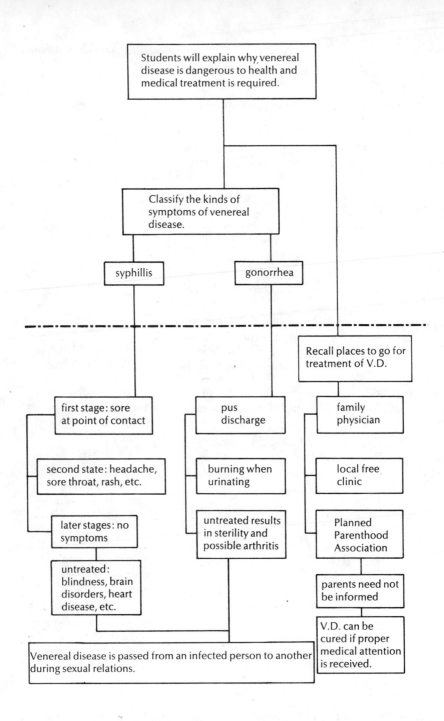

Figure 9–1   *Learning hierarchy of the concept venereal disease*

discovered, there is a confusing variety of materials, many of which are quite costly.

What are "commercial" materials? They are materials mass produced by a publisher or development center to reach an often broad or poorly-defined learner audience. They may be subject specific (SRA Reading Program, 1971) or skill-oriented (Barnell Loft Reading Comprehension Series, Boning, 1970; Peabody Language Kits, Dunn & Smith, 1968); they may be highly specialized or may extend across a number of subject and skill areas.

Evaluating commercially developed materials is similar to the process used for teacher-developed products. Three steps are involved.

Step I. Establish whether the product is an *instructional system*. Does it contain learner objectives and a matching set of evaluation procedures? Does the product claim to be an instructional system when it is in fact a "dressed up" instructional element? Has the developer provided an adequate psychological structure to justify the cost of the product? Remember expensively produced and packaged instructional elements may present information no better than a teacher with a blackboard or a magic marker.

Step II. If the product is an instructional system (or claims to be) apply the criteria for each stage of the curriculum process. Examine:

1. Goal statement
2. Educational assessment
3. Learner objectives
4. Learning activities
5. Evaluation procedures

Determine if the product meets the criteria for judgment.

Step III. Since the commercial system being considered has been produced elsewhere, there are several other factors to consider before selecting and purchasing it.

Cost factor. Most commercial systems are expensive. Those systems that have materials such as books, audio tapes, and records, for example, are quite costly. The cost vs. benefit question is always difficult to resolve. The issue should be transformed into a question: "Will I use the product frequently enough to justify the outlay of funds? Will these materials be of benefit to my students?" It is always a good idea to try out an expensive system before you make your purchase. The local Regional Resource Center is an excellent source of materials. In some states, it is quite easy to borrow a system from an Instructional Resource Center to determine its value for your particular class.

Fit. Does the system fit well with the existing curriculum or course of study? Will students be confused or agitated when they

Billy listens intently as Darrel demonstrates his reading skills.

move to and from this system to others in the same classroom or in other classrooms they attend? Can the instructional system be used in a normalized and/or mainstreamed curriculum program? Too often only direct effects are considered in making adoption decisions. In those cases, there is always a danger that unanticipated effects on other teachers and the administration may diminish the positive direct effects of a particular instructional system.

Utilization. Another factor to be considered is who will use the system. If it is an expensive system, is it possible or probable that several teachers may need to use it? There are times, particularly with handicapped learners who have very special needs, that large outlays of funds are required for a system to be used by only one child.

The usability factor has several dimensions: (a) number of students who may potentially benefit from the commercial system, (b) application and use of the system for several areas of the curriculum, and (c) adaptability of the system to children of varying age levels. These factors should be in direct proportion to the cost (except, of

A pencil-and-paper activity allows Diane to show the teacher what she has learned.

course, in isolated cases of specially determined need). For example, if a commercial system is the most expensive item purchased by a teacher, can its purchase be justified because it will be used frequently?

Training requirements. The training required to use a commercial system effectively must also be considered. When reviewing selected commercial materials that result from careful research and analysis, one quickly discovers that they must be employed with skill and understanding. Unless the teacher understands the theory underlying the development of some systems, they will have limited benefits.

On the other hand, those materials evolved from a carefully and thoroughly researched theoretical framework are potentially the most beneficial to children. But even the most carefully developed materials, when improperly implemented, lose their power as teaching tools.

Portability. Some systems are large, cumbersome, and require a permanent place in the classroom. Other systems come with carts, carrying cases, or other similar means for moving them from place to place. Here again you must consider who is going to use the system and where they are going to use it before the importance of portability can be determined.

Evaluated effectiveness. Can the developers of the instructional system provide formative and summative evaluation data to demonstrate learning success? Has the system been field tested with learners who have characteristics similar to those of the children you teach? How many years of development were needed to produce the system? Many complex systems, whose conceptual framework is rich in thought and resources, may take 5 years to complete. Generally, the longer the development process, the greater the developer's attention to quality—that is, unless the terminal goal that originally excited the developers has lost its timeliness or importance.

Has the system been compared to other products? Have authorities in the field provided testimonials to the quality of the system? In many cases, the director of the Regional Resource Center may have evaluation information about a commercial system. Finally, you can consult the professional literature to determine if the system has been reviewed or used by others.

Availability of comparable teacher-made systems. Can you make a similar system that is more appropriate for your students? Since no commercial system can ever really meet your students' needs as well as those you design with your own students' needs in mind, can you create a system that would be comparable?

Some materials lend themselves easily to individual, private use.

Keeping the Teacher Involved

Instructional materials, whether systems or elements, should not be implemented mindlessly. It is very important that teachers not become totally dependent upon them to the point that the teacher's ability to evaluate instruction is diminished. The evaluation of instruction was discussed in detail in Chapter 8, but we need to reiterate a few key principles. Quality instruction always rests on repeated and careful evaluation. This is especially important when using materials produced elsewhere. A careful evaluation process ought to include:

1. Assessment of learning success in response to predetermined objectives.
2. Assessment of the instructional process to determine long-term and/or unanticipated outcomes.

The assessment of predetermined outcomes has been thoroughly discussed earlier. Assessment of the instructional process often involves assessing student attitudes. Observing the students as they use materials is one source of data. Asking students what they think (and requiring them to give clear, concise reasons for their reactions) is another technique for obtaining data. It provides students with practice in expressing ideas and feelings.

The teacher's reaction to some systems is one factor in the system's overall effectiveness. A system may be appropriate, may enable

Jennifer listens carefully as Evelyn reads braille.

students to reach objectives and meet the criteria stated earlier; but if the teacher doesn't enjoy using it, its value is diminished. The teacher's attitude toward a system, either overt or covert, influences the students. Teachers will sometimes say, "I can always teach children to read when I use the X reading system. I know it always works." This kind of statement can become a self-fulfilling prophecy and have a very positive effect on instruction.

Commercial Materials in a Functional Life Curriculum

Remember the Curriculum Centers that comprise the Functional Life Curriculum discussed at length in Chapter 4.

I. *Gaining insight into contemporary life.*
II. *Becoming a responsible adult.*
III. *Understanding oneself and others.*
IV. *Education for independence.*

The next section of this chapter presents many materials organized into the four centers. We do not endorse these materials, but present them only to show that a Functional Life Curriculum is practical, given the wealth of commercially prepared materials available for use.

These materials represent only a small fraction of the number that are presently on the market. Some are very expensive, and some are quite inexpensive. What is of major importance in the analysis and review of these materials is the degree to which they will assist your student to attain their objectives. Of equal importance is their usefulness. Can the materials be used for individuals and small or large groups? Do they present a multisensory approach to learning? Can they be integrated into your curriculum for multiple uses? These questions can only be answered by teachers who have reviewed the materials carefully. It is the teacher's responsibility to send for catalogues, read about new materials, and experiment with materials from Special Education Resource Centers or curriculum libraries in universities or local boards of education.

Some of the materials that follow are programs, some are games, and some are supplementary workbooks. Teachers must keep in mind the three steps for evaluation already discussed. Establish whether the product is an instructional system; establish if one can apply the judgment criteria in each stage of the process; consider cost, fit, utilization, training requirements, portability, and evaluated effectiveness.

An individual, quiet, seated activity is preferred after lunch.

Unit I   Functional Life Curriculum

Gaining insight into contemporary life

A. Applications of science and technology into everyday life

ME NOW! Life Sciences: A special Education Program (Hubbard Scientific Company)

This program is specifically designed for special education, but has extended usefulness in elementary programs. The curriculum is well designed so that concepts and facts are sequentially taught in four complete units. Filmstrips and practice exercises accompany each unit which teaches body operations. It was conceived under the rubric of Hubbard's Biological Sciences Curriculum Study Programs.

Beginning Concepts/Science (Scholastic Book Services)

This program for young learners contains two units. Unit 1 introduces children to the Life Sciences, and Unit 2 involves children in the Physical Sciences. Each unit contains five full-color filmstrips, five soundtracks on records or cassettes, and a teacher's guide.

Scholastic Health and Safety Series (Scholastic Book Service)

This program contains four units on health and safety, each containing four filmstrips and cassettes or records plus a 64-page teacher's guide. Grade K–3 Health Unit: Watch Your Health; 4–6 Health Unit: Stay Healthy; K–3 Safety Unit: Safety Day; 4–6 Safety Unit: Play It Safe.

Health and Nutrition (Hubbard)

Included in this series specially designed for mildly handicapped learners ages 10 to 18 are:

"Dudley"—3-foot high functioning torso that houses models of five functioning body systems and helps explain their interrelatedness.

Tommy Torso Discovery Pack—Torso body that provides a visual reference for tape-directed investigation of the structure and various systems of the body and how they work separately and together.

"Grow and Go Game"—Game teaches food classification and nutrition.

"Food Chain Game"—Cards with living things that can be placed in the food chain.

"Circulation Game"—Game simulates circulation of blood throughout body as it carries nutrients and waste materials to and from cells.

*The Basics of Nutrition (Butterick)

This is a multimedia program for adolescents and young adults. It includes two cassette filmstrips, six transparencies, eight duplicating masters, and a teacher's guide. It shows how food affects height, weight, and strength.

*Buying Health Care (Changing Times)

This multimedia kit presents open-ended dramatizations of teenagers confronted with decisions about health products and services. The program contains two cassette filmstrips, 12 pages of reproducible activities, facts, and posttests, and a teacher's guide with discussion questions.

*Nutrition Reading Module (Relevant Productions)

Students listen to a cassette lesson and follow along word-for-word in booklets. Geared for grades 7–12, this module consists of one cassette, 30 read-along booklets, 30 four-page activity booklets, and a teacher's guide.

---

* All items designated by an asterisk can be ordered through J. Holcomb.

B. Appreciating aesthetics

American Short Stories (Educational Insights)

This is a high interest/low readability program that consists of 36 short stories, open-ended questions, and spirit masters for activities.

The Sea Wolf Mysteries (EMC Corporation)

This program includes four paperback books, four read-along cassettes, and a teacher's guide. Reading level: grade 3.

Early Childhood Original Stories and Songs (Exceptional Child Development Center)

These five records or cassettes and guides offer opportunites for teaching basic concepts through words and music.

C. Ecology/environmental education

The Environment (Hubbard)

This program is specially designed for mildly handicapped learners:

Some Cycles—A look at repetition in the environment. Set of 22 cards includes a pictorial sequence showing the development of a dandelion, a trout, butterfly, and aspen tree.

Some Houses—A look at varied environments. This filmstrip provides students with a basis for comparing their houses and surroundings with other types of houses around the world.

I'm the Very First Link—A look at recycling. Students learn, via a filmstrip, to identify and demonstrate how to improve the immediate environment through participation in a group or individual recycling project.

"Relationships in My Environment" booklets—The three booklets use thought-provoking illustrations to stimulate environmental thinking and discussions.

"Nature's Delicate Balance" deals with the interdependence of wildlife, using deer as an example.

"The Long Journey" conducts students through a series of illustrated events in nature and human activities which demonstrate the transfer and cycling of materials.

"The Fate of the River" looks at the causes, effects, and controls of water pollution.

The City as an Ecosystem (Interpretive Education)

This program includes five color filmstrips, five audio cassettes, 30 student workbooks and a teacher's manual. This program is designed to help students understand the city as an ecological system.

D. Morals and values

Scholastic Book Services provides several kits that contain books, posters and records and deal in depth with the following areas:
Drugs,
Maturity,
Prejudice.

Values in the News (Westinghouse Products)

Eighteen news photographs illustrating social issues, world events, and famous personalities are used to explore 18 different aspects of the value-clarifying process.

Values Activities (Educational Insights)

Puzzles, games, and fill-in-the-balloon cartoon strips help students think about and clarify values related to getting along with others and investigating goals.

Life Goals: Setting Personal Priorities (Sunburst)

These multimedia kits consist of three cassette-filmstrips and teacher's guide. These kits help students develop the skills they need to make competent decisions about values and life goals.

Winners and Losers (Argus)

This paperback book with concise observations of human behavior with illustrations helps students examine their own values.

E. Mass media communication and appreciating the human experience

Violence USA: What Kind of People Are We? (AVNA)

Two cassette filmstrips and a guide acquaint students with the history and causes of violence in America.

Television and Values: Exploration Kit (Learning Seed)

Kit consists of 1 cassette filmstrip, 24 research project cards, 128-page TV Action Workbook, TV on Trial simulation, reproducible observer form, *TV Sponsor's Directory,* and a teacher's guide. It encourages students to actively investigate the impact of TV on their own lives.

Kids in Crisis (Zenger Productions)

This kit gives students insight into the problems confronting millions of juveniles and the institutions designed to deal with them. The kit consists of role profiles, role tags, probation reports, an activity booklet, and a teacher's guide.

---

* All items designated by an asterisk can be ordered through J. Holcomb.

Unit II   Functional Life Curriculum

Becoming a responsible adult

A. Participating in a democratic society

You Decide: Opposing Viewpoints (Greenhaven)

For secondary learners, this set consists of 35 booklets presenting pros and cons on crime issues. Each booklet contains articles and essays written by leading criminologists, psychologists, lawyers, judges, religious leaders, and sociologists.

Confrontation in Urbia: A Legal Simulation (Classroom Dynamics)

Secondary students simulate a jury trial to decide a case and gain realistic understanding of constitutional rights, due process of law, and the problems faced by police in urban crises.

Innocent Until . . . A Criminal Justice Simulation (ABT Associates)

This kit helps students understand how the law works by having them simulate a courtroom trial to determine innocence or guilt, assuming roles of judge, jury, lawyers, defendant, defendant's wife, witnesses, law officers, and courtroom personnel.

About Your Community (Steck-Vaughn)

Two paper booklets in the Family Development Series specifically related to two topics:
"Being an Informed Citizen,"
"Where to go, Who to see, What to do."

B. Career choice

Explore (Scholastic Book Services)

For elementary grades, this sound/filmstrip program relates career awareness to the hobbies and interests of children. Three units cover the areas of (a) Work? Play? (b) Who? What? When? Why? (c) Career Connections. Each contain four filmstrips with sound on records or cassettes, five student workbooks, and a teaching guide.

Preparing for the World of Work (F.R. Publications)

The fourteen areas in this 138-page worktext designed for secondary retarded learners were developed to provide instruction in the area of work preparation and work study.

---

* All items designated by an asterisk can be ordered through J. Holcomb.

Turner Career Guidance Series Reading Level 5–6 (Follett)

These 138 structured daily lessons in six workbooks present a cohesive and integrated program in career planning. Many jobs are documented as to qualifications, education, training, working conditions, and salary ranges.

I Want To Be MINIPACS (Children's Press)

An elementary school career awareness program featuring classroom and community student career activities, these six minipacs can be ordered separately. Each includes a booklet, filmstrip, cassette, hand-held filmstrip viewer, student interview sheets, and teacher's guide.

Multimedia instruction programs for secondary education materials for special needs students (Interpretive Education)

All of the following programs have filmstrips, cassettes and teacher manuals:

Finding a Job
Career Education Series A & B
Office Worker Series
Applications and Forms
How to Read the Classified Ads in the Newspaper

Career Awareness (Educational Activities Inc.)

This is an elementary program in three parts, each containing four filmstrips and four records/cassettes and guide. The filmstrips illustrate specific responsibilities, educational background needed, and advancement opportunities.

*Job Survival Skills Complete Multi-Media Program Reading Level 5.5–6.5 (Singer Career Systems)

For secondary learners, 15 program units with filmstrips, cassettes, and booklets help students develop personal and interpersonal skills not ordinarily covered in an educational or vocational training program.

*First Jobs Reading Level 4.5–5.5 (Educational Design)

For secondary learners, this program consists of 9 filmstrips, five cassettes, 12 duplicating master activities, plus a teacher's guide divided into two units that covers working part-time while still in school. It also shows how to make the transition from part-time to full-time work.

---

* All items designated by an asterisk can be ordered through J. Holcomb.

The Job Hunting Game Reading Level 4.0–5.0 (Interactive Media)

Students simulate actual job-hunting activities to practice looking for and finding a job.

Get that Job! Reading Module Set Reading Level 3.5–4.5 (Holcomb's)

Three modules each contain one cassette, 30 student booklets correlated word-for-word with the cassette, 30 four-page posttests, and a guide.

Critical Skills for Getting a Job Involvement Kit. Reading Level 3.5–4.5 (Media Materials)

For secondary learners, this kit contains 10 cassettes, 300 four-page activity booklets, and 10 reproducible posttests to check competency and comprehension. Self-directing activities take students through all the steps of finding a job and developing on-the-job skills.

Selling: A Good Way to Earn a Living Reading Level 4.5–5.5 (Educational Design)

This is designed to stimulate interest in selling and prepare students to find and get sales jobs. It contains two cassette-filmstrips, 24 copies of a student booklet, 12 duplicating masters, role-playing and simulation activities, and a guide.

People Talk: Selecting a Vocation Listing Too Reading Level 4.5–5.5 (Coronet)

On-the-job interviews with people working in different occupational areas give students the information they need to make career choices. It includes eight cassette filmstrips and a guide.

The Job Box Reading Level 3.5–4.5 (Fearon)

Simply written booklets with photo illustrations provide detailed descriptions of 70 entry-level jobs: e.g., hospital orderly, laundry worker, messenger, and file clerk.

C. Production and consumption of foods and services

Multimedia Instruction (Interpretive Education)

The following programs have filmstrips, cassettes, and a teacher's manual:
Using the Telephone Book,
Applying for Credit,
Automobile Insurance,
Clothing Care,

* All items designated by an asterisk can be ordered through J. Holcomb.

Apartment Hunting,
Income Tax,
What Are Company Benefits,
Bills—How and Why We Have to Pay Them.

The Tuned-In Consumer: A Complete Multimedia Consumer Education Program Reading Level 4.5–6.5 (Butterick)

These five units for secondary learners are available separately. The complete program has 15 cassettes/filmstrips, 52 duplicating masters, 40 activity cards, 30 student magazines, 4 transparencies, 5 gameboards, and 5 teacher's guides.

Consumer Sense Reading Level 4.5–5.5 (Coronet)

This high-interest format encourages students to teach themselves important consumer skills. The multimedia kit consists of 10 cassettes and 30 student response books with questions and activities and a guide.

Let's Go Shopping Program Reading Level 4.0–5.0 (Changing Times)

Two cassette filmstrips show young adults participating in the consumer process, the mistakes they make, and the lessons learned from their mistakes.

Buying a Used Car Reading Level 3.5–4.5 (Relevant Productions)

Students strengthen reading skills while learning things to look for and questions to ask when buying a car. The kit includes one cassette, 30 booklets, and 30 posttests plus a manual.

Financing and Insuring a Car Reading Level 5.5–6.5 (Unigraph)

Self-directing activities let students learn for themselves how to deal confidently with the process of buying and insuring a car.

What Is Credit Reading Level 5.5–6.5 (Visual Education Consultants)

Units help to simplify the world of credit with captioned filmstrips, programmed learning booklets, and reproducible activities.

Establishing Your Credit Reading Level 3.5–4.5 (Relevant Productions)

This teaches students step-by-step how to establish credit for the first time, build a credit rating, and maintain a good credit rating. It includes one cassette, 30 reading modules, 30 posttests and a guide.

So You Want to Use Credit Reading Level 4.0–5.0 (Changing Times)

Six real-life case studies get students involved in resolving common credit problems; they contain two cassette-filmstrips, 8 pages of reproducible activities, and a guide.

---

* All items designated by an asterisk can be ordered through J. Holcomb.

332

Housing: Finding a Place to Live Reading Level 4.5–5.5 (Changing Times)

Four self-contained units help to prepare students to make wise decisions about housing. The program contains 120 student booklets, a house-hunting simulation game, a record of interviews from housing experts, 20 reproducible activity pages, pre- and posttests, and a guide.

What You Should Know About Insurance Reading Level 4.5–5.5 (Relevant Productions)

This program explores two basic categories of insurance coverage: protecting people and protecting things. The cassette and booklets allow students to read along word-for-word; it also contains 30 skill sheets and a teacher's guide.

React: Violated Consumer Rights Reading Level 3.0–3.5 (Relevant Productions)

This cassette presents a dramatization of two young consumers whose rights in Truth-In-Labeling have been violated. Students are asked to consider what they would do in this situation and then check the cassette to learn channels of action open to them.

D. Managing money

Math for the Young Consumer (Educational Activities Inc.)

These four units presented with cassette filmstrips and activity dittos present simple, practical approaches for using money and math in daily situations.

Multimedia Instruction (Interpretive Education)

Materials designed for secondary learners with special needs, the following programs contain filmstrips, cassettes, and teacher's manuals.
Money Handling,
Budgeting,
Banking,
Using Arithmetic When Shopping for Groceries,
Mathematics and You.

Using Consumer Math Reading Level 3.5–4.5 (Media Materials)

Students practice basic math skills while teaching themselves step-by-step how to cope with everyday living needs. Units consist of 10 cassettes, 300 four-page activity booklets, 10 reproducible post-tests.

---

* All items designated by an asterisk can be ordered through J. Holcomb.

Daily Math Application Program Reading Level 4.5–5.5 (ESP Inc.)

Twenty-four lessons on 12 cassettes allow students to listen to lessons and apply basic math skills for everyday life on corresponding activity sheets.

Math for Living Skillbooks Reading Level 4.5–5.5 (Mafex)

These 10 separate skillbooks provide lessons and activities that give students the math-related skills needed for successful daily living. Single sets may be purchased. The titles of the skillbooks are: *Math for Family Living, Math for the Worker, Math for Citizenship, Math for Banking, Math for Employment I and II, Math for Adult Living, Math for Everyday Living, Your Daily Math I and II.*

Today's Consumer Math Problems Reading Level 5.0–6.0 (Home-making Research)

Word problems teach students how to use credit, shop wisely, and budget.

Budget Ideas for Teenagers Reading Level 3.5–4.5 (AVNA)

This captioned filmstrip provides humorous illustrations and easy-to-read captions on budgeting techniques geared to the income and expenses of teenagers.

The Big Buy Reading Level 4.0–5.0 (AVNA)

This captioned filmstrip dramatizes a teenage girl shopping for a stereo set. It deals with comparison shopping for quality, price, guarantees, and financing.

Payday Game Reading Level 4.5–5.5 (Parker Brothers)

This game simulates the adult world of budgets, wages, and bills. The game includes a gameboard, tokens, dice, expense cards, opportunity cards, payday money, savings-and-loan interest chart, and directions.

Shopping Bag Game Reading Level 4.0–5.0 (Creative Teachers Assoc.)

Four high-interest games challenge students to strengthen basic math and reading skills while learning how to shop. It includes four gameboards, 100 problem-solving cards, and a teacher's guide.

E. Family living

The Follett Family Life Education Program/Elementary (Follett)

Six books (3 primary, 3 intermediate) deal with children's questions concerning sex and reproduction. They also help clarify what

---

* All items designated by an asterisk can be ordered through J. Holcomb.

it means to be a man or a woman and to be a member of a family. The books can be purchased separately.

Baby Sitting Program (Interpretive Education)

This filmstrip/cassette program introduces the student to the basics of taking care of a child in the baby-sitting situation.

About You and Others (Steck-Vaugh)

For secondary learners, these three booklets with activities and stories relate to family living. The titles are "Your Family," "Communicating with Others," and "Working with Others."

Unit III Functional Life Curriculum

Understanding oneself and others

A. Understanding oneself

Becoming Yourself (Scholastic Book Services)

For elementary learners, the three units—exploring my identity, expressing myself, understanding myself and others—stress the concepts of self-respect and respect for others. Each unit has four filmstrips with records or cassettes and a teacher's guide.

Going Places with Your Personality: A Guide to Successful Living Reading Level 2.7 (Fearon)

This booklet uses information, observation, and discussion to help students develop desirable attitudes and habits; it has a strong emphasis on interpersonal skills.

ACCENT/Personality Reading Level 3–4 (Follett)

This series of four booklets is designed to teach social skills and encourage the social attitudes needed in our society. The four titles include: "You and They," "You Are Heredity and Environment," "Taking Stock," and "You and Your Needs."

Focus on Self-Development, Stage One: Awareness, K–2; Stage Two: Responding Reading Level 2–4 (SRA)

This development program leads children to an understanding of self, others, and the environment and its effects on them. It contains activities for whole group, small group, or individuals. The program contains a set of five 36-frame color filmstrips and records, four activity records, 20 photoboards, pupil activity book, and a teacher's guide.

The Social Learning Curriculum (Charles E. Merrill)

This very comprehensive kit is designed to give the special student knowledge, skills, and behaviors that will enhance his opportunities for success in his environment. Physical, social, and psychological elements of the environment are taken into account so that the child receives a balance of stimuli to develop and reinforce important social learning concepts. The kit contains 10 phases and has the following components: 10 phase books, 72 stimulus pictures, 10 spirit duplicating books, an assessment and record for each phase, transparencies, supplementary books in physical education, mathematics, and science, a 32-page teacher's guide, and a scope and sequence chart.

Got To Be Me!—A Self-Awareness Program for Elementary Students (Argus)

This program helps develop positive self-images by providing opportunities for students to talk and write about themselves. It includes workbooks, 48 cards, and a teacher's guide.

Lifeline—Education in Human Relations for Grades 7–12 (Argus)

This kit has three major areas subdivided to deal with situations that involve a variety of value decisions that are part of the growing-up years. The three content areas are: In Other People's Shoes, Proving the Rule, and What Would You Have Done. Situational cards and/or booklets are provided for each area.

Making Sense of Our Lives (Argus)

This program for self-expression includes six units with six exercises in each unit. The goal is to help students become more aware of their strengths and more respectful of the strengths of others. Each unit has six posters, six spirit masters, and six teacher's guides. Unit titles are: Learning About Myself, Expressing Feelings and Emotion, Self-Concept, Sensitivity to Others, Goals, and Decision-Making and Social Issues.

Developing Understanding of Self and Others (DUSO) (American Guidance Systems)

Two kits, D1 and D2, are programs of activities with accompanying kits of materials designed to encourage healthy social and emotional development. For grades K–4, these programs are instructional and highly motivating. Kits include very structured manuals, story books, group discussion cards, posters, puppets, play props, role-playing cards, and cassettes or records.

Toward Affective Development (TAD) (AGS)

TAD, designed for grades 3–6, focuses on real-life experiences and on developing patterns of motivation, feeling, understanding, and participation. TAD is organized and presented in five sections, comprising 21 units or 191 lessons. Materials contained in the kit are a manual, feeling wheels, 44 illustrations, color chips, shapes, and objects cards, duplicating masters, cassette, filmstrip, posters, and career folders.

The Awareness Center (Children's Press)

This is a multimedia unit to help children (K–3) understand their feelings and emotions. Included are a teacher's guide, eight life situation books, two poster sets, 10 stories from children's literature and eight cassettes.

B. Establishing social relationships

C. Working successfully in groups

All of the materials listed under A—**Understanding oneself**—can be used in these two subsections. Additional materials are:

Am I O.K.? (Argus)

This higher level reading book with spirit masters offers helpful, practical exercises in Transactional Analysis.

If You Don't Know Where You're Going, You'll Probably End Up Somewhere Else (Argus)

This paperback book and spirit masters for secondary learners outlines major factors such as skills, education, friends, motivation, family, experience, and health, that influence choices.

All About Manners (Interpretive Education)

These filmstrips and cassettes show, via situations, the options an individual has in displaying acceptable behaviors.

What It Takes—Developing Skills for Contemporary Living Reading Level 2.4 (Fearon)

This is a paperback book about an urban family's day-to-day problems. It is designed for grades 7–12.

D. Multicultural awareness

Learning About Religion/Social Studies (LAR/SS) (Argus)

This is a nondenominational, multimedia program for grades 1–6. The three levels covered are cross-cultural family studies, cross-cultural community studies, and ethnic studies in an urban setting.

*Man: A Cross-Cultural Approach Listening Level 5.5–6.5 (Educational Design)

This comprehensive cassette filmstrip program explores the activities, interactions, needs, and attitudes of all mankind. Four modules are People and Cultures, Daily Life, Basic Needs, and Social Organization.

*Comparative Cultures Listening Level 5.5–6.5 (Learning Corporation)

Four cassette/filmstrips compare an American city, small town, factory, and family with their counterparts in other parts of the world.

*The Peoples of America Reading Level 5.0/6.0 (Educational Design)

This is a multimedia look at our pluralistic society. It provides an overview of multicultural studies as well as in-depth coverage of 19 American ethnic groups.

*La Raza (English Version) Listening Level 6.5–7.5 (Multi Media)

This provides, via several media, an insight into the history and culture of Mexican Americans from pre-Columbian Mexico through Cesar Chavez and the success of the United Farm Workers.

Hispanic Heroes of the U.S. Reading Level 5.5–6.5 (EMC Corp.)

These four paperbacks correlated to cassettes present the lives and achievements of 12 successful Hispanic men and women.

*Black Americans at Work Listening Level 5.0–6.0 (Coronet)

Six filmstrip/cassettes give students insights into the goals and problems shared by many Black Americans.

Afro-American Contributors to American Life (Benefic)

This is a book of 20 biographies of high achieving Afro-Americans. Their collective lives are written in three versions for three levels of reading difficulty: 2.0, 3.5, and 5.5.

---

* All items designated by an asterisk can be ordered through J. Holcomb.

Power of My Spirit: The American Indian Listening Level 5.5–6.5 (Denoyer-Geppert)

Two cassette/filmstrips show how Indians are reaffirming old tribal customs and values while, at the same time, seeking access to better educational and occupational opportunities. They are narrated by Buffy Saint Marie.

E. Broadening understanding through travel

Transportation (Interpretive Education)

This cassette/filmstrip gives students with special needs an awareness of the different modes of transportation that are available within the city.

Bicycle Safety (Interpretive Education)

This cassette/filmstrip explores the safety concerns in riding a bicycle.

How to Read a Map (Interpretive Education)

This cassette/filmstrip illustrates the legend and index of a map and how to read them.

How to Read Schedules (Interpretive Education)

This cassette/filmstrip deals with schedules for trains, planes, buses, and other local transportation.

Travel Planning Kit (Interpretive Education)

This program takes the students through a simulated trip where the students themselves calculate the costs involved.

F. Human sexuality

Understanding Our Growing Up (Ages 10–14) (Mafex)

The three cassettes in this program deal with the reality and dignity of growing and maturing. Topics include Learning to Love, Girl Grows Up, Boy Grows Up, and Becoming a Young Adult.

Understanding Ourselves as Adults (Mafex)

Four cassettes discuss sexuality, its importance, confusions, and responsibilities.

---

* All items designated by an asterisk can be ordered through J. Holcomb.

Sol Gordon (John Day)

This author has written several books and illustrated comic books expressly for retarded people that deal in a straightforward manner with sex and teenagers.

Everything a Teenager Wants to Know About Sex . . . and Should (Mafex)

This book honestly answers the questions boys and girls may have about their own bodies and their relationships with others.

A Baby Starts to Grow Ages 4–8 (Crowell Crocodile Series)

In clear and simple language, this book presents a forthright description of the growth of a baby in the mother's womb.

Unit IV   Functional Life Curriculum

Education for independence

A. Fostering thinking and problem-solving skills

A Direction for Tomorrow (Bowmar)

This kit of filmstrips and booklets looks at basic areas of life survival skills. Included are such topics as Compassion for People, Jobs for the Now Generation, Money Tree, The Nation's Builders, Age of Electronics.

Databank (Holt, Rinehart and Winston)

This comprehensive, multimedia program deals with social studies and component skills.

Action (Scholastic Book Services)

This kit is for severely retarded secondary learners. Booklets begin at 2.0 reading level and stress scope and sequence, comprehension, and thinking. Also included are 11 open-ended plays and 20 fiction stories.

B. Mastering the basic skills

There is a concerted effort today to improve all children's basic skills. This movement is often called "back to basics" in education. Several states have passed laws that, in order to receive a high school diploma, students must achieve a certain level of proficiency in reading, mathematics, and handwriting, usually referred to as Minimal Competency Testing (MCT).

This movement seems to be positive; however, the ways children are being taught the basic skills appear to be the same ways used during the 1950s. The goals themselves are legitimate, but the objectives and strategies for attaining them are usually not clearly stated and often do not account for individual learning styles. Many parents are reverting to old answers such as "He'll learn it if you drill hard enough." "He's lazy, but extra homework in math will help him." And much of the back to basics movement is, in reality, oriented toward punishment.

Mastery of basic skills is certainly necessary for people, especially the retarded, to survive in society today. What is of utmost importance, however, are the methods and materials used to teach the basic skills.

The following programs are currently being used to teach basic skills. Several of them involve unique ways of teaching old subject matter.

New Phonics (Lyons and Carnahan)

This series of workbooks deals specifically with letter sounds in relation to formulating words. Any or all of these materials can be purchased to provide an alternative means of teaching.

REACH (Singer Visual Education)

This multimedia program stresses phonics. It has its own pre- and posttests that involve the auditory as well as the visual modalities in learning.

Multiplication Rock (Xerox)
Grammar Rock (Xerox)

These filmstrips, cassettes, worksheets, and spirit masters present math and grammar in tune to a rock beat and teach new concepts as well as give practice exercises.

Skillpacers (Random House)

This is an individualized approach for teaching reading that includes instruction and practice exercises. The skillpacers encompass 15 vital reading areas and can be used for elementary and secondary learners.

Comprehensive Skills Lab (American Learning Corporation)

This is a multimedia program labeled a *prescriptive* reading program. The books, which utilize the visual and auditory modalities, emphasize comprehension skills. The booklets range from A to H and can be used as supplemental information for students throughout the elementary and secondary school curricula.

Veri Tech (Educational Teaching Aids)

This program has a wide range of usefulness. It extends from pre-primer level to grade 8 and includes practice exercises in both reading and math. This program also includes manipulative materials and provides excellent supplemental exercises.

Glass Analysis (Walker Corporation)

This is a relatively new approach to reading. It presents a system of booklets that build word power and sentence structure in what is called a "cluster" approach. It differs from linguistic readers to some degree, but a structured, almost programmed approach is utilized. Word families are used as a basis and then the words are expanded with the beginning and endings of a main word built.

Skill Boosters (Modern Curriculum Press)

This program provides five booklets dealing specifically with reading comprehension. They are: "Building Word Power," "Increasing Comprehension," "Working with Fact and Detail," "Organization," and "Using References."

Sprint Series (Scholastic Press)

These high interest/low readability books are designed for adolescents with reading problems. Library I has five short books with a reading level range from 2.0 to 2.4. Library II has five books with reading level ranges from 2.5 to 2.9.

Reading is always given special preference because it is so necessary a skill. Commercially prepared basal reading programs have been and continue to be the most widely accepted and commonly used materials for teaching reading. These programs are basically acceptable and have met the needs of most children for many years. Publishers have been sensitive to the changes in society and have provided stories that are multicultural and multiethnic. Nearly all the basal reading series, however, present a strictly visual approach to learning. This restricted approach is often of concern to teachers of retarded children.

Another factor to consider is that publishers are currently deviating from the grade levels of books. Previously, all major series started at a preprimer level, continued to primer, grade 1^1, grade 1^2, 2^1, 2^2, and so on. Many publishers now include as many as eight levels in the programs before a child even reaches the second grade.

Strong consideration, then, should be given to the level of readability of a story or a book. Readability is measured by the length of sentences and the number of syllables in words in a given passage. If the words or sentences are too long, often the content of the reading passage will be too difficult for a child and will only frustrate the child's attempts at reading and comprehending the material. Commercial publishers often are not accurate or reliable in their estimates of the readability of some of their materials. Quite often a reader labeled "third grade" has stories more applicable for fifth grade reading books.

Therefore, teachers of retarded learners should be able to evaluate the readability of instructional materials themselves. A competent teacher can use either the Fry or Spache techniques for determining readability.

The Fry Technique. The Fry technique uses two language factors: number of sentences and number of syllables per 100 words. This technique provides the quickest way to determine the difficulty level of a book. The formula is very easy to use, and the results of the sentence and syllable counts are easily applied to the Fry Graph for Estimating Readability. The Fry Graph and its directions are shown in Figure 9–2.

The Spache Technique. This technique is very useful with retarded learners because it was designed to assess materials written at or below the fourth grade level. Since many retarded learners are reading within these levels, the Spache has been used by many special educators. The Spache formula uses two language factors: word difficulty and sentence length. Although the Spache is more time-consuming than the Fry, it is sometimes more reliable. Coleman (1977) comments on the Spache:

> The Spache has a major advantage for the special education teacher. The formula is specifically intended for materials at grade level 3.9 or below. . . . Another advantage is that the Spache formula uses a list of words to compare against words in the story one is evaluating. The list enables the teacher to locate words that may be difficult for a class. The list also supplies you with a quick summary of vocabulary which students generally need to know if they are to advance beyond third grade reading. This list can be used as a basis for designing a word study program, for a diagnostic test, or for constructing or adopting reading materials. (p. 341)

Other techniques that are readily available are the Dale-Chall, which was designed to be used with adult reading materials (fourth grade level and above), and the Harris-Jacobson Technique, which

Figure 9–2   *Fry Readability Test*

Directions for Using the Fry Readability Graph

1. Select 100-word passages from near the beginning, middle, and end of the book. Skip all proper nouns. Skip all numerals (329, 8). Count hyphenated words as two words except those divided because of lack of space at the end of a line.

2. Count the total number of sentences in each 100-word passage (estimating to the nearest 1/10 of a sentence).

3. Count the total number of syllables in each 100-word sample. There is a syllable for each vowel sound; for example: cat (1), blackbird (2), continental (4). Don't be fooled by word size; for example: polio (3), through (1). Endings such as -y, -ed, -el, or -le usually make a syllable, for example: ready (2), bottle (2). Since there is at least one syllable in each word, some find it convenient to count every syllable over one in each word and add 100.

4. Average the total number of syllables for the three samples.

5. Average the total number of sentences for the three samples.

6. Plot on the graph the average number of sentences per 100 words and the average number of syllables per 100 words. Most plot points fall near the heavy curved line. Perpendicular lines mark off approximate grade level areas.

Example

	Sentences per 100 words	Syllables per 100 words
100-word sample page 5	9.1	122
100-word sample page 89	8.5	140
100-word sample page 160	7.0	129
	3 $\overline{24.6}$	3 $\overline{391}$
Average	8.2	130

Plotting these averages on the graph, we find they fall in the fifth grade area; hence the book is about fifth grade difficulty level. If great variability is encountered either in sentence length or in the syllable count for the three selections, then randomly select several more passages and average them before plotting.

---

employs two formulas for readability. Formula one is for materials below fourth grade, and formula two is for third grade level materials and above.

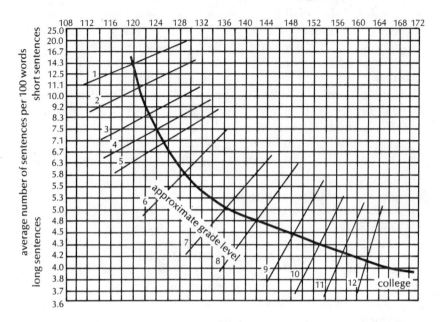

From Edward Fry, Rutgers University Reading Center.

These readability techniques, if properly and cooperatively used, help teachers select materials that will provide instruction rather than frustration for the individual students. Once the readability has been considered and assessed, a major block to instructional planning has been conquered.

A second area that teachers must carefully analyze is the modalities used by the commercial materials. Modality learning has become a widely discussed phenomenon in education, but many teachers do not allow for a child's learning preference when selecting commercial reading materials. For example, if a child is not a visual learner, then a basal reading program such as the Ginn series would not be appropriate. If the child is an auditory learner, then reading could be taught using an auditory program such as the Reading Attainment Series (Grolier). This would allow the teacher to teach reading using the child's modality strength and thus allow for more success for the child.

Some programs allow the student to use a multi-sensory approach to learning. Some reading programs have created new symbols that aid the child in learning. The DISTAR Reading Program (Englemann & Brunner, 1969) is a good example of one system that creates new symbols in language and then allows the student to transfer to standard language symbols following success with the symbols.

To help keep very aware of the modalities and readability levels of the programs they are considering, teachers can chart their children's modality strengths and reading levels and then match them with available commercial materials. Table 9–3 shows how this can be done. The chart organizes reading systems by modality type.

Table 9–3   *Basic skills programs*

Modality Type	Reading system
Auditory modality	Listen & Think (Troll Assoc.) Reading Attainment Series (Grolier) Language Master (Bell & Howell) Audio-Tronics (Fryan)
Visual modality	Ginn Reading Series Allyn & Bacon Reading Series Houghton & Mifflin Reading Series MacMillan Reading Series SRA Kits (SRA) Specific Skill Series (Barnall Loft)
Integrated modalities	DISTAR (Reading & Math) (SRA) Alpha One (New Dimensions in Education) Singer Modules (Singer Visual Ed.) Systems 80 (Borg-Warner) Craig Reader System (Craig)
Linguistic	Merrill Linguistic Readers (Charles Merrill) Lippincott (Lippincott)

C. Using leisure time productively

Commercial Games

Almost all games such as *Sorry* and *Monopoly* and card games can be taught to children. These games reinforce basic skills by allowing the individual to generalize reading, math, and motor skills to social situations.

I Can! (Hubbard)

This physical education program is designed for retarded children.

Recreation and Leisure Time Series (Interpretive Education)

Five filmstrips and cassettes with workbooks explore possible recreational activities in terms of expenses, places to go, things to do, how to cut costs, how to utilize community facilities, and how to get there.

D. Homemaking/home maintenance

Clothing Care Series (Interpretive Education)

Five filmstrips and cassettes deal with clothing care and the use of washers, dryers, and dry cleaning machines.

Kitchen Measures (Interpretive Education)

This filmstrip/cassette lays the groundwork for all measuring done in the kitchen, from a quarter-teaspoon to a cup.

Using Arithmetic When Shopping for Groceries (Interpretive Education)

This filmstrip/cassette covers fundamental areas in shopping such as comparing sizes and prices, unit pricing, costs per serving, reading labels, and using coupons.

Inexpensive Apartment Decorating (Interpretive Education)

This filmstrip and cassette highlight how to find inexpensive furnishings and how to decorate or fix them up and select curtains, rugs, slipcovers, and cushions, as well as plants and pictures.

The Kids Kitchen Take Over (Mafex)

These recipes allow kids to read directions and prepare foods by themselves.

The Easy-To-Cook-Book (Mafex)

This book includes simple to make, four-step recipes for breakfast, lunch, dinner, snacks, and parties.

Young Homemakers at Work Series (Fearon)

Three booklets on reading levels 2.5, 2.8, and 2.9 deal with three topics: Planning Meals and Shopping, Getting Ready to Cook, and The Young Homemaker's Cookbook.

E. Expressing one's individuality

Developing Understanding of Self and Others (American Guidance Systems)

Reviewed in Section III.

Toward Affective Development (American Guidance Systems)
   Reviewed in Section III.

Social Learning Curriculum (Charles Merrill)
   Reviewed in Section III.

Lifeline
   Reviewed in Section III.

Making Sense of Our Lives (Argus)

Conclusion

The evaluation and selection of curriculum materials is a confusing, multifaceted problem. Teachers face this problem each time they attempt to select materials that are appropriate for the pupils they teach. The concept of the instructional system can be used to classify curriculum materials that can be used effectively in EMR classrooms.

The curriculum process developed throughout this book is useful as a framework to evaluate instructional systems. The curriculum process, goal selection, assessment, learner objectives, learning activities, and evaluation procedures, when accompanied by the relevant criteria for judgment, can be helpful in developing and evaluating teacher-made products as well as those produced commercially.

Commercial products must also undergo an additional set of tests. They must be examined for cost, utilization, fit with existing curricula, portability, required in-service training effectiveness, and availability of teacher-made substitutes.

The final section of this chapter describes a number of commercially produced products under each of the broad goals of the Functional Life Curriculum. It remains the responsibility of the teacher to evaluate these products, using the criteria already developed.

REFERENCES

Boning, R. Barnell Loft Reading Series. Baldwin, N.Y.: Dexter and Westbrook, 1970.

Coleman, L. J. An examination of seven techniques for evaluating the comprehensibility of instructional materials. *Education and training of the mentally retarded,* 1977, *12,* 339–344.

Dunn L., & Smith, J. Peabody Language Development Kits. Circle Pines, Minn.: American Guidance Systems, 1968.

Englemann, S., & Brunner, E. S., DISTAR: *An instruction system for reading instruction.* Chicago: Science Research Associates, 1969.

Sarason, S., Levine, M., Goldenberg, I. I., Cherlin, D., & Bennett, E. *Psychology in community settings: Clinical, educational, vocational and social aspects.* New York: John Wiley, 1966.

SRA Reading Programs. Chicago: Science Research Associates, 1971.

Educational materials
sources

Achievement Products, Inc.
P.O. Box 547
Mineola, NY 11501

Allyn & Bacon, Inc.
470 Atlantic Ave.
Boston, MA 02210

Allyn & Bacon, Inc.
Longwood Division
470 Atlantic Ave.
Boston, MA 02210

Alpha II, Inc.
2425 Alama Ave., S.E.
Albuquerque, NM 87106

American Art Clay Co., Inc.
4717 W. Sixteenth St.
Indianapolis, IN 46222

American Guidance Service, Inc.
Publishers' Building
Circle Pines, MN 55014

American Printing House for the
  Blind
1839 Frankfort Ave.
Louisville, KY 40206

Ann Arbor Publishers, Inc.
P.O. Box 388
Worthington, OH 43085

Argus Communications
7440 Natchez Ave.
Niles, IL 60648

Arista-NDE
83 Keeler Ave.
Norwalk, CT 06854

ATC Publishing Corporation
P.O. Box 5588
Lakeland, FL 33803

Barnell Loft & Dexter Westbrook
  Publications
958 Church
Baldwin, NY 11510

Beckley—Cardy
1900 No. Norragansett Ave.
Chicago, IL 60639

Bell & Howell
7100 N. McCormick Rd.
Chicago, IL 60645

Bemiss-Jason Corporation
3250 Ash St.
Palo Alto, CA 94306

Benefic Press
10300 West Roosevelt Rd.
West Chester, IL 60153

BFA Educational Media
P.O. Box 1795
Santa Monica, CA 90406

Binney & Smith, Inc.
1100 Church Ln.
Easton, PA 18042

Dick Blick
P.O. Box 1267
Galesburg, IL 61401

Borg-Warner Educational Systems
600 West University Dr.
Arlington Heights, IL 60004

Bowmar Publishing Corp.
4563 Colorado Blvd.
Los Angeles, CA 90039

Broadhead-Garrett Company
4560 E. 71st St.
Cleveland, OH 44105

Bureau of Education for the
    Handicapped
400-6th St.
S.W., Washington, D.C. 20202

CEBCO Standard Publishing
9 Kulick Rd.
Fairfield, NJ 07006

Centron Educational Films
1621 West Ninth St.
St. Lawrence, KS 66044

Centurion Industries, Incorporated
167 Constitution Dr.
Menlo Park, CA 94025

Changing Times Education Service
1729 H St. N.W.
Washington, D.C. 20006

Childcraft Education Corp.
20 Kilmer Rd.
Edison, NJ 08817

Childhood Resources, Inc.
1150 Connecticut Ave. N.W.
Suite 74
Washington, D.C. 20036

Childrens Press
1224 W. Van Buren St.
Chicago, IL 60607

Classroom World Productions
14-22 Glenwood Ave.
Raleigh, NC 27603

Cleo Living Aids
2957 Mayfield Rd.
Cleveland, OH 44121

Cole Supply Company
103 E. Bird
Passadena, TX 77501

Communication Skill Builders, Inc.
817 East Broadway
Tucson, AZ 85719

Community Playthings
Rifton, NY 12471

Constructive Playthings
1040 East 85th St.
Kansas City, MO 64131

Consulting Psychologists Press
577 College Ave.
Palo Alto, CA 94306

The Continental Press, Inc.
520 East Bainbridge St.
Elizabethtown, PA 17022

Ken Cook Education Systems
12855 W. Silver Spring Rd.
Butler, WI 53007

Creative Playthings
Princeton, NJ 08540

Creative Publications, Inc.
P.O. Box 10328
Palo Alto, CA 94303

Thomas Y. Crowell Co.
666 Fifth Ave.
New York, NY 10019

Curriculum Associates, Inc.
6 Henshaw St.
Woburn, MA 01801

Cybernetic Systems, Inc.
E III, Inc.
9615 Acoma S.E.
Albuquerque, NM 87123

John Day
666 Fifth Ave.
New York, NY 10019

Developmental Learning Materials
7440 Natchez Ave.
Niles, IL 60648

Didax, Inc.
P.O. Box 2258
3 Dearborn Rd.
Peabody, MA 01960

Dragstrem, Inc.
2710 Walnut Way
Marion, IN 46952

Early Years Magazine
P.O. Box 1223
Darien, CT 06820

Eckstein Bros., Inc.
4807 West 118th Pl.
Hawthorne, CA 90250

The Economy Company
1901 N. Walnut
Oklahoma City, OK 73125

Educational Activities, Inc.
P.O. Box 392
Freeport, NY 11520

Educational Design, Inc.
47 West 13th St.
New York, NY 10011

Educational Insights
20435 S. Tillmon Ave.
Carson, CA 90746

Educational Patterns, Incorporated
63-110 Woodhaven Blvd.
Rego Park, NY 11374

Educational Performance Associates
600 Broad Ave.
Ridgefield, NJ 07657

Educational Progress Corporation
4235 S. Memorial
Tulsa, OK 74145

Educational Service, Inc.
Box 219
Stevensville, MI 49127

Educational Teaching Aids
159 W. Kinzie St.
Chicago, IL 60610

Educators Publishing Service
75 Moulton St.
Cambridge, MA 02138

EMC Corporation
180 East 6th St.
St. Paul, MN 55101

Encyclopaedia Britannica
  Educational Corporation
425 North Michigan Ave.
Chicago, IL 60611

Erca-Enrichment Reading Corp. of
  America
Iron Ridge, WI 53035

Everest & Jennings, Inc.
1803 Pontius Ave.
Los Angeles, CA 90025

Exceptional Child Development
  Center
725 Liberty Avenue
Pittsburgh, PA 15222

Exceptional Play
P.O. Box 1015
Lawrence, KS 66044

Family Communications
4802 Fifth Ave.
Pittsburgh, PA 15213

Fearmon-Pitman Publishers, Inc.
6 Davis Dr.
Belmont, CA 94002

Flaghouse, Inc.
18 West 18th St.
New York, NY 10018

Follett Publishing Company
1010 West Washington Blvd.
Chicago, IL 60607

FR Publications
1103 St. Paul Dr.
Merrill, WI 54452

Gallaudet College
  Office of Demographic Studies
7th & Florida Ave. N.E.
Washington, D.C. 20002

Gamco Industries, Inc.
P.O. Box 1911
Big Spring, TX 79720

Game Time Inc.
900 Anderson Rd.
Litchfield, MI 49252

George Washington University
Special Education
Early Childhood
Washington, D.C. 20052

Globe Book Company
175 Fifth Ave.
New York, NY 10010

Gould Athletic Supply Co.
3156 N. 96 St.
Milwaukee, WI 53222

Grolier Educational Corporation
575 Lexington Ave.
New York, NY 10022

Grosset & Dunlap, Inc.
51 Madison Ave.
New York, NY 10010

Grove School, Inc.
Box 646
Madison, CT 06443

Grune and Stratton, Inc.
111 5th Ave.
New York, NY 10003

Guidance Associates
757 3rd Ave.
New York, NY 10017

The Delmer F. Harris Co.
Box 278
Concordia, KS 66901

Harvest Educational Labs
Pelham St.
Newport, RI 02840

HC Electronics, Inc.
250 Camino Alto
Mill Valley, CA 93941

Hester Evaluation System
120 S. Ashland Blvd.
Chicago, IL 60607

High Interest Teaching Systems
32158 Camino Capistrano
San Juan, CA 92675

Highlights for Children, Inc.
2300 W. Fifth Ave.
Columbus, OH 43216

The Highsmith Co., Inc.
Box 25
Fort Atkinson, WI

J. R. Holcomb
3000 Quigley Rd.
Cleveland, OH 44113

Hopewell Books, Inc.
730 Jefferson Dr.
Pittsburgh, PA 15229

Horton Handicraft Co., Inc.
P.O. Box 330
Farmington, CT 06032

Houghton Mifflin Co.
One Beacon St.
Boston, MA 02107

Howe Press of Perkins School for
  the Blind
175 N. Beacon St.
Watertown, MA 02172

Hoyle Products Co.
302 Orange Grove
Fillmore, CA 93015

Hubbard Scientific Co.
1946 Raymond Dr.
Northbrook, IL 60062

Human Behavor Magazine
12031 Wilshire Blvd.
Los Angeles, CA 90025

ICT-Instructional Communications
  Technology, Inc.
10 Stepar Pl.
Huntington Station, NY 11746

Ideal School Supply Co.
11000 S. Lavergne Ave.
Oak Lawn, IL 60453

Incentives for Learning, Inc.
600 W. Van Buren St.
Chicago, IL 60607

Independent School District
   No. 129
6th and Grove
Montevideo, MN 56265

Instant Buttons Machine Mfg. Co.
18 Selden St.
Woodbridge, CT 06525

Instructional Fair/Taskmaster
P.O. Box 1650
Grand Rapids, MI 49501

Instructional Industries, Inc.
Executive Park
Ballston Lake, NY 12019

Instructo/McGraw-Hill
Cedar Hollow & Matthews Hill Rd.
Paoli, PA 19301

Interpretive Education Co.
2300 Winters Dr.
Kalamazoo, MI 49001

Janus Book Publishers
3541 Investment Blvd.
Hayward, CA 94545

Jayfro Corp.
P.O. Box 400
Waterford, CT 06385

The Judy Co.
250 James St.
Morristown, NJ 07960

Kellogg Co.
235 Porter St.
Battle Creek, MI 49016

Kimbo Educational
86 S. Fifth Ave.
Long Branch, NJ 07740

Lakeshore Curriculum Materials
   Centers
16463 Phoebe St.
La Mirada, CA 90638

Learning Products, Inc.
11632 Fairgrove Industrial Blvd.
St. Louis, MO 63043

Learning Research Asso.
1501 Broadway
New York, NY 10036

Leicestershire Learning Systems
Chestnut St.
Lewiston, ME 04240

Library of Congress
Division for the Blind and
   Physically Handicapped
1291 Taylor St. N.W.
Washington, D.C. 20542

J. B. Lippincott Co.
East Washington Square
Philadelphia, PA 19105

Love Publishing Co.
6635 E. Villanova Pl.
Denver, CO 80222

Mafex Associates, Inc.
90 Cherry St.
Johnstown, PA 15902

Magnus Craft Materials, Inc.
304-8 Cliff Ln.
Cliffside Park, NJ 07010

Manson Western Corp.
12031 Wilshire Blvd.
Los Angeles, CA 90025

Market Linkage Project for Special
   Education
829 Eastwind Dr.
Westerville, OH 43081

Keystone View Div. of
   Mast/Keystone Co.
2212 E. 12th St.
Davenport, IA 52803

Charles Mayer Studios, Inc.
168 E. Market St.
Akron, OH 44308

CTB/McGraw-Hill
Del Monte Research Park
Monterey, CA 93940

EDL/McGraw-Hill
1221 Avenue of the Americas
New York, NY 10020

McGraw-Hill Book Co. (College
  Division)
1221 Avenue of the Americas
New York, NY 10020

McGraw-Hill Films
1221 Avenue of the Americas
New York, NY 10020

Webster McGraw-Hill
1221 Avenue of the Americas
New York, NY 10020

McKnight Publishing Co.
808 Eldorado Rd.
Bloomington, IL 61701

Media Marketing, Inc.
5307 Lee Hwy.
Arlington, VA 22207

Media Materials, Inc.
2936 Remington Ave.
Baltimore, MD 21211

Melody House Publishing Co.
819 N.W. 92nd St.
Oklahoma City, OK 73114

Melton Book Co.
111 Leslie St.
Dallas, TX 75207

Charles E. Merrill Publishing Co.
1300 Alum Creek Dr.
Columbus, OH 43216

Midwest Publications
P.O. Box 129
Troy, MI 48099

Milliken Publishing Co.
1100 Research Blvd.
St. Louis, MO 63132

Milton Bradley Co.
Springfield, MA 01101

Modern Curriculum Press
13900 Prospect Rd.
Cleveland, OH 44136

Modern Education Corp.
P.O. Box 721
Tulsa, OK 74101

Monroe Educational Center
The American Rd.
Morris Plains, NJ 07950

The C. V. Mosby Co.
11830 Westline Industrial Dr.
St. Louis, MO 63141

Motor Development Equipment Co.
P.O. Box 4054
Downey, CA 90241

L. Mullholland Corp.
1536 Los Angeles Ave.
Ventura, CA 93003

NASCO
901 Janesville Ave.
Fort Atkinson, WI 53538

National Audiovisual Center
NARS/General Services Admin.
Washington, D.C. 20409

National Committee on Arts for the
  Handicapped
1701 K Street N.W.
Washington, D.C. 20006

National Institute of Education
1200 19th Street N.W.
Washington, D.C. 20208

National Tutoring Institute, Inc.
6314 Brookside Plaza
Kansas City, MO 64113

NCS
4401 W. 76th St.
Minneapolis, MN 55435

New Dimensions in Education
Harpster A-V Inc.
2550 Medina Rd.
Medina, OH 44256

New Readers Press
Box 131
Syracuse, NY 13210

North American Recreation
  Convertibles, Inc.
P.O. Box 758
Bridgeport, CT 06880

Novo Educational Toy and Equipment Corp.
585 Avenue of the Americas
New York, NY 10011

Opportunities for Learning, Inc.
8950 Lurine St.
Chatsworth, CA 91311

Ortho-Kinetics, Inc.
1610 Pearl St.
Waukesha, WI 53186

Theraplay Division of PCA Industries, Inc.
29-24 40th Ave.
Long Island City, NY 11101

Paramount Communications
5451 Marathon St.
Hollywood, CA 90038

Pendulum Press, Inc.
Saw Mill Rd.
West Haven, CT 06516

Phonovisual Products, Inc.
P.O. Box 2007
Rockville, MD 20852

Plastics Manufacturing Co.
2700 S. Westmoreland
Dallas, TX 75233

Playground Corp. of America
Catalogue E
29-16 40th Ave.
Long Island City, NY 11101

Prentice-Hall, Inc.
Sylvan Ave.
Englewood Cliffs, NJ 07632

Prentke Romich Co.
RD 2
Box 191
Shreve, OH 44676

Prep, Inc.
1575 Parkway Ave.
Trenton, NJ 08628

Pre-School Publications
P.O. Box 272
Commerce, TX 75428

J. A. Preston Corp.
71 Fifth Ave.
New York, NY 10003

The Psychological Corp.
757 Third Ave.
New York, NY 10017

Psychotechnics, Inc.
Glenview, IL 60025

Random House
457 Madison Ave.
New York, NY 10022

Reader's Digest Educational Division
Pleasantville, NY 10570

Relevant Productions, Inc.
319 Gulf Blvd.
Indian Rocks Beach, FL 33535

Research Press
2612 N. Mattis Ave.
Champaign, IL 61820

Responsive Environments Corp.
Englewood Cliffs, NJ 07632

Frank E. Richards Publishing Co., Inc.
Box 66
Phoenix, NY 13135

Frank Schaffer Publications, Inc.
23770 Hawthorne Blvd.
Torrance, CA 90505

Scholastic Magazines, Inc.
50 W. 44th St.
New York, NY 10036

Scholastic Testing Service, Inc.
480 Meyer Rd.
Benesenville, IL 60106

School Specialty Supply Inc.
3525 S. 9th St.
Salinas, KS 67401

Science Research Associates, Inc.
155 N. Wacker Dr.
Chicago, IL 60606

Shakean Stations
Farley, IA 52046

Singer Career Systems
80 Commerce Dr.
Rochester, NY 14623

Skill Development Co.
1340 N. Jefferson St.
Anaheim, CA 92807

Society for Visual Education, Inc.
1345 Diversey Pkwy.
Chicago, IL 60614

S.W. Iowa Learning Resources
  Center
401 Reed St.
Red Oak, IA 51566

Special Education Materials, Inc.
484 S. Broadway
Yonkers, NY 10705

Special Learning Corp.
42 Boston Post Rd.
Guilford, CT 06437

Special Olympics, Inc.
Let's-Play-to-Grow
170 K St. N.W.
Suite 203
Washington, D.C. 20006

Special Press
724 S. Roosevelt Ave.
Columbus, OH 43209

Spellbinder, Inc.
Interactive Systems
Bradford St.
Concord, MA 01742

Spoken Arts Children's Catalogue
Pre-School and Elementary
1945 Hoover Ct.
Birmingham, AL 35216

Stallman Records, Inc.
P.O. Box AL
Rolynh Heights, NY 11577

Steck-Vaughn Co.
Box 2028
807 Brazos
Austin, TX 78767

Step, Inc.
South Complex-Paine Field
Everett, WA 98204

Syracuse University Press
1011 E. Water St.
Syracuse, NY 13210

Teacher Magazine
866 Third Ave.
New York, NY 10022

Teachers College Press
1234 Amsterdam Ave.
New York, NY 10027

Teaching Resources Corp.
100 Boyington St.
Boston, MA 02116

Telex Auditory Trainers
9600 Aldrick Ave. S.
Minneapolis, MN 55420

Charles C Thomas, Publisher
301-327 E. Lawrence
Springfield, IL 62717

Threshhold Catalog
Macmillan Co., School Division
Riverside, NJ 08075

Tomahawk Corp.
6900 220th S.W.
Mountlake Terrace, WA 98043

Trend Enterprises, Inc.
300 9th Ave. S.W.
New Brighton, MN 55112

Triarco Arts & Crafts
4146 Library Rd.
Pittsburgh, PA 15234

Troll Associates
320 Rt. 17
Mahwah, NJ 07430

University of Illinois Press
Urbana, IL 61801

University of Washington Press
Seattle, WA 98105

USC-United Canvas & Sling, Inc.
155 State St.
Hackensack, NJ 07601

Vocational Research Institute—JEVS
1624 Locust St.
Philadelphia, PA 19103

Vort Corp.
385 Sherman Ave.
Palo Alto, CA 94306

Voxcom Division/Tapecon, Inc.
10 Latta Rd.
Rochester, NY 14612

Walker Educational Book Co.
720 Fifth Ave.
New York, NY 10019

Wayne Engineering
4120 Greenwood
Skokie, IL 60076

Western Psychological Services
12031 Wilshire Blvd.
Los Angeles, CA 90025

Albert Whitman & Co.
560 W. Lake St.
Chicago, IL 60606

John Wiley & Sons, Inc.
605 Third Ave.
New York, NY 10016

B. L. Winch & Associates/Select-Ed.
45 Hitching Post Dr.
Building 2
Rolling Hills Estates, CA 90274

Xerox Education Publications
245 Long Hill Rd.
Middletown, CT 06457

Zaner-Bloser
612 N. Park
Columbus, OH 43215

Publications for teachers
of retarded children

American Journal on Mental Deficiency Mental Retardation
American Association on Mental Deficiency
Washington, D.C.

Child Development
The University of Chicago Press
11030 Langley Ave.
Chicago, Illinois 60628

Childhood Education
3615 Wisconsin Ave., N.W.
Washington, D.C. 20016

Educational Technology
Educational Technology Publications, Inc.
140 Sylvan Ave.
Englewood Cliffs, NJ 07632

Exceptional Children
Teaching Exceptional Children
Education and Training of the Mentally Retarded
Council for Exceptional Children
1920 Association Drive
Reston, Virginia

Exceptional Teacher
Philips-Allen
1330 S. State College Blvd.
Anaheim, CA 92806

Focus on Exceptional Children
Love Publishing Co.
6635 E. Villanova Place
Denver, CO 80222

Instructor
P.O. Box 6099
Duluth, MN 55806

Journal of Learning Disabilities
Executive Office, The Professional Press, Inc.
Publishers, Room 1410
Five North Wabash Avenue
Chicago, Illinois 60602

Journal of Special Education
111 Fifth Ave.
New York, NY 10003

Language Arts
National Council of Teachers of English
1111 Kenyon Road
Urbana, Illinois 61801

Learning
Education Today Co., Inc.
530 University Ave.
Palo Alto, California 94301

Teacher Magazine
866 Third Ave.
New York, NY 10022

Author Index

Author Index

Subject Index

TEXAS A&M UNIVERSITY-TEXARKANA